WORD IS OUT

Stories of Some of Our Lives

NANCY ADAIR
and
CASEY ADAIR

New Glide Publications/A Delta Special

A DELTA SPECIAL

Published jointly by
Dell Publishing Co., Inc.
1 Dag Hammarskjold Plaza
New York, New York 10017

and

New Glide Publications, Inc.
330 Ellis Street
San Francisco, California 94102

Produced in San Francisco by David Charlsen & Others
Editorial Services: Gail Larrick
Composition: Zoe Brown

Delta ® TM 755118, Dell Publishing Co., Inc.

ISBN: 0-440-59709-0

Manufactured in the U.S.A.

First Delta printing—September 1978

To the twenty-nine men and
women who are the book.
To the Mariposa Film Group.
And to each other.

Contents

Prologue

You are reading the book which we have put together from
the material collected for *Word Is Out,* a film presenting the
life stories of twenty-six homosexual men and women.

Each person you will meet is represented in the movie by an
average of eight minutes screen time; for each, we have many
additional pages of transcribed interviews. In locating and
selecting the best people to be in the film, the six filmmakers
(Nancy Adair, Peter Adair, Andrew Brown, Rob Epstein,
Lucy Massie Phenix, and Veronica Selver) videotaped about
one hundred fifty interviews with homosexuals from many
areas, classes, and backgrounds. After carefully reviewing
these tapes, they chose the people they wanted to appear in
the movie and returned (much later) to reinterview them on
16-millimeter color film.

In the long history and gradual evolution of the making of
Word Is Out lies a fascinating story: how the film was first
conceived by Peter; his asking Nancy to join him to make
the initial videotapes; the addition first of Veronica, then
Andrew, and later still of Lucy and Rob—and how these six
people slowly, joyfully, and painfully grew into a collective
entity. The usual professional roles of cameraperson, sound-
person, director, and others were shared by all, making the
process of creation of this film unique.

In assembling the book we were confronted by so much
material: all the videotapes, all the film "outs," all the tape-
recordings of the meetings of the six filmmakers. These meetings often included screaming conflicts and confrontations
but usually ended with constructive decisions about what the
film should say and how to say it, and almost always with
consensus and an increase of love and trust—the essential
ingredients of a successful collective production. Looming
in the wings was that seemingly irresolvable question: How

does one apply his or her talents, experience, and skills without exercising personal power when everyone is "equal"? The film itself testifies to the success of the cooperative effort and the individual sensibilities. This particular work could have been made in no other way.

Nancy has written her perception of the making of *Word Is Out* and woven into it the comments and views of the other five filmmakers so the reader will have a sense of the whole project. I look at her piece as a bonus portrait because it is really also the story of Nancy learning to relate to her homosexuality.

I really can't separate "The Film" from my relationship and love for my children, from my responses to two homosexual children, from my growth and development through close contact with them and their friends, from my irresistible urge to communicate what I have learned to my straight friends and relatives. Somehow it is all one undifferentiated ball of yarn—collected from leftover bits and strands of many colors and textures wound together in a spirit of conservation (they may come in handy some day).

In looking back, I think that when Peter and Nancy first talked to me about their homosexuality, my strongest single response was curiosity. How else could I deal with what they were telling me? I needed to know how they felt, what they did about it, what their individual problems and responses were. But I also wondered what I could learn about the phenomenon in general. How did I feel about it for society? Did one think about the matter in terms of how one individual (my child) copes with homosexuality within an unaccepting and oppressive society? Of course. But also I needed to know *what* homosexuality was—how would it fit into any viable society one might construct as an ideal? And, realistically, what could now be done to improve the immediate situation for homosexuals in our culture today?

Perhaps the underlying force which has affected my judgments and consequent emotions has been the increasing emphasis on the positive by both Peter and Nancy. Early on, I was not privy to their struggles and self-doubts, and I think when I first became aware, they had already dealt with much of their confusion and anxiety. So for me, it was easier. I learned from them and was never put in a position of offering parental advice out of ignorance. As they discovered who they were and began to feel the enormous relief and strength of their self-recognition and honesty—and freedom—that was conveyed to me with a sense of acceptance, and my faith in their abilities to cope, to deal fearlessly and with integrity with themselves and their lives, created in me an overpowering sense of pride and love, plus an appreciation and gratefulness for our growing communication.

When the film production began and Peter and Nancy were joined by the other four, I followed the group's progress avidly and with enormous pleasure and satisfaction. For a time I came into San Francisco to the film office a couple of times a week to do what I could to help—primarily bits and pieces of office work. I was able to follow the progress of the work, to feel a small part of it, and to observe the meetings in which the collective method of operation evolved. I felt privileged to share the excitement, the anxieties, and some of the work. All of the filmmakers were unfailing in their generosity with their time (explaining things I wanted to understand about making a film) and in making me feel I was some part of the group. Occasionally, I looked upon myself as a kind of "groupie"—I couldn't get enough of screenings, listening to taped meetings, gleaning every detail I could from the process and the progress.

During this process I grew to know each of the filmmakers better and to love them—as my friends, as the friends of my children, as part of my family, and as very special and exceptional human beings. They are incredibly bright, with refined and varied sensibilities and unbelievable energies. Such an opportunity for a woman in her sixties to work in this way is, I believe, a rare gift. But also, perhaps, a danger. Is my

immersion vicarious? Am I a contributor or an observer—
a sort of parasite?

When the possibility of doing a book was mentioned, I agreed
to take the project on. When I got bogged down and discour-
aged with the enormity of the task, Nancy joined me. At first
I felt that the material gathered on the some one hundred
fifty videotapes which had *not* been directly used in the film
should not be buried in an archive but should form the basis
for this book. Later we decided instead to expand the interviews of the people included in the film and to save the other
material for another book.

One of my primary concerns in these past few years has
been the responses to homosexuality by the larger society—
"the straights." My concern first emerged as a defensive reaction in terms of my children. Then, as I worked alongside the
filmmakers, I felt the group was ignoring the heterosexual
world to a large extent. The movie was primarily geared for
the gay audience. When it was finished, the emphasis in the
group's public relations and publicity was likewise directed.
This tendency was not only natural and understandable, but
it was also what the group *wanted.* All the while, concern
about this direction has been in the back of my mind.

For me, the most elementary and perhaps unsophisticated
way to express my feelings is in the one word "love." Real
love cannot exist without understanding and communication.
So I want to say to all those people with homosexual children, relatives, friends, or whatever, "If you love them, keep
the lines of communication open. Learn from them. Don't
panic and shut them out." But this gross oversimplification
will open no eyes or hearts or minds. How can I explain—
briefly, directly, clearly—how this can be done? Composition
teachers say, "Start with what you know."

As a young graduate student, I had a friend (and father con-
fessor) who was homosexual. In our circle of mutual friends,
the subject was never mentioned in front of him, or directly
to him, yet I felt curious, titillated, shocked, and, most of all,

tolerant! I saw myself as a sophisticated, broadminded woman-of-the-world because I was his friend, and *unprejudiced!* I have a feeling that (without the youthful overtones) this attitude is basically the one my straight friends hold. Most old friends who still love Peter and Nancy, whom they've known since babyhood, still will not directly confront the fact that they are homosexuals. The subject seems to be taboo, and they refuse to deal with it; it is ignored, as if it didn't exist. My friends can't seem to realize that my children's homosexuality is not just a statement of sexual preference. It is their identity—who they are—and if this fact is overlooked and avoided, my children are invalidated. To me, this attitude forms a large part of the oppression of homosexuals: making them *invisible* is degrading and incapacitating.

And herein lies a paradox I wish I could deal with at greater length. The very concentration on such labels as "homosexual," "gay," or "lesbian" in the film, the book, or among activist groups defies the greater long-term goal—which is, in another sense, to point out the irrelevance of such labels, and to point to the reality that homosexuals are human beings with some sexual preferences, lifestyles, or sensibilities different from ourselves. The unnerving and wasteful human failing of making scapegoats of those who don't conform in some ways is what we should all fight against. Has there ever been a film, a book, or an individual described as "heterosexual"? Any such designation should be of no consequence. What is of importance is that people are people, and neither "hetero" nor "homo." But we all fall into the trap—particularly in these times when so many are attempting to do away with the oppression. In order to deal with positive identification, we find *ourselves* doing the labeling. Our first phrasing of the dedication to this book was "To the gay men and lesbians . . . ," until we realized that we ourselves were perpetuating this definitive and imprecise labeling.

So much of the behavior of homosexuals (and of all of us) is the result of the traumas and anxieties suffered because of the attitudes of society. Were there no biases and prejudices, the problems of gays would be solved. Homosexuality *per se* does not create difficulties; it is the widespread fear, ignorance, and condemnation of it.

I am not unaware of the other horrors homosexuals are subjected to, which are clearly documented in the interviews in this book. I simply feel that my own experience, more immediate and understood by me, qualifies me as a spokesperson to those who are unable to accept the homosexuality of people around them.

Casey Adair

Acknowledgements

I would like to thank the following people for their support while I was working on this project.

Syreeta	Sandy Boucher	Rene Dustman
Gwyn Metz	Treelight	Trish Nugent
Kathy Glaser	Lucia Valeska	Deanna Hanson
Tracy Gary	La Rosa	Lynn Landor
Ann Hershey	Penny Doran	Arina Isaacson

Casey and I would like to especially thank:

Gail Larrick	Vicki Hochberg	Brian Bullard
Margie Brown	Ann Kent Rush	Bob and Priscilla Bunker
Roland Dickey	Janet Cole	
Gloria Frym	Barbara Price	

We both want to express our strong feelings of love and indebtedness to our family:

Margo, what would I do if I didn't have a sister I could yell with, and Casey didn't have a daughter she could confide in. You are always there for us, and always our friend.

John, you are the rare father who truly supports his kids, the rare husband who supports his wife, the rare man who believes in his own changes.

Peter, your phenomenal dedication to this project still astounds me. Your unlimited trust in Casey and me has forced us to meet ourselves as well as each other.

Both Casey and I would like to thank David. Who ever heard of getting a book out in three months? Only you—with Brian—could have done it. What we value most, though, is our new friendship.

I must also express heartfelt gratitude to all the women of the meditation retreats which gave me the strength to acknowledge myself.

It was often difficult to write in the confusion of our living situation. I stayed in the homes of many people while they were away. Each of your homes gave me the extra energy I needed, and I thank all of you.

Lucy Massie Phenix, Rob Epstein, Andrew Brown, Veronica Selver, Peter Adair, and myself—the Mariposa Film Group—we did it, and I am proud of us.

Casey, where did you find the strength to see this project through, to work with me for a year? As much as you have encouraged your children to express themselves, you have encouraged the twenty-six gay men and lesbians to express themselves.

And what can I say to those of you who so candidly and courageously shared your lives with us on both film and video tape, except thank you, thank you, thank you. And we all love you. All our lives have been enriched as we have participated with each other to bring more understanding into the world.

Special Acknowledgement

Jan Williams died in January, 1978. Jan, your spirit has always, and will always, touch so many. I love you very much.

Nancy Adair
June 1978

INTERVIEWS

Whitey

NANCY: *Tell me about your childhood.*

WHITEY: "God will punish you!" was my mother's favorite saying to me. She—and my father, too, I guess—were very church oriented, very Lutheran. I remember going to Sunday school at a very early age—it was a must. Sunday school can be heavy for a child. You are taught to believe strongly in a kind of heaven-and-hell thing—and in the wrath of God. You tend to think that every little thing you might do is wrong, or that every little thing you think about that's not right is punishable in some way; so you are always fearful. If you do *anything* that isn't right, you are terrified you'll be struck by lightning or go to hell. It caused a lot of fear. You never knew exactly what form the punishment would take, so you were always anticipating that something terrible would happen to you. It's a pretty heavy trip to put on a kid.

N: *Do you remember when you stopped believing in that stuff?*

W: I was pretty well brainwashed, so it was quite a while before I didn't believe it completely. I realized I could never live up to all the things you were supposed to do, and that caused me a great deal of guilt and fear. As I grew older—and mostly on an unconscious level, I guess, because I couldn't have survived had it been on a conscious level—for a long time I believed God would take pity on me and change me, or help me out. I prayed a lot because I believed if I had enough faith I would get over this . . . this sickness. I remember those years of confusion—trying to do what was right but not quite knowing what that was; being made to carry around guilt for something that was quite natural to me.

As I developed as a human being, I felt I was somehow stunted because I spent all that time grappling with that problem when I could have been learning how to live.

N: *When were you first conscious of being gay?*

W: In grammar school—even though I didn't know what being gay was. I didn't know it was anything strange at the time. I was enjoying crushes, until I found out they were considered abnormal. I was about twelve, and at that age girls were getting interested in boys. I heard someone remarking once that "so-and-so was acting like a lesbian," and I wondered what that was, and so I asked and everybody laughed. "That's a woman—or a girl—who likes other girls instead of boys." I thought, "Oh-oh, that sounds like me." It scared me a little because that was the name for what I felt, but I didn't know whether it was bad. I thought about it and started to get a little worried. I read a pocket book that was going around school about homosexuals—males—so I realized it could happen to a boy too.

N: *Why weren't you into boys?*

W: I have no idea. I just liked girls.

N: *Did you talk to anyone about it?*

W: I was still very naive about the whole thing, so I decided to ask my mother just what a homosexual was. My God!—her reaction was so violent that it really scared me. She screamed, "Where did you hear that word?" and I said, "In this book." She took the book, tore it up, threw it down the incinerator, and said, "I don't ever want to hear you repeat that"—*without telling me what it was.* So I thought it must be really horrible—and I didn't push it.

My mother told my father about it, and he just laughed. That made me more confused. I didn't really have a good grasp on what the whole thing meant in terms of my life. About a year later I did learn what it meant and thought, "I really am a homosexual—*for real.*" But I thought it was some kind of disease that could maybe be cured. So again, I mentioned this to my parents. My mother didn't want to believe it and my father, again, didn't take it very seriously. But my mother was so terrified she talked my father into taking me to see a psychiatrist who was connected with the Church. I was full of expectations that going to a psychiatrist was going to solve all my problems; I would be fine, and my mother would be happy. The psychiatrist put me on a diet of green salads.

N: *A diet of* what?

W: Two green salads a day. What this had to do with any-thing I don't know, but I figured she knew what she was do-ing. I had a schedule of green salads interspersed with prayer but obviously it didn't do any good. I blamed myself for its not working. I was made to feel I was disgracing my family—that it was a reflection on them. My father wasn't around much at that time, but my mother would look at me strangely; all of a sudden it was like a wall had dropped, and I was some kind of freak thing that wasn't supposed to have happened.

N: *Did it have to do only with your homosexual tendencies?*

W: Well, that's when all this change took place in people's attitudes towards me. I realized I could not say to somebody, "I am a homosexual," because they then no longer related to me as they had before—which made me think it was some-thing to be ashamed of and to hide.

N: *How old were you?*

W: Thirteen. Eventually the pressure got to be so great that I decided I could no longer talk to anyone about it—my mother or anybody—because they had such a negative reac-tion to me and to the whole thing. There was no point in dis-cussing it. I decided the best thing I could do would be to leave so as not to disgrace my family, and they wouldn't have to deal with it. At this point I felt I was doomed to this life. It was like my whole life was just turned around. I didn't know what in the world to do—it was such a drastic thing. I resigned myself to the fact that I guessed I should find peo-ple like me and live my life shut off from everyone else. I had no idea what type of life homosexuals led. I just knew my parents' reaction to me and the psychiatrist's . . . people's reaction just to the *word.* The word "pervert" was always attached to it, and this meant something horrible for me.

The whole thing was devastating. All of a sudden I had sunk to the depths. I had heard about the Village by then—not much, just that that's where homosexuals were. So I left, got on the train, and went down to the Village determined to find other homosexuals and learn to live however they lived. I didn't feel like I had any other choice. There was the trip—sleeping on roofs, rooftops, and under stairwells. You have to know New York . . . you could do that. I was actually glad to be found because I knew, by that time, I would—could never survive like that.

N: *So your father found you in the Village?*

W: Yeah. I was walking by the Westside subway entrance when who should come up but my father. He grabbed me by the neck, and all of a sudden police cars were pulling up. I don't know how they got there so fast, I was in such shock seeing him. My father was more sympathetic; to him these people were perverts, but I don't think he really thought I was—he just thought I was sick and he wanted me someplace where I could "get well again"—which meant hospitals and doctors.

N: *Then what happened?*

W: I was put in a police car and whisked off to Kings County Hospital, which is —like Bellevue, only in Brooklyn— for observation. At the end of thirty days, they sent me home. It was strange because nothing was settled one way or the other. I was in limbo. It was unbearable living at home. It would have been unbearable in the Village too. I was just too young. I wouldn't have known where to get a job. Consequently I went back and forth to Kings County. If I had been smart enough, I would have played their game and pretended I was OK, but I was too upset and miserable, and I couldn't lie to my mother. She kept trying to get me to do things that everyone else did—to have the normal relationships that kids have at that age, the whole trip. I got dragged to church and had to talk to the minister periodically. We all had to get down and pray for my affliction.

Finally they considered me incorrigible, and I was sent to a state hospital, which was an entirely different number. I went willingly, thinking that there I'd get intensive care—which, in retrospect, is really funny since I saw a doctor maybe two or three times the whole time I was there, which was four years. Being in there at that age and being as naive as I was, I had a really rough time.

I saw mostly other patients and attendants. Later I was on tranquilizers; they almost killed me with them. You were given no other treatment of any kind, so I don't know how they expected you to get any better. There were lots of other homosexuals; that's where I actually learned the facts of life. I was completely changed from what I was when I went in there. I was full of hate, angry at the world. I was a totally different person, mainly because of the kinds of things you had to do in there in order to survive. It was a totally different way of living. It was a shock—something you either adapted to or you went crazy. It was a horrible, horrible experience. I saw things in there that no one who hadn't been in a state hospital in the fifties could have allowed themselves to believe was happening in this country. But it was like a horror movie. I would like to think it doesn't happen anymore, but I don't know.

N: *Did you have shock treatment?*

W: No, I didn't personally, thank goodness, but you were threatened with it all the time to keep you in line. That kind of treatment was used as punishment.

N: *Did they try to prevent you from being gay?*

W: The strange thing was that most of the attendants were gay. But very sadistically—rapes—and they just enjoyed seeing people squirm. They had so much power!—which they exercised. This situation was totally frustrating to the patients. They were totally powerless. You were locked up and had no way of getting back at people for the things that were happening to you there. You came out like a keg of dynamite ready to go off! You had all this anger and hatred, which to me now is the scariest part of the whole thing. If you feel that kind of hate, it is really dangerous—to yourself and to other people.

N: *Where did you go when you got out?*

W: I was eighteen, but I didn't have much choice. Being in the hospital had interrupted my education, so I had to go back home and try to find a job. I took any kind of work I could get—factories, bars—the whole job scene was so depressing most of the time. For a good part of the time I had to live with my mother because I couldn't afford anything else.

N: *Did you have friends?*

W: I made friends—mostly in gay bars. That was really the only place that anybody could go.

N: *After you got out of the hospital, was it long before you had a good relationship with a woman?*

W: It was a long time. I don't think any relationship I had was good—or beautiful.

N: *Did you have a lot of them?*

W: Oh, no, not really. But when I got out of the hospital I wasn't in such good shape myself. Naturally, I couldn't digest all the stuff that went on. I was really kind of freaked out . . . .

N: *Did you say to yourself, "I'm a lesbian, and it's all right," or "It isn't all right," or . . .?*

W: No, I said to myself, "I'm a lesbian, but it isn't all right."

N: *Didn't you like being a lesbian?*

W: I didn't like it because of what had happened to me— or because from what I could see, it wasn't going to get any better.

N: *Did you ever attempt to be straight?*

W: No, I couldn't . . . somehow that never occurred to me. By the time I got out of the hospital, I guess I considered myself set off totally from normal life . . . or what at that time was considered normal life.

N: *How did you feel about the butch-femme scene? How did you fit into it?*

W: It was . . . I didn't. I always felt really funny about it— but that was what was happening. I never felt comfortable with that kind of thing, but that was all there was. Being as tall as I am, and being athletic, I naturally fell into the butch thing: I looked the way everybody else did at that time—shirt, pants, tie—the whole bit.

N: *So you wanted people to think you were a man?*

W: Yeah, most of the time. I can understand how people got into that because at the time you didn't really want to look like a dyke—you wanted to look like a man so you wouldn't get beat up on the subway. You didn't want to look like a faggot either, because then you would surely get beat up. So it was mostly to protect yourself. It was really scary working like that.

But finally I got lucky. The small electronics company where I was working moved out of New York City to a small fishing village on Long Island, and I figured I had nothing to lose so I went along with the company—which was probably the beginning of getting halfway together. It was like night and day from New York—totally different—but I went, and I even liked it. I began to laugh a little bit; I didn't have the pressures and I didn't have to play roles. So I stayed about four years. In the meantime I began to realize that I was situated in the middle of the Hamptons, and during the summers I met a lot of people who were mostly rich and well known—a totally different class. It felt good, because they were like nothing I had ever known in my life, and I realized that not everybody in the world was the same. In New York I got the feeling that—God!—I had no way of knowing that there were other types of gay people in other places. So it was the beginning of a hope that those people I'd met in the City were not what I had to live with the rest of my life.

N: *When and how did you decide to come to California?*

W: I met several people during the summertimes who had been to San Francisco, and it sounded really good to me. So I saved up some money and bought a car and thought, "It's time," and I came. It was an exciting thing—scary, too—but I made it. It was very strange to me. Everything looked flat, but after a few months I began to relax a bit, and I realized all the things I didn't like about New York were missing here. I didn't have to be afraid to walk down the street. It was much freer. People weren't so cold—they were friendly. You didn't have to be suspicious or so defensive.

N: *Did you begin to have fuller relationships with women?*

W: My relationships got continually better as I began to be more open and less afraid—not having to be such-and-such, or to live up to a certain image. They've become more and more meaningful. They don't end on violent notes like most had in the past when I was still very touchy and feeling very threatened about a lot of things. They just ended because we were going in different directions, and there's still a good feeling between myself and ex-lovers—a lot of warmth. I've changed a lot in the years since I came out here—more every year. My relationships became different because in the relationships I was finding out more about myself—about how I really felt with other people—so it was very revealing to me. I really hadn't known much about myself or about the things I really like to do. I was also finding out how people reacted and related to me—which was different, because I was different.

N: *Why did you decide to move to the country?*

W: I hadn't really ever been in the country—or exposed to country types of living before. When I was, I reacted very positively—very quickly. It felt to me like a really good place. In fact, being in the country was the first time I felt myself to be a part of something bigger. It was a space in that larger universe that felt good to me—as though I belonged there and felt at peace with myself and my environment.

So I began planning to go up to Humboldt County and build a house. I worked on plans for a small cabin—nothing spectacular, but one I could build myself with the help of some friends. I wanted to live in the country and raise some animals. Last year I was able to do it. I got some land a few miles from some gay women friends of mine who have also built, and we helped each other.

N: *How do you feel about your relationship to your old friends in the city?*

W: I've been so into what I'm doing here, and there is so much still left to do, that I haven't really had time to sit back and reflect—or to think about my friends in the city. A lot of them don't understand it—that I would come up to a place as far away and isolated as this. It's something they would never think of doing. But I feel better up here in every way. It feels more natural, and I don't feel that my particular place is in the city—too much is going on, and it has a paralyzing effect

the saw and women to chop these using the chainsaw to the
wood. Women call for courage, and women working with hard
sand, and hurl and hurling with...

on me. Most of the people I know hang out in bars—it's a whole lifestyle—and I'm glad to be out of that. For me it wore itself out—and it wears you out too.

N: *Do you enjoy being alone? Do you get lonely?*

W: I enjoy being alone. There's a difference between being lonely and being alone. I don't really get lonely—not the kind of being alone I felt in New York. *That* was loneliness—terrifying, being shut out and hiding from things. Being alone here is a good experience for me because I have seldom been alone, and you can be lonely with a whole lot of people around. I like being alone because it's quiet and I can read or just relax and reflect. It enables me to think and see things more clearly without being influenced.

N: *So you feel good about yourself now?*

W: Yeah, I do, because I've gotten older and had enough time to realize that I'm not necessarily the horrible person that I was told for years that I was. It's so deep. You believe for so long that you are not a worthy person. You are so geared to failure because everything that happened and everything you've been told makes you think of yourself as wrong and not good. If you are made to feel unworthy and not a whole person, you've lost before you can begin. You arrange your life so things will work out that way—so that feeling is reinforced. Now I'm able to do things that I would not have attempted to do before because I would not have believed them possible—and I think that's a big thing. I feel now I am able to take some control over my life, whereas before I was just reacting to things that were happening and I was afraid to rock the boat. I didn't feel I had any effect on anything; I was being affected. And now I'm not afraid to take myself with me wherever I go. That's a relief.

Elsa

NANCY: *Do you mind saying how old you were when you were born?*

ELSA: How old I was when I was . . . ?

N: *No, how old are you now?*

E: I am seventy-seven; I was born in December, 1898.

N: *How long have you been a lesbian?*

E: I never understand what that means, because as far as I am concerned I was born that way. I never had that crossing-over crisis that people talk about these days—the feeling that you have to have some kind of an indoctrination or trauma, or a coming-out ritual. I just knew that I was different in many ways from what was usually accepted. I was always interested in why I am here and what I am, what it is all about in a larger sense. But my difficulties and problems were in other directions—from a family point of view. We all had difficulties of survival when we came to Canada—difficult climate, under poverty conditions—there are things you don't worry about until you have solved a few of these problems.

N: *Tell me something of your childhood.*

E: I was born in a rather ordinary—in terms of economics— middle-class family environment. While I had rapport with my mother and to some extent with my father and with siblings, nevertheless I felt that I had all kinds of feelings and aspirations that I couldn't share. When we came to Canada, my mother was doing everything under the most primitive conditions for three, four, five, six, and finally seven children. I helped, and my younger sisters helped, but she was the one who was doing most of the work. She was very unsophisticated, but she was a great reader. My father had a sense of adventure, and my siblings were all interested in some kind of art—they all had visions of becoming famous in one way or another.

I felt utterly alienated from what was presented as the culture and the religion and the general social attitudes around me, growing up in a poor French-Canadian village. What I remember of my first six years in England was much different, more physically comfortable. I remember my beautiful, loving maternal grandmother. I remember two busts on the mantelshelf above the fireplace. My mother told me that when I was still a baby in arms, if they were shown to me, I would cry at the sight of one—Beethoven—and laugh and put my arms out to the other—Mozart—who was a pleasant, somewhat feminine-looking man. But my mother's awareness of songs and poetry, dance and music—even though on a very unsophisticated level—made me aware such a world existed and that it was what I was looking for.

I was interested from a very early age in poetry. I started to read poetry just as soon as I could find books to read. Art seemed to be on the periphery of possibilities, always. It was something to aspire to. I felt I just didn't belong where I was. There was something else, some place where I could belong better, and there were people with whom I could relate—my kind of people—quite apart from all the family attachments.

N: *Was most of your childhood spent in that small village?*

E: We left when I was about sixteen and moved to Montreal, where we lived in a very lower-middle-class flat in the French-Canadian section. But at least there were libraries! The first thing I did was haunt bookshops. With my first dollar-a-month allowance, I bought Samuel Taylor Coleridge's *Collected Poems;* I still have that book and I love it very much.

N: *How did you come to realize that you were a lesbian?*

E: When I was about seventeen, I'd been working for a year and a half in tiresome jobs, and I just couldn't see myself going through life that way. So in search of my people—of where, perhaps, I might belong—I had an inspiration one day. Under an assumed name I wrote a letter to the editor's column in the Montreal *Daily Star,* asking, "Is there in Montreal any kind of an organization to which writers, or prospective writers, might belong?" I forget the exact wording, but that was the gist of it. I wrote under an assumed name; then, under my own name, I sent an answer, saying, "The undersigned knows of no such organization, but one is in the process of being formed and anyone interested should write to . . .," and I gave my name and address. I received all kinds of letters, and I called a meeting at my parents' house for the formation of this group. One of the men who came was a young man who these days would be called gay, a homosexual young man, Roswell George Mills—the most extraordinary being I'd ever seen in my life. He was beautiful. About nineteen, exquisitely made up, slightly perfumed, dressed in ordinary men's clothing but a little on the chi-chi side. And he swayed about, you know. We became friends almost instantly because we were both interested in poetry and the arts.

Roswell apparently recognized immediately my temperament. He said, "Do you know about Sappho?" I don't remember if I'd heard anything about her, but I went to the library, found writings about her and translations of her fragments, and immediately became interested. Through Roswell—all blessings— I started to hear about some literature that would lead me to some knowledge about myself and other people like me. Other than the literary, I think the first books I read were Edward Carpenter's *The Intermediate Sex,* and Kraft-Ebbing, and Lombroso—and all these were revelatory to me because I could have no doubt, having read them, of where my orientation lay. Though they wrote on a level of morbid psychology, and I couldn't accept the morbidity side of it, it was very interesting to read all this and at least find out there had been other people like me in the world—and a great many of them, a large number distinguished and outstanding, even if they weren't acceptable in ordinary life. Here is where I feel I won for myself, through my intellectual curiosity and passion for reading, a tremendous advantage over young people who grow up with movies (now television) and popular magazines which mainly reflect back to them the prejudices and limitations of middle-class society. As contrast to the often sordid dullness of lower-middle-class life, its bourgeois morality and indifferences—as I saw it—to the arts and high thought, books opened up worlds of beauty, adventure, tolerance, and respect for diversity of ways of being and the promise that I should be able to find people with wisdom beyond the ordinary, with whom one might share dreams and explore what life was all about.

N: *Do you think a relationship exists between being a lesbian and creativity?*

E: I believe part of the lesbian temperament is that we are—those of us who are conscious of it, at any rate—more creative in our souls than in our bodies. There are people, from as far back as they know, who feel more creative on some other level than the physical or the maternal. With men, I'm sure it isn't confined to whether they're homosexual or heterosexual, but with women, it seems to me it's more apt to be. Maybe it's sublimation. Certainly it was not a conscious sublimation for me. I never wanted to have children, never felt the desire to be a mother. But from the earliest time that I can remember, I wanted to write poetry. That was my creative expression. That was what meant most to me in life. And the difficulties I have encountered in that have been my primary frustration.

N: *At the time you discovered that you were of this particular temperament, did you identify with any particular women?*

E: No. I was very much alone. If there *was* a problem connected with my temperament of being lesbian, before and even after I became aware of its connotations, it was the loneliness—the fact that I didn't know anybody like me. I felt that I had all kinds of feelings and aspirations that I couldn't share. That was the first thing I realized under those circum-

stances. But I cannot stress strongly or often enough that the feelings of difference, of aloneness, were not due simply to the difference in emotional orientation. A. E. Houseman wrote: "I, a stranger and afraid/In a world I never made." I was not particularly afraid, but I did feel myself a stranger among the majority of people with most of the acceptable ambitions to get on, make it, have a family, acquire "things," all that. As an aspiring poet, artist, I believe I should have felt the same if I'd been heterosexual. Who were the others, if there were any? Where were they?

N: *Did you find them?*

E: Over the years, I did find some people that I could relate to, yes. But it doesn't happen overnight. I don't think that you realize what it means to be cast out upon society with no real education, no fitness for any kind of profession, no means of earning a living other than in menial jobs. Those things become predominant, even though in your deepest soul you know that your searchings are in other directions. I don't at all feel that the most difficult thing at that time was my awareness of my erotic temperament. The most difficult was survival, and how I was going to earn a living as a woman.

When I first learned to know about myself, I was mainly in association with homosexual men. They were very nice people; I liked them. Some were various kinds of artists, so I had companionship there. But I used to wonder where the women were. I didn't know any lesbians. Not for years did I ever meet a lesbian. I fell in love with women who now, I suppose, would be called straight.

The first woman I was profoundly interested in I met when I was sixteen. We were best friends, but there was no question of a lesbian relationship or anything of that sort. I'm sure she was devoted to me as a friend, but it never occurred to her what might be the nature of my interest in her. I hardly knew myself, except that it hurt a great deal when I realized that she was much more interested in boys.

N: *Had you yet had any physical experiences with women?*

E: No. I had had no physical experiences whatsoever. I had never even kissed this woman whom I was in love with. Then, through my homosexual men friends, I met Estelle. I was on the verge of being eighteen; she was probably thirty-four or thirty-five. I felt extremely drawn to her. At one of our gatherings, I read some of my poetry. Later I went into the bedroom, and Estelle was there. She said, "Your poetry is so intense! You're a dear girl," or some such expression. And she put her arms around me and kissed me. Well, this was like putting a match to oil as far as I was concerned—she was the first person who had ever kissed me in that way. I realized later that it was not an intentional lesbian kiss, but my interest in her flared up much higher.

I was desperately in love for a time, but it was very unrewarding so far as any fruition went because she was totally heterosexual. I don't think she intended to be a tease, but it turned out that way because she let me caress, and she let me embrace, but nothing more, and I was getting more and more frustrated. This went on for three years.

But in the meantime, I met another woman in the same group. A very lovely French-Canadian woman, Marguerite. I suppose now she would be called bisexual. Marguerite was somewhat charmed by my ignorance and unsophistication, or innocence, or who knows what. She and I were lovers for a while, and it was delightful. Estelle gave me my first kiss, but Marguerite gave me my first love experience with a woman—with anybody.

N: *When did you leave Canada?*

E: When I was twenty-one, I went to New York to seek a career as a writer there. I was really too busy, too preoccupied with that to think much of love and, for that matter, still in love with Estelle in Montreal. From the age of sixteen, I had to earn my living, and I felt an obligation to help at home even after I left. For the first three years it was at the dullest imaginable office chores. But gradually I found opportunities to learn ways to fit me for slightly less boring jobs. I was secretary for a time in a place where motion pictures were assigned to theaters. Then for a time I was assistant editor of an industrial house organ where I began to learn some journalistic skills. Then I spent about a year as English secretary to the consul of the Serbians, Croatians, and Slovenians (brought together as an aftermath of World War I). I resigned from there with a wealth of one hundred Canadian dollars (reduced by inflation to eighty American) when I decided to go to New York.

While still in Montreal, I had much admired a magazine, *Pearson's,* published by Frank Harris (whose "Portraits" of poets and other greats and of Oscar Wilde and "The Man, Shakespeare" I also admired). Arrived in Manhattan, I wrote to him, sent along some of my poetry and reviews already published in *The Canadian Bookman,* and said I needed a job. He invited me to come see him, praised my writing highly, gave me a job as poetry editor. Later, I became associate editor. *Pearson's* was a World War I-depression casualty. When it failed, I did a little freelancing for a time, but after four years there, I had had enough of New York. In the meantime I had met a Scottish woman who had been living in British Columbia. She was about fifteen years older than I was. A beautiful person, one with nobility of character. We became friends, soon, lovers.

N: *Did you live with her for a long time?*

E: For thirteen years. Until she died. When I first realized that I was going to be involved with her, she had several gold rings on her hand. She took one off and said, "Marry me for tonight." Of course, by then we were being a little intimate. But no commitments of any sort were being made. She put this ring on my finger, and as far as I was concerned, it was just temporary. I wore it for thirteen years.

I don't think either she or I made love with anyone else more than two or three times in those thirteen years. It wasn't due to any commitment. There wasn't any "I'll love you forever, and I'm the only one"—none of that. It just happened that's what we wanted. As for what I feel about fidelity, if that's what the two persons are happy with—yes. If they don't, let that be too. But be honest.

She died of cancer of the lung. It was a horrible experience. I was shocked and deprived. It was a deep, dark period. But about a year after that, I met a woman whom I fell very much in love with. I was then about thirty-five, and she was some sixteen years younger. I was faithful to her for six years. She was physically faithful, as far as I know, but ultimately she started a relationship with a woman a little younger than herself. She wouldn't continue afterwards in a friendship, and that is a sorrow for me. With everyone but her I've always continued in a friendship after the love relationship ended.

N: *Do you suppose that's true of most lesbians?*

E: Yes. They do continue. My feeling about lesbian relationships is that—if they mean anything at all—they're total. While the erotic part, the sexual part, is important, I feel that the friendship in the relationship—the total relationship—is more important. Even though for one reason or another the erotic part of it may cease to work, or fades out of your needs, very often there is enough love and respect for one another so that the friendship remains.

N: *Rather than being a negative experience for you at any time, has being a lesbian been basically a positive orientation?*

E: Definitely. As far as I'm concerned, it's an advantage. I've always had a positive feeling about being a lesbian. Of course, I knew what the social attitude was. Couldn't escape it. But I always felt I had the right to be me. No regrets, no guilt, no apologies. For women, being lesbian is liberating.

N: *How were critical social attitudes manifested toward you?*

E: They were not manifested toward me at all, because I didn't go out with a placard on my breast. I never hid, and I never advertised. I was myself as I was. I realized that if I wanted to keep my job or not have difficulties and unwanted pryings into my life, I had to keep my own counsel. It never occurred to me to feel that it was anybody's business. That's the way it was. Maybe it's the English in me. We feel we have a right to our private life. In the United States, you want to know all.

N: *How do you feel about the younger women accepting their lesbianism and being open with it?*

E: I think it's excellent to the extent to which a person who wishes to be open can be open and still survive in society in terms of employment, family, or whatever. It's entirely up to the individual. I don't think there should be any pressure one way or the other; we should accept whatever degree of openness the individual feels willing and able to exercise. I was always open with close friends, and for a long time now, due to my writing, anyone interested knows my orientation.

N: *Did your parents ever know that you were a lesbian?*

E: I don't think they would have known what it was. They were not sophisticated in those realms. My mother wouldn't have known the meaning of the word "lesbian." She knew I had close women friends I lived with, but I didn't want to disturb her by spelling it out. I don't know if it would have done any good. Why enter into useless controversies? It does nobody any good. Anytime it's significant and would do any good, I will offer the greatest frankness, but I don't believe in sticking under people's noses what they're not ready for. To me it's also kindness. Why embarrass people when no good is served? No good for me, no good for them, no good for the general populace. To say, in effect, to others, "You have got to love me no matter how I affront your values or feelings" appears to me to be a sort of arrogance or aggression.

(Veronica joins the interview.)

VERONICA: *Can you describe what you mean by lesbian temperament? Is it different from the lesbian experience?*

E: The lesbian temperament, which I feel comes with us, so to speak, is being described in this day as that of "a woman-identified woman." It's thinking of oneself as a woman—certainly not as a pseudo-male, as some people seem to think it might be—as a woman who relates positively to other women, regardless of erotic orientation. And that seems to be happening, at least verbally, these days. I see it as more of a commitment to women—not a commitment to the race in terms of potential motherhood or wifehood. To me, also, a woman having what to me is a lesbian personality is one willing to take full responsibility for herself. I've always thought my basic commitments—other than those to woman— are to my work, to writing and poetry, to doing what is in me to do as a creative person.

V: *Why do you think society holds the attitude it does toward lesbians?*

E: If I could answer that, I'd be some sort of a seer. But I wonder if it isn't really in the fact that before the world became so populous, it was felt necessary to concentrate more on procreation. Maybe that is still in people, in their deepest emotional orientation. Most men certainly don't like the idea of lesbianism. They would have to say why, but it seems as if they feel threatened by it in all kinds of ways. After all, it takes some desirable women out of the arena for them. And it also is a kind of affront to their idea of their masculinity that another woman—a mere woman—could prove more satisfying than they could. I don't know. These are just speculations. As for the male side of it, men—at least Western men—seem to be very, very afraid of the necessary residue of their own female elements. They're scared of the feminine in themselves.

V: *Elsa, you mentioned that when you started out as a child, a young woman, you had a feeling of being alone. Has that feeling ever left you?*

E: I think it is still there. And I think it will always be there to some extent. There's always been a rather deep sense of aloneness. Even in love. Maybe it's just my temperament. But on the other hand, I've had endless friends, I must say. Beautiful friends, and loving friends. But there always seems to be an area where you don't touch.

I think it's temperament. I tend to feel alone and separate in crowds, even if I enjoy them. Don't get the impression that I don't enjoy people; I do very much and always have. But I've always had a rather deep sense of the solitude of the human individual in the cosmos. I have felt probably less alone and separate in nature, and with nature, than any other time. A lot of poets and artists always feel like stepchildren of society, in a way. We don't necessarily fit in, because the majority of people have different concerns.

N: *How do you feel about what's going on today within the lesbian and feminist culture?*

E: It's utterly wonderful! I often stop and think how different my life would have been if some of this courage and openness had occurred earlier. It's impossible to really visualize or imagine that, but it would have been entirely different, obviously. With all my heart, I hope that women never retreat from the re-emerging vision of our dignity and spiritual power. It goes far beyond sexual orientation and belongs to all women. That is why I hope to see trivial prejudices with respect to some personal and private predilections swept aside: so that we can get on with helping to make life better for everybody.

Rick

PETER: *What are some of your recollections of your child-hood?*

RICK: When I was about six my family moved to a small town in Oklahoma. We lived there for three or four years, and I remember it as being a very negative period. I was very much overweight, not at all a part of the community. I didn't belong. I'm sure much of it was my own projection—almost wanting to be rejected, and therefore I was. I had some early sexual relations with other little boys—mostly show-and-tell situations. But then at nine my family moved to a farm again, and within a year I met Joe, with whom I fell in love. I was ten, I guess, and Joe was twelve.

P: *How did you meet him?*

R: I think it was in the school bus. I first became aware there were four or five other kids getting off at the same place I did. And he was everything that I wanted to be physically and felt that I wasn't—dark and handsome, with great athletic ability.

Across the road from where we lived there was a fairly wealthy individual who had a lake and a little private boat. Joe and I went over one night to go swimming in the lake. We didn't bother to wear bathing suits or anything—of course, it was night and dark, and we were in the water. We climbed up in the boat, and I just reached over and took hold of him and kissed him on one shoulder.

P: *So it didn't even begin as normal adolescent games. The fact that you kissed him seems to me to be unique. I mean, young adolescent boys don't kiss each other. How do you think your feelings differed then from sex with other boys—doctors, circle jerks, or whatever?*

R: Well, I can remember doing things like that with other little boys—and maybe a little mutual masturbation. But with Joe it was different.

P: *Immediately?*

R: Yes. There was an incredibly strong attraction. He was really a Greek god for me. I finally went on the football team when we were in high school, primarily to do his homework—to see to it that he was eligible to play.

P: *Were you particularly affectionate?*

R: Ah, yes. A lot of oral sex, a lot of touching—a great deal of touching. Something that I carry through as a part of me today in that I like to touch people and be touched. We rode horseback a lot; we worked together a lot to earn money, and we drank fairly heavily.

P: *So how long did the two of you continue this relationship?*

R: Ten years.

P: *My God! Was it always a secret between the two of you?*

R: Yes. It's interesting to me that I didn't realize that the society would have quite as much of a problem with it as they did, and yet I obviously knew enough to know you didn't tell anyone about it.

But at seventeen he married a young woman who lived on the corner between our two homes and . . . well, backing up a bit, she first came into his life when I was about fifteen. They began to date, and then of a night I would sit up on the hill and wait for him to walk her home, and then he would come back and we would go to the nearby barn. We had sex almost every day for those years.

P: *Didn't anyone discover your secret in all that time?*

R: Not until after I was married. But before that . . . when he got married that was a real problem for me to deal with, so I went into the service—partly, I think, as a way of striking back.

P: *Do you think he was genuinely attracted to women?*

R: Yes. I don't think it was a feigned thing for women. I don't think he ever stopped to realize that what we were doing was gay. We were just doing what felt good and natural. I think that if there had not been such strong pressures on him to be straight, he would have been able to have lived and loved with me for years and never had any problems with it at all. Had he moved away from that environment, had he not been going with a girl who became pregnant, probably we would have lived out life together as a gay life. But he got married because that was what boys were supposed to do when girls got pregnant.

And then, coming home one time on leave, I met a young woman from a wealthy family, and we began to go together. I thought, "I've finally grown up and become like all the other kids I've grown up with." I was going to be straight. So we got married. I told my wife before we were married all about Joe and about the other fellows I had met in the service. Like so many women, she assumed that once we were married and living together, that would take care of all the sexual needs that I had. That, of course, wasn't the case.

P: *Do you think that your relationship with Joe had anything to do with your being gay? Or the other way around?*

R: Umm . . . no. He didn't create the attraction in me for boys. That was there before he came along. He just made life a lot nicer to live during a particular time of it.

P: *When you were in the service did you have much gay sex?*

R: Yes, a lot. I met a lot of other fellows and discovered that, rather than being in an isolated situation, I was one of thousands of gay people in the world. I met a lot of older gay men who took me to theaters and movies, and bought me clothes, and helped me learn what kind of colors go together and what knife and fork to use. A lot of socialization that normally occurs in the home took place for me as older gay fellows did these things for me. I found out that a lot of life out there was like I thought it would be. As a kid from a rural family, what I saw around me was not the kind of life I wanted. I knew that there was a world out there where exciting people did interesting things, and I wanted to do those kinds of things, and I didn't want to live in Oklahoma. I came home on leave one time, and my mother asked when I was going to bring a girl home. I told her that I probably never would. If I were lucky, I would bring home another boy sometime, but not a girl. I wasn't really prepared for her inability to really understand. I obviously naively assumed that somehow my parents would be supportive, but they weren't. Although my mother wasn't terribly critical, my father understood less than she. He, like most fathers, assumed that the other boy had been the aggressor and that I'd been the passive bystander. I tried to make them understand that everything that had happened had happened as a result of my wanting it to happen, and determining that it was going to happen, and making it happen. He probably grappled as well as the average father would. They just didn't deal with it very much at all.

P: *Your description of your relationship with Joe sounds very apple pie and American somehow. Just like a Norman Rockwell painting except, instead of a boy and a girl up on the hill, there are two boys.*

R: Well, I think about going through four years of service having his picture set out on my foot locker where other kids had their girls' pictures. Of course, you told everybody this was your friend—at a time when this just wasn't done. It blows my mind looking back at it. To think of the things I was audacious enough to do and just assume that nobody would be disturbed. Amazingly enough, for me it was all right in most of the situations. If you are naive enough to assume that people are going to be friendly and loving and accepting, lots of times they are.

P: *Why do you think you got married if you were basically gay?*

R: Peter, I think probably one of the reasons—if not the principal reason—why I got married was that I hadn't received any support for my gayness at all. My folks didn't give me support. There was no support from the Church. There wasn't any encouragement for my making it with the young man that I had already loved, or for trying to find some other man. Everything around me told me that ordinary little boys grow up to meet ordinary normal little girls and get married. That's the way it's done. There isn't any other alternative.

Then when this gentle woman came along whom I liked very much, and liked her family . . . I guess it was a sigh of relief— I really am normal after all.

But we didn't have any premarital intercourse. I've always felt that was most unfortunate. Once we were married and began to have intercourse, I discovered what a terrible mistake that had been. Like something was missing. You can only go so far in fantasizing and being able to convince yourself that what you're doing is really rewarding. If you've never really had good sex, I guess you might be able to make that period of time last longer, maybe indefinitely. But I had had really good, satisfying sex with a man. I knew what that was all about, and I knew what I was having with her differed drastically from that. I was limited as to how long my desire to be a successful husband could overcome the desire to be fulfilled sexually. That lasted for almost five years before I was able to say, "I want to get out. This is not going anywhere for anyone."

P: *So she thought she'd cure you? Do you think that ever works?*

R: Oh, you may have some people who have enough of a component of bisexuality in them so that, if it's encouraged and developed, the person may be able to sublimate the homosexual aspect. In that sense, I think, a person may be—quotes—"cured." But if you're basically homosexual, as I seem to be, there's just no way. The only thing you could do is deny it, pretend that it's not there, convince yourself that you're just not going to have any sex life. In that sense, one can be cured. I question, though, the cost of the "cure."

But I think my wife began to realize that despite her beliefs about marrying me, it wouldn't work. At that time, my father-in-law found out I was gay, and he couldn't cope with it. He was a very strong man who had never had a son, and I was "his boy"; I was the son he had wanted all those years. He had all of the hopes and expectations that I would eventually take over the corporation. He had great difficulty with the fact that his "son" liked other boys, so they were looking for a doctor who would cure me. It all wound up with my mother- and father-in-law going to my parents and telling them that unless they signed papers to have me treated in a mental sanatorium, they would have me committed to the state mental hospital—the insane asylum, literally. When I first went to see the doctor in the sanatorium, he told me, "Well, we could castrate you, but let's try some treatments and see what we can do there." It's a frightening thing to have a man you're going to as a doctor lay that sort of trip on you.

P: *So then what happened in the mental institution? How old were you?*

R: I must have been about twenty-three then. I underwent a fairly lengthy series of shock treatments. That was a very frightening experience—ah, that's the understatement of the year. I mean it was a terrifying experience. You would wait for maybe an hour or two for your turn, and then I remember, with utter terror, how the clock would go, and you'd have people—someone would call the individuals, and you knew when your turn was coming . . . and how each time you would hope against hope that it wasn't your turn yet, that there would be one more time before you had to go into the little room. You would go into a fairly small cubicle which had a gurney—a bed—in it, lay down on the bed, and at that time they were using Ambytal or Nembutal—my recollection was most clearly of their using always the left arm . . . lying on the back with the left arm extended, and the nurse would come in her little white suit—uniform—and give you a shot.

About the same time that she was giving you the shot, the little machine would be wheeled into the room from where it had been used in some other room on some other person. And this little brown box was a frightening, terrifying little thing. It's a little innocuous box with a couple of wheels on it and lots of dials. And I remember the nurse playing with the dials at the same time that the shot is beginning to take effect, and I'm about to go out. That would be the last thing I would recall . . . just spinning wildly out of control until you lose consciousness. And you are aware constantly of this little box over there and what it's going to do to you after you go out. I just can't tell you what an utter feeling of terror it was to have that wheeled in and know that they were going to do something to you that you had no control over while you were asleep and out. My mother had bought me a new watch at that time, and I recall one time I had a treatment, and we forgot to take off the watch. We went to the jewelry store, and the watchmaker put the watch on whatever machine it was—he was trying to see what was wrong with it. The sparks flew from it—very visible sparks. The realization that this was happening to your brain while you were out made a real impression on me.

P: *How many did you get?*

R: I really don't know, Peter. It would be somewhere between ten and fifty—probably twenty-five, somewhere along in there—and again, I'm not certain of the number.

P: *What were you hoping to get out of this? Were they hoping they would make you a heterosexual?*

R: At the time, I don't think I had any hopes. It wasn't my idea to go through all of this. But at least during the periods of treatments, I was cooperating to the utmost. I tried to block out attractive men, to be unaware as I walked down the street that there were men who were nice to look at, who might be interesting individuals to get to know. To some degree I succeeded—literally blocking them out, not being aware that my world had these people in it too. But a realization—I'm not sure exactly what caused it—made me suddenly say, "What are you doing to me? And what's the price that I'm paying? What am I supposed to get out of this, for blocking out what's positive, pleasant, and a delightful part of life? And what are you giving me in return?"

I couldn't see anything I was getting in return. Because of my relationship with Joe, I had the belief, the knowledge, that life really could be good. By just being natural and doing what was natural, it *was* good. And I believed there was somebody out there for me, a guy that I would love and do all the good things in life with . . . an underlying belief that that was out there for me.

P: *You mean it was the fantasy that saved you?*

R: Maybe.

P: *. . . or maybe Joe?*

R: Maybe. I'd tried to play the game by their strange rules—I'd gotten married, I'd had children, I'd tried to block out men—but it just wasn't me. All it produced was unpleasantness and fear.

P: *It's ironic that the same thing that caused you to have the treatments saved you in the end, I suppose.*

R: The thing that caused me to have them, though, wasn't the gayness, I don't think at all, Peter. It was the other people's inability to deal with the fact—to accept the fact—that Rick happens to be gay, and happens to like men.

P: *I'm sure that there are thousands of people who went through experiences like yours—many less traumatic—who didn't come out well on the other end. Try to think a minute on why you did.*

R: I think the experience with Joe was a major part of it. That was a good experience for me. If it hadn't been Joe, it would have been somebody else, because I had the belief that there was a guy out there. And coming to California and looking for him, and being lucky enough—a year later—to find David, the person with whom I've loved and lived for the past sixteen years. He provided the stability I needed after the emotional roller coaster I'd been on during that year of looking.

(David joins the interview)

P: *What was your impression when you met David?*

R: I was aware that sitting across the room from me was a young man who looked very interesting and that I was very interested in meeting him. It was a place where people were dancing—it was a home. So I went over to ask him to dance, and he told me that he didn't dance. That sort of took me aback a little bit. So I went back over and sat down, trying to figure out just how I was going to get around to meeting this young man. As the evening wore along, and it came time to go, I let him get all the way to the front door. With his hand on the door, he was trying to look back over his shoulder at me. I jumped up and ran over and asked him if I couldn't take him home, and he said "Yes." So we went out and sat and had coffee or tea or something, and then went home, and it was very good.

P: *What are your early recollections of Rick? Do you remember when he asked you out?*

DAVID: Yes, I remember all that very vividly. After meeting at the party, we went out to a drive-in, and I rather immediately felt very much attracted to him. I had come out of the type of background that was very traditional and emotionally somewhat conservative, and I grew up with the expectation that someday I would meet somebody and that I would fall in love with that person and get married and settle down. I never had any doubts when I met Rick that that's exactly what was happening.

P: *Instantly?*

D: Yes.

P: *Like right out of a Hollywood movie?*

D: Well, yes. So much so that Rick said, "Slow down— you're going too fast." And he got a little bit frightened that I was so certain so early in the acquaintance.

P: *Then you sort of moved in together and set up house- keeping?*

D: At that particular time I was living with an unmarried older sister and with my father, who was several years retired. Rick had had ulcers for a long time, and they had finally got to the point where they had to be operated on. My sister was going to Japan for the summer, and she suggested that Rick should come and stay after he got out of the hospital. Some of the others in the family went down and bailed him out of the hospital, brought him home, and he became a member of the household through the summertime—and never left.

P: *Were they aware of your relationship?*

D: Well, yes, they just surmised. My brother knew that I was gay, and I'm sure they knew that Rick was gay, and they knew what our relationship was. We are very much a family unit. I have nine brothers and sisters, and whatever you do is accepted within the family, and anyone you bring into the group immediately becomes a part of the family. It's been a very significant factor in my life, and in our life together.

P: *Rick, how did your family feel about it?*

R: I was going to say, from my side, my family were put on notice, if you will, if they wanted to relate to me and to have me be a part in their lives, that I was married to David, and that was the only way in which I existed as a person. I was not a unit anymore, but I was a part of a unit—the other half being David.

P: *Do you follow traditional roles?*

D: To begin with, there are changing patterns in heterosexual lifestyles too, at the present time. But we don't follow the traditional man-wife roles. That's one of the advantages of being a same-sex couple. There are no expectations that one of you is going to do the housework and one of you is going to repair the car. There are no set roles. Some of the things in maintaining a life together come easier for one, as opposed to the other one, so naturally we divide chores up, and the things that both of us find unpleasant we share. As far as sexual activity goes, there's no one person who is supposed to be dominant and one person who's supposed to be passive. Over the years our sex roles have been varied, to say the least.

P: *How about monogamy?*

R: I've never accepted the wisdom of monogamy and certainly not the requirement that it be the *sine qua non* of a relationship for it to be successful. It doesn't feel comfortable for me; there are needs that I have that are not met in the one-and-one relationship. I've never felt that "I love you" means that "I own you" means that "I have a wall around you," that "I'm the only one that has a key to that wall." That's not what love has anything to do with.

P: *How was the decision made that you would both go into the same profession?*

D: When I first met Rick I was already a member of the California State Bar, and Rick had some college work—but a long way to go before completing college. We just decided that we'd have a better chance of making it together if both of us had similar backgrounds, and that he should go back to college. I just said to him, "What did you always want to do?" He said, "I've always wanted to teach Spanish—that's been my first love." I said, "Fine, then you should get a degree in Spanish." He proceeded to do that, and then went to Spain and studied for a year and came back and taught Spanish in the public schools in Sacramento for a couple of years. Then he decided, as we became more and more politically aware and active, that he could do more for gay liberation if he were a member of the legal profession. So he went to law school at Davis, and when I had an opportunity to take a position as an attorney for the San Francisco Neighborhood Legal Assistance Foundation under the Office of Economic Opportunity, we moved down here.

P: *How about your law practices. Are they different?*

D: In the subject matter we deal with. Rick does criminal law almost exclusively for our office of five lawyers; I do a variety of civil cases.

P: *Is the office exclusively gay?*

D: No.

P: *Both in and out of your practice, you spend a lot of your time on gay rights. Rick, you seem pretty much without bitterness about your early experiences. Is that true? I would have a hard time not being extremely angry about that.*

R: Maybe I am angry, but the anger has taken the form of being strong, of saying that I am me, that I'm going to be me and do the things that I know are worthwhile. And if you—

straight world—if your world doesn't have room for gay people out there, can't accept that, then *you've* got a problem. And you're going to have a real battle on your hands with me. Because I'm not fighting just for me, I'm fighting for all those other people who may be too frightened or too timid or who, for whatever reason, haven't been lucky enough to feel good about who they are. I'm angry in that sense. And the anger comes out anytime I hear gay people put down, oppressed in the thousand ways that they are oppressed in this society, by people who are just uncomfortable with their own straightness.

Pam and Rusty

NANCY: *Why don't you tell me about your marriage, Pam.*

PAM: I was seventeen and pregnant when we got married.
He was in the navy at the time. I loved him very much. I
thought he was a typical Prince Charming, but when you're
seventeen, everything is Prince Charming, I guess, really. He
was comfortable to be with and very gentle and understanding. But after we were married, things changed. Actually, it
was kind of cute. He either called me a nymphomaniac or
said I was frigid. And I couldn't figure out how I could be
both. One or the other I'd buy. I mean, I don't mind being
cold, but when you live with a man, and after six months he
doesn't even turn over to kiss you goodnight, I guess you could
be called frigid. I don't mind being Boston in the parlor and
French in the bedroom, but just let me know what you want.
I was three months pregnant with my second child when he
left, when he walked out. We'd been married a little over
fifteen months. He was too young to settle down, and he
wasn't ready for children. I think he is just now growing up;
he's thirty-one and working on his third marriage. He left his
second wife when she came home from the hospital with
their first son.

N: *So he essentially deserted you. How did that make
you feel?*

P: Oh, it's bad enough to be in a situation trying to support your two children and have no means of support except
to go begging to your parents, but it's another thing when a
man has completely destroyed every belief you had of your
self-worth. I mean, after all the time we had been together,
by the time he got through with me I was not only convinced
that I was a lousy woman but a bad lover, a funky mother,
and no damn good to anybody for anything. And that took a
long time. If I hadn't had some really nice friends, I would
have been over the edge somewhere. But I had the kids, and
that's the only thing that kept me going.

I needed a babysitter, so I told the Avon Lady, "If you know
anybody that wants to take care of kids, that loves kids, I
need a good one." She introduced us. I called up Rusty and

she came over. She was fine people—warm, friendly—and I didn't think I had a thing to worry about with the kids. She was very capable—a little bit on the shy side and very withdrawn, but a very warm person. She was lonely, and so was I. And her husband didn't get home until very late at night. So I'd come rushing home from work to somebody who was probably my best friend after about the first five hours I'd known her. And we just sat and rapped and rapped and fed the kids, and after they'd had their bath and everything, we'd have a very enjoyable evening. And it was too late for me to go home, so I'd bed down on the couch. We went on like that for weeks sometimes.

N: *Rusty, tell me something about your marriage.*

RUSTY: I had been working in Tahoe as a change girl, even though I was a little bit young. He was in the service, and he called me from San Diego. Being young and living in an atmosphere in Tahoe that was really fast, I just took up one day and split. I went down to San Diego, and we went down to Mexico and got married—it was a few days before I was eighteen, actually. Then we came back to the States, and he was out of the service. We came up to San Mateo County, and right away my children started being born.

When I left my husband, I just simply . . . . We had had an argument, quite involved; it doesn't need to be gone into. On a Sunday evening he came back to the house after sobering up a bit and was having a cup of coffee, and I just walked into the kitchen and said, "Tomorrow, when you go to work, I'm leaving, and I'm never coming back!" and that's exactly what I did. I walked out with the children and about half of our clothing, and that's all I took. And I left. I don't have anything against the man. I mean, he's a nice guy. We just had a nothing marriage for ten years—and four children later.

N: *Let's get back to your story, Pam.*

P: So we were first together as friends. Then New Year's Eve—the first year we had known each other—Rusty had a

party. Everyone was kissing everybody, and I went into the kitchen where she was cleaning up or taking in some dishes or an ashtray or something and said, "Happy New Year, Sweetheart," and gave her a big lip lock. I thought she was going to pass out! I really didn't mean it any other way than how I greet you or anybody else who comes into my house. That's just the way I am. I'm a very forward and very affectionate person, always have been. But I guess that's what started her bright eyes.

N: *Rusty, did you have a crush on her before then?*

RUSTY: Oh, absolutely. From the minute after I met her. I thought she knew everything right then and there. All that time I had a very severe crush on Pam, very severe. And yet we had no contact until one night I just . . . my husband and I hadn't been getting along for several months before I even met Pam. I just told him that I was leaving, and I wasn't coming back. And I did exactly that. I left with the children and moved in with Pam.

P: We had been friends for a good time, and I had her move in with me because of the way her husband was treating the kids. When she finally told me, you know, what she was thinking, I told her she was sick. I really couldn't understand it. I said, "Sweetheart, you're just misunderstanding the fact that you've been lonely and you need somebody to care about and somebody to pay attention to you and talk to and be with. You're mistaking it for a different kind of love. Sure, I love you; I love everybody that I care about." I didn't want to hurt her. I figured that when she got this funny idea out of her head, if I didn't hurt her feelings, then it'd be all right. She'd be OK.

R: But I was realizing up to this point that any kind of gay feelings I had were really very real, yet very inexperienced. I mean, you simply don't go around and tell all your friends or the morning coffee klatch that you have affectionate feelings toward women. We had little enough time to spend together, and the time we did spend was spent talking, understanding one another, getting to know one another better. Pam and I have been together almost seven years now.

P: Seven years?

R: We're not going to go through that again. It's eight Easters but seven years.

N: *A lot of people might feel that you two may exemplify typical types of lesbian relationships—a butch and a fem,* *someone who's more masculine and someone who's more feminine. Do you think you fit that stereotype?*

R: Sure. We do.

P: You are more masculine in many ways than I am, and I am more feminine in many ways than you, but it depends on how you're going to talk about it.

R: When we were first together, it was almost a constant thing. I think what happened was that we really did fall into the heavy role playing. I was definitely in the very gung ho butch-type role, and I wore suits, sports jackets, and ties—and I even cut my hair so I had actual sideburns. With sunglasses and my hair combed back, I was always approached as mister.

N: *And you liked that?*

R: I didn't dislike it, let's put it that way.

P: It made it easier for me to cope with my new-found life.

R: . . . and of course then I was also getting into a life that was brand new to me, and the person who influenced me the most in being gay, outside of Pam, was a stone-drag butch. I mean, this woman looked like a guy all of the time. And I loved her, and she was my friend, and I stereotyped right after her.

P: We didn't have any ground rules. We didn't know how to play this game. All we knew was we were in a different place, and we had to find our way through it.

N: *Do you get hassled by gay people?*

R: Yes, very much. I've been approached on different occasions, and they said, "Don't you think you're being a bit masculine?"

P: "Phony!"

R: Phony—that's a good word, because they use it. "Don't you think you're being phony dressing in slacks and a sport shirt and wearing a binder?"—or whatever it is I do. I am not being the least bit phony. My only reply is, "I'm supposed to accept your thing, wearing no bra and a tee shirt and levis all the time, and yet I am expected to live by your standards rather than my own."

N: *Pam, are those pictures on the wall of your children? They're very cute kids.*

P: Yeah. They're all beautiful. Every one of them. I'm very proud of them. The family has always been my life. I've never had anything but family. That's all there is for me. Our household is kind of a drop-in for everybody who doesn't have family. You come around at Christmas or Thanksgiving or Easter and you'll find every kid that we've known who doesn't have any family, and you'll find probably twenty or thirty people at the table or around the tree. To be a human being takes more than water and sustenance. It takes an activeness in the mind, a feeling in the heart. You have to touch somebody. You can't just sit back and say you're the only one and suffer and all of that. You're not the only one. You're not the only one in anything. And I think that's probably how I felt when I first had gay feelings, that—God!—I was the only one. And I had heard all these bad stories about all these people.

R: That's probably the one strength that Pam and I have had from the very beginning. From our very first time in court, we talked at great length about what we were going to do. We could have totally denied our relationship and moved away from one another, broken up what we thought was a pretty stable home for the kids, but we really believe in where we're at. We believe in the love we have for one another. It's not just a stand, it's not just a crusade; it is where we are. And we plan on staying here, no matter what they try to do to us—if they took my children away too. Our children—we very seldom distinguished between my children and Pam's children until we lost . . .

N: *How did you lose Pam's children?*

P: Well, after nine years—six years with Rusty—my husband decided he was now going to be a father and make up for all the time and practice the loving affection that he hadn't shown the kids. And he took me to court. He didn't really charge me with lesbianism or being a homosexual, but it was definitely in the court.

I was very confident at that point. We'd already been with the county, and probation officers were fighting for us. All these letters and interviews were made by employers and our families, friends, and neighbors and all, and the juvenile people had said, "There's nothing wrong there. The children are well balanced, and everything is going fine." And I really—honest to God!—thought you could go into a courtroom and say, "Hey, look. You got two women and six kids beating their asses to death trying to make a living, give these kids a place where there is love and affection, and nobody's going to run out on them—someplace where they know that it's going to be a forever thing—and give them the strength to live and grow up and be individual human beings and have self-respect and be able to love and cry and laugh and do all the things that most people are so blasted hung up on they can't do them when they get older."

And, I don't know, everybody in the world seems to think that queer, homosexual, gay—whatever it is—is some kind of a goddamn orgy on the living room rug. If there are two straight women living together in an apartment, they don't call them names; they don't take their kids away; they don't do nothing. But had I moved out by myself, I couldn't have afforded to live and raise my children. Had I gotten a roommate, if it wasn't a man, I would have been accused of lesbianism. So again I would have lost my kids. So what's in a word? I'm thirty years old, I'm blond, blue-eyed, of supposedly high intelligence—if you want to believe those dumb tests they give you. I don't know. I'm just me. I write poetry, I do ceramics, I play with plants, I love animals, I dance, I draw; whatever it is around here, I do it.

But after seven years!—and he knew about Rusty and me for five years and supposedly was very happy about the whole thing. . . . But he was approaching it in the way, "I've been a real bad father. I haven't seen the kids for all this time, so now I want to take them back and make it better."

N: *And did you think up until the last minute you would get the kids?*

P: Not after they let us wait a full year before they gave us a decision. I didn't have the kids for that period of time. They took the kids the minute the thing went to court. They pulled the kids out. My son—my baby—had an asthma attack the day that they were supposed to take the boys, and they allowed me to keep him home for two days. And that was before we even went to court. That was when I got my papers. The county can do anything they damn well please.

N: *So when it comes to children, you don't really have . . . they were just taken away from you?*

P: Yeah. They were ripped out of my arms, as a matter of fact.

N: *. . . and put them in foster homes?*

P: No, their father took them. Richard was holding my arms and crying, and Johnnie had his arms wrapped around my legs, and they had to go. I said, "I'll do what I can. It will only be for a little while until I get the court thing figured out." I figured he never supported the kids, he visited an average of once a year, twice a year maybe. He didn't give a damn about the kids until all of a sudden, so why should I figure that I was the one in the wrong?

N: *Did you resist giving them up?*

P: No. I couldn't. It would have killed the kids. I had to make it as easy on them as I could. It's been that way since they've been there. I've had to make them happier where they are at. They know there's no way in hell I'm going to get them back now. But they keep saying, "You promised." Now Richard's going to a psychiatrist. He's lying and stealing and cheating with his dad, thinking that if he's bad enough there, they'll send him home.

You can't live a normal life in the gay world with children, because somebody is always taking pot shots at you. Somebody is always saying you're unfit, or you're sick, or you're not worth a damn, or you're a bum, or you're perverted. And all we're trying to do is say, "Hey, look, world. We're two human beings who love each other and are trying to get a good household for our kids and be able to afford for them to have some of the things in life that they richly deserve. And we haven't hurt anybody in the process."

R: I have outside pressures that affect me because I am a homosexual, but I do not have the problem within me, fighting this or trying to cure myself. I'm not going to "cure" myself because there is no cure for one who is not ill. And I am not sick.

P: God's up there. He knows where you're at. You're not crazy, you're not sick, you're just plain flat a number one human being, and honey, that's the most beautiful thing in the world. It hurts, it's happy, it's beautiful; it's like listening to a dandelion; it's gorgeous. But it's life, and that's all there is. You live with it, you get hurt with it, you may even drown with it. Any relationship worth its salt—be it a friendship, be it a working relationship, or one with your children, your pets, whatever it is—you've got to work on it. I mean, nothing comes easy in life.

N: *Did either of you ever think that you're wrong, that you're abnormal or something?*

P: I think sometimes that it's wrong that a relationship as nice . . . that has given so much fulfillment and so much happiness to so many kids, a stability and a family to two families that weren't stable . . . . My children hadn't had a father for five years before I met Rusty, and her children had a father but not a stable factor at all. They never knew one minute from the next whether he was going to be there, or what was going to happen when he was. But they always know that we're going to be here. And they always know we both love them. I think it's wrong that we would have to suffer because we're doing right things for our children and because we love each other. That's the only wrongness in it.

Honey, if I'm abnormal, I love it. I've never worked so hard in my life to make something work. I've never been happier, and I've never been treated with more respect in my life.

R: There are a lot of fears involved in being gay. Letting your parents know how you really feel is one of those fears. The second fear was being able to explain myself to my God. That was very hard for me. My mother and . . . I have one of the world's worst mother-hangups, because I love that woman with all my heart, and I have got to live up to a certain standard for her. I just have to. And my God. But once I'd made peace with those two people, there just wasn't any more fear. There was no more "You're wrong." There just wasn't. And these kids—these are one of the biggest reasons why I don't believe I'm wrong, because I believe that they're basically happy children. I think the good thing about this is that they will have lived with us. They'll know what we are. They know we love them, and they can go out in their lives and honestly say to their friends, "Hey, listen, it may not be your cup of tea, but it's their life, and they can live it."

N: *Do you think you'll be together forever?*

P: I hope not.

R: I don't think forever . . .

P: . . . because forever for us is only until tomorrow. That's what we came into this life with, and that's what I've given her as my promise, and that's what she's given me as hers. Only until tomorrow. Because I came out in life with very definite views about what I was going to be and what I was going to do. If you'd told me eight years ago I was going to be queer, I was going to be living with a woman and give up my children, or give up anything else, I would have said you were a lousy liar. So now, I say only until tomorrow because I will never say forever again.

N: *But you're not sorry?*

P: I'm sorry that we had to suffer for a beautiful thing. I'm sorry that my kids had to suffer because they had the best family relationship going. They had to give it up for a lot of the supposedly creature comforts—more money and all kinds of neat things. I'm sorry for all the kids in the world that would prefer to be in one place and can't be. It's a shame, and it may take two more generations before people can honestly look at another human being and say, "You're fine, even if you are gay." But I'm not sorry.

Pat

PETER: *Tell me about your childhood.*

PAT: Early on, I decided that the only way I could make much of an impression on my world or on myself was to be a great actress, but I really didn't know anything about that, so I decided to be totally different. I officially gave a picture of myself to my grandmother when I was twelve. I autographed it "To my darling Grandmother, with love, Denise Darnell," and underneath, in parentheses, I put my name in case she didn't know who I was.

My mother always said, "Well, Pat's ugly, and she's mean; but—Jesus!—is she smart!" So I had to be the intellectual, right? I would go to the library and check out all these adult books that I really didn't understand. I wanted to impress my mother that I was reading grown-up books. It was a terribly lonely period; I was an only child, and I didn't have a hell of a lot to do. I was always looking for friends, for people. I was terrified of boys. They chased you and beat you up. I wasn't really attracted to girls either. Loneliness was my whole battle. Maybe gays feel different very early on? I don't know. I just knew somehow that I was terribly different, an outcast. I think most human beings are lonely. And kids don't know how to interpret that. They're not prepared for their loneliness, so they think it's them. "I must be a bummer because I'm so lonely," you know.

P: *What were your earliest gay feelings?*

PB: I don't think I felt any gay feelings until I was in high school. By then my mother remarried. She was, I think, in love with my stepfather, and I was sort of left alone. I began transferring my feelings for my mother to one of my high school teachers. I used to go over and sit in front of Miss Blackman's house. She was my French teacher. I even read the book to impress her, but it was worth it—I remember some French, anyway.

After Miss Blackman, Mary came along. She was a stripper who got stranded in Davenport. She was a very plain lady and terribly cultured. Affected. She read Omar Khayyám all the time; I thought that was just great. She would let me go with her and pick out her clothes—which bent my mother's mind because she thought I had absolutely no taste; why any full-grown woman would trust me to pick out clothes was beyond her.

I would double-date with a girlfriend and two guys so I could sit in the back seat and watch her neck with the guy and get my kicks. Then I'd go home and practice with her. I'd pretend to be "him," and she'd pretend to be Mary, and we'd neck. That whole trip, you know—"Oh, Mary, let me touch your breast." Then we'd giggle for hours. Never occurred to us that we were both queer and fondling each other.

P: *How was all this making you feel?*

PB: I was in love with Mary, I suppose, in a first branching-out kind of way. I remember I wrote in my diary, "I don't know what's wrong with me. Women just don't go around falling in love with women. I guess I'm crazy." And there were big tear splotches on the page. My mother found that and, of course, had a semi-fit. But anyway, it didn't come to much. Mary finally got herself a lover—a guy—and had me write poetry that she gave to him saying that she'd written it—which was pretty weird.

P: *When did you say to yourself, "I'm a lesbian"?*

PB: I guess almost right away. I think I kind of wished to be. I liked the whole idea because it's like belonging to a secret society. I wanted to be Jack Armstrong, the All-American Dyke, or whatever. I had the certain knowledge all the while that no one would ever want me. So it would be groovy to be a dyke because then you could take the initiative. You wouldn't have to sit around and wait for anybody to ask you to dance, to have a date, to be in love. You could do it. That seemed to me pretty great. Like who wanted to be a woman, for Chrissake? Boring! When we were kids, we used to play Tarzan, and we were forever look-ing for a Jane because all Jane could do was lay there, right?

P: *Did you have any woman you could relate to for a role model?*

PB: I guess not. Except Radcliffe Hall and her book, *The Well of Loneliness.* And I didn't even know who Radcliffe Hall was. I guess I had the certain knowledge that most gay women have: that you are forever alone. Our parents hated us for what we were. You were divorced from parents, from family, from everything. You were just kind of out there. I looked for some place that I belonged. Always.

Then I decided that I was in love with this woman who was obviously not in love with me, and the thing to do was to escape into the Women's Army Corps. I thought I could go to Paris, where Gertrude Stein had been! Little did I know that I was never going to get to see Paris. I remember I went down to the Blackhawk Hotel in Davenport, Iowa, where the recruiting sergeant was—and she was just darling! She looked sort of like all my old gym teachers in drag. Stock-ings, little earrings, her hair slicked back and very daintily done so you couldn't tell she was a dyke, but *I* knew! I tried to show her how smart I was, asked her if she liked Carlos— I knew "L'Internationale" and some of the Spanish march-ing songs—but I didn't get anywhere. She didn't even give a blink. She didn't know what I was talking about. I had thought that all officers were smart and all enlisted people weren't. So I was showing off for the officer, and I got nothing.

P: *Were most of the women gay?*

PB: About 99 percent. It was sort of a man's role—being in the army. It attracted a lot of women I knew. They came down for their interviews in drag.

P: *What do you mean?*

PB: Wearing men's clothes—wearing argyle socks and pin-striped suits and the hair cut just like a man's with sideburns shaved over the ears—the whole bit. And they let them in like that—much to the credit of the army psychiatrists. They would say, "Have you ever been in love with a woman?" You would say, "Of *course* not! What's a woman?" sitting there in your pin-striped suit. I remember when I came staggering into the mess hall with my suitcase, and I heard a voice from one of the barracks say, "Good God, Elizabeth, here comes another one!"

P: *Do you think you were distinctively dykey then?*

PB: No, not at all. Never was, really. One short period. When I was first in the army I tried it, and I looked so weird. I'm just not shaped like a man.

P: *Was there pressure to look butch?*

PB: Yeah, there *was* a lot of pressure to look butch if you were. And, of course, you wanted to, cause you wanted to be identified as a dyke. I was never too good at it. It was frightening because if you weren't really like that, then you were acting all the time. And there was no way to counter so you could really be yourself. I tried running the baseball team, and the first time they threw a baseball at me I ducked. So that was a total loss. And I looked really funny trying to look like a man. Men's pants look funny because I'm very short-waisted and big busted. Trying to wear the short haircut with sideburns shaved over the ears, I looked like the missing link. So I would affect how I stood, and you learned to walk like a man (*gets up and demonstrates*) with a grim look on your face—that suggested maleness, somehow, being grim. Stomp, stomp, stomp. You always stood, if possible, with one foot up like this (*foot on chair and arm resting on knee*), and when you sat you'd cross your legs like that, not like a woman

crosses her legs. You had to learn to sit like that, and you affected the way you held your hands so you'd look butch. I remember holding a cigarette. You had to hold it like this (*demonstrates*), and of course you got a lot of smoke in your eyes because you tried to hold it in your mouth—I would cough and sputter. I remember sneaking into the bathroom and putting on cologne—cause you were only allowed to wear Old Spice after-shave lotion. And you had to wear men's jockey shorts, which never fit me. It was terrible. You were always adjusting the damn things (*shows how—and laughs*).

P: *Did the army know this was going on and look the other way?*

PB: Yeah, at that time, until they decided to crack down, and then it was hell on wheels.

P: *What happened? Why did they crack down?*

PB: Well, I think several officers who were gay themselves got scared. We got sent overseas—to Tokyo. The "Mitsubishi Main." We were all gay, with one or two exceptions. There we all were, locked up together, everybody trying to find a loved one, trying to find out about their own sexuality. You invented it as you went along from books you read, bits and pieces from your idea of what romance was like. You were courting a woman the way you would really like to be courted— with presents and perfume and that whole trip. It was fool- hardy. Sooner or later, the shit had to hit the fan.

When you went in the army, you were interviewed, you know—a lot of women in drag. Once they got you in, they decided they wanted you out. Nobody could understand that, since most of our officers were gay—and kind of openly. They. started an incredible witch hunt in Tokyo. Unbelievable!— sending 500 women home for dishonorable discharges. Practi- cally every woman I know who was in the army has a dishon- orable discharge. Every day there were court-martials and trials. You were there testifying against your friends, or they were testifying against you—yes, they had seen you necking with a woman, or they had seen you dancing with a woman too close, or whatever—until you got afraid to look your neighbor in the eye. Afraid of everything!

They called up one of our kids—Helen. They got her up on the stand and told her that if she didn't give the names of her friends they would tell her parents she was gay. She went up to her room on the sixth floor and jumped out and killed herself. She was twenty.

And now—twenty, thirty years later—they're still going through the same kind of hell in the army. They drive forty or fifty miles to go to a gay bar so they won't be seen. They don't talk to anyone on the base, and they date guys to fake it up.

P: *Did you have friends who were given dishonorable discharges?*

PB: Yeah, about twenty or thirty.

P: *Did you have to testify?*

PB: No. When I was aware that we were all going to get busted, I got out of the army. Before I had gone into the army, I had married a gay guy—he wanted to please his family, or something. So when I realized what was going down in the army, I decided to go home to my husband. At that time you could get out of the army if you were married. So I went to my C.O. and said, "Ma'm, I would like to go home to my husband." And she said, "You WHAT?" I produced my marriage license, and they let me go home.

P: *San Francisco, even then, was known as a gay town?*

PB: Oh, yeah. Especially right after the war. There were five gay bars on Broadway and dancing—you could go from bar to bar. The GIs would wait outside and try to beat you up. They got mad that they couldn't dance with girls—the girls were gay. We would announce this to them. "Go away, I'm a lesbian, I'm a queer. Get out of my life." We all lived on Bush Street in this old two-story house. It was a very exciting place to be, because, as I said, we were in bars every night. You never wanted to work because you might miss something. But you had to work in order to get money to go to bars at all. So we worked part-time.

I remember—oh, God!—Blum's fruitcake factory. You couldn't work in any office job because there you were in your costume. I was in my shaved-over-the-ears, sideburn stage, and you could hardly go down to work in an office in that garb— nobody would hire you. And you'd look pretty funny on the street. So we went to work in the factory. We got bandanas and tied them over our heads so nobody could see our short haircuts. There were about three of us. Nancy—a tiny, diminutive type who had to have all her clothes made for her, like itsy-bitsy pin-striped pants and infinitesimal suspenders with her initials in gold—even had a little itsy-bitsy tuxedo. She was barely five feet tall, very blond, with short, short hair. And she would stomp, stomp. She really wasn't butch at all, but it was a good act. When we got out of work at the fruitcake factory, we got into a cab and went to the gay bar. You'd rip off your bandana, and there you were!

P: *Did you live in a sort of communal way?*

PB: Yeah. It was fun because we were allowed to be together and to have fun and play with being gay and to put on our different costumes for being gay. We had a big loyalty code. If anyone said anything bad about one of your buddies, you took her outside and got into a fight with her. We shared our money, and if you came home in the middle of the night with a woman that you'd picked up at the bar and you wanted something to eat, we had a basket on a pulley. You'd scream out of the window, "Eggs," and somebody in the house would have eggs and put them in the basket. You'd pull up the basket and get your stuff to share with your girlfriend or whoever else you managed to drag home.

P: *Was there much role playing?*

PB: Yeah, we each had our own room, but we all lived in the same house, so we were in each other's rooms and were together a great deal. And some of the girls were butches, like Nancy, and others were femmes, like me. Everybody had their allotted tasks; butches had to do all the heavy work. They didn't have laundromats, so I'd wash the sheets in the one bathroom and put a board across the bathtub and sit on it and (*stamping her feet up and down*) read and wash the sheets—that was the femme's job. Then the butches would take over and wring out the sheets. So there was itty-bitty Nancy wringing out the sheets, and then the butches would hang them up. We femmes were supposed to be too weak to do that.

Femmes were few and far between. It was hard to get a good femme, because once she was around dykes for a while, she turned into a dyke, anyway. It was fierce for me because I didn't belong either place, really. I might have belonged more in the traditional women's role, but who needs that? If you were going to be gay, you wanted to be like a guy because they were the ones who could get things on. The masculine role was the one to play—to do all the asking, all the picking and choosing.

(Nancy joins the interview)

NANCY: *What were the differences between gay relationships then and now?*

PB: I think now the attempt is being made to be women together rather than man and woman. Kids today say, "There's no need for role playing in a modern society." But it's terribly confusing. The longest relationships were the butch-femme ones. They were the ones that lasted twenty, thirty years. Everybody knew what she had to do. Now we say, "I'm not butch or femme; I'm just me." Well, who the hell is me? And what do I do? And how am I to behave? At least in role playing, you knew the rules. You knew your mother and father. You knew what they did and what their lives were like. You tried to do the same thing; you got a house, right? Now nobody knows how to behave in a lot of areas. It's harder.

N: *Do you think if society accepted lesbianism, you would have a different sense of yourself?*

PB: I might become a great criminal, who knows?—something that was not in the mainstream of society. One of the depressing things about gayness being accepted is that we'll lose that sense of the in-group, the adventure of being different in a straight world, which was always exciting to me, anyway. You know, having your own language, your own terminology, secret places where you go. It was like belonging to the Elks, I suppose. I'll miss that a lot—that secret society.

N: *It makes you kind of sad to see that?*

PB: Yeah. I'll miss that a lot, that secret society—Little Orphan Annie's decoding society. Ah, I belong somewhere that nobody knows about. It's very secret, you know.

N: *Is there an equal trade-off? Are you able to feel more free?*

PB: I would prefer that we be accepted, yeah, because it carries over into your life. You know, how do you have a career? How do you do anything if you can't be yourself? I know we are oppressed by our society—good God!—the times when we've been beaten up, run over by the cops, persecuted by police. So many times. There was no recourse; you just had to put up with that crap—and being called names by the police, being rousted out of bars for no reason when you were just sitting having a beer . . .

N: *It's incredible to me that you lived with that on a daily basis—accepted it!*

PB: You had to. What else were you to do?

N: *What kind of toll has that taken? That's a number!*

PB: I don't know. I suppose it takes a terrible toll. You never—*I* never felt, anyway—that I was really worth very much. Whatever I did had to be done to make a secret little safe place in my life for myself, somehow. Without any help at all from any quarter, except perhaps my dogs (*smiles*) and perhaps a couple of very good friendships. That's about it.

What if the whole thing reverses in ten years, and we're all on some list or another? I was around during the McCarthy era, and it scares me. I was around in the army inquisition era, and *that* scares me. I just don't know about teachers coming out—and they are, you know—and people in the army coming out. And they are. I know they're helping—my God! they're helping—but what will be done to them in the future? I don't know.

N: *Have you ever come out of the closet?*

PB: Yeah, a couple-three times! I'm coming out now, right? Here I am on television. Big white face on the screen saying, "Yeah, I'm gay." Ah, it scares me a little. There's that little reserve somewhere in my mind of "Oh, I'm going to get swatted down for this." You know?

George

PETER: *As a kid, did you have any feelings of being different?*

GEORGE: Yes, I definitely felt different from other kids—
there's no question about that. I felt somehow—in the whole
physiognomy of my body—uniquely different from other
children. But also I felt like society itself was already bringing pressures—as it does toward very young children. Certain
things were expected of you. For example, I was interested in
journalism; I was interested in dramatics; I was interested in
student government—way back in elementary school—and
most other students weren't. I just sort of stepped out in a
leadership role early, and leaders are often lonely people—
as I found out later in life—because most people are followers.
I never could take that role. I always had to lead, no matter
what I got into, and I felt that way back in those early, form-
ative years—I felt different in that sense. And sexually—I
became aware that I was supposed to like girls. My sexual
orientation at that time wasn't too well developed, but I
remember in the fifth or sixth grade I was more curious
about boys than I was about girls. I wasn't interested in girls
sexually, and I was interested in guys sexually. At that early
age it didn't reach any conclusion except maybe a little
monkeying around now and then, but very minor—no more
than other boys were doing, though I can remember hanging
around a restroom and looking at guys' penises.

P: *How did it go later on, in your adolescence?*

G: As an adolescent, I was interested in having sex with
men who were older than I. In junior high and high school
and even college I was interested in men in their thirties and
forties. And I can remember being fourteen and fifteen, and
I would go out and seek sex with men in their thirties and
forties. I'd hitchhike to school and hope that some guy would
pick me up who I could have sex with, maybe in the car.
Even when I was ten or twelve years old . . . . Imagine a ten-,
eleven-, or twelve-year-old (*laughs*). You pick up a young kid
you've seen hitchhiking to school or something and he says—

ah, you know—and he puts his hands on your leg or something, and at least you know he is sexually interested. Some
guys just absolutely panicked, you know. I would have sex
with a guy, and then he would say, "If you ever see me again,
don't come near me—and I don't ever want to see you again.
Goodbye! Get out of the car!" and off they'd go. They'd be
scared to death. I always thought it was strange that I couldn't
establish a relationship with anybody. I was interested in older
guys, and they were not interested in having any relationship
with me. I couldn't understand. And it was never explained
to me until I was older that these people were afraid of the
law, which is very restrictive. The laws say that children don't
have sex. (*laughs*) And if they do, they are being forced into
sex with adults—which is a bunch of baloney, you know, certainly in my case, and I can mention others. So when you
talk about child molestation, what are you talking about? I
was an adult molester! (*more laughter*) Most people think
children aren't sexually active—which is an outrageous farce.
Where I was raised, in a typical small neighborhood, kids
were very interested in sex and very sexually active.

P: *When you were having that sex as a young kid, did you
think that was a passing phase, or did you know you were going to be gay, or that you were gay?*

G: Homosexuality was never discussed in school. I didn't
have any education about it, though I had heard about queers
and always considered them to be people who walked effem-
inately or had a limp wrist or something like that. They were
queers to me, and I never felt like I was one of those people.
In junior high I felt like I was sort of "sissy"—in quotes—
because I was doing things that weren't considered by other
guys to be the masculine things. Girls were supposed to be
interested in dramatics and public speaking, and girls were
supposed to be interested in art and things like that—things I
was interested in too. And I wasn't interested in sports. But
I never considered myself effeminate because I never had that
perspective on myself, and in my entire schooling I can never
remember once being called a queer. In fact there were some

effeminate males that I really loved seeing on campus when I was in high school because I could step back and say—not in an aggressive way—but I could say to myself, "Well, *they're* the campus queers. I'm not like them." I dated girls and went to a lot of school dances and was very social and had girl friends. As I look back on it now, the girls were like sisters to me, and I think that they felt that I was not really a sexual threat to them. We would just always have real fun together, and I enjoyed their company very much, but I didn't think about them sexually.

P: *When were you first aware that you were gay . . . that you were attracted to men?*

G: At some point in high school I had a buddy who said he went to a bar in downtown Long Beach even though he was only seventeen. One night he told me it was a gay bar. I knew what the word meant, but I sort of avoided it. I really hadn't committed myself to being gay or being straight or being anything but just me, and I didn't like to dub myself as being a gay person any more than I would dub myself as being a Catholic or Unitarian or anything else. I later went to this bar—when I was about eighteen—and I learned that it was a bar full of people all of whom liked to have sex with each other. It really opened my eyes. I said, "Wow! Look at all these people relating to each other, and they're having fun . . . this is for me! I'm one of these people." I really identified, because they weren't the effeminate kind that I had been associating with gay things. I was delighted that I had finally found that there are other people like me, and I was very excited by this. I think I sort of thought, "Gee, I'm gay."

P: *Did your parents know? Or do they?*

G: In a half-assed way, my parents know. I was busted having sex with a marine in an all-night theater at 4 A.M. — my senior year in college. The probation officer told my parents that I had had a homosexual experience, and my father, then for the first time, confronted me with it. He said, "How much do you pay these guys to go down on you?"

There was no money involved; I was the one going down. It was very interesting to me that he had that concept, and I confronted him with the possibility of his own homosexuality, because he'd been in the navy for eight years, and I figured he must have had some homosexual experiences. He became very maniacal and denied it emphatically.

One of the traumatic things about this was—I get very emotional when . . . here I go! . . . I get very emotional when I talk about this because . . . . One of the great tragedies in our society is that it doesn't expect children or people even in junior high to be thinking about and having sex, which they do. I mean . . . they just do. And you cannot relate to your parents on this level. Being homosexual, and knowing I was, made it even . . . you know . . . . If I had been dating, my dad would have liked that, as he did when my brother dated girls— or even fooled around with them. It was a big thing, and my dad used to joke about it. It was a very "in" thing, and it was fun and everybody accepted that—but I couldn't bring that home, and as a result I very early realized that I had to lead a double life.

Society in general did not accept me or my kind, and so, in relationship to school, teachers, to organizations, and in regards to my parents, I had to separate all of that. I was enjoying the company of girls, but my personal sex life was all homosexual, and that I had to conceal. That was a game that I learned to play—and a lot of us do very early in life— and it was a very difficult game. I found it frustrating, and it wasn't all happy times because I had to play this fine line, and there was no one I could confide in. There was no counselor I could tell—even in high school. I sort of fringed on talking about this a couple of times and immediately there was—oh, wow! I knew I was in dangerous territory, and I got off it right away and never went back because there was no attempt to help anyone like me.

P: *What toll do you think it took—leading a double life?*

G: I felt a great demand for respect from my parents and other students and teachers—and I got lots of it because of all my extracurricular activities and all the other things I was doing like service clubs and so on. But I also wanted respect for being me in every sense, including my sexual orientation—and that was a whole area where I could not get respect, so I couldn't feel like a worthy person. I felt like an unworthy person in that whole area, so it made it something dirty and degrading—something that just wasn't nice. I look back on it now, and it *was* nice. There was nothing degrading about it except that I was in search of my sexual reality, and I was forced into an impossible situation.

P: *What was the next stage?*

G: After high school I went to college. I got very involved with my studies and got interested in going into education. I became a conscientious objector and was very involved in the cause of pacifism—during the Korean War when it was very unpopular not to go to war. After I graduated I went to work. After my arrest in the theater in my last year, just before graduation, I thought it was rather obvious that I could not go into education with that on my record. So I withdrew and got a job in public relations with Coca Cola Company in Los Angeles.

P: *How about your sex life?*

G: When I was about twenty-three I met a guy who was about ten years older than I, and we really fell in love. That's the only person that I ever had a sexual and emotional relationship with, and it was terribly traumatic to me. He decided he wanted to go straight and get married, so he ended the relationship, but he ended up with another guy, and they lived together for twenty, twenty-five years.

P: *How did you end up in San Francisco?*

G: I felt the need to get out of Los Angeles, so I just took a Greyhound bus for San Francisco with thirty dollars in my

pocket. I didn't know a soul when I came to town, and I
wandered around, ran into a police officer, and I said, "Where
is a gay bar?" (*laughs*) He told me about this bar called the
Black Cat. And so that year I began to get oriented to the gay
community, and I used to go to the Black Cat every Sunday
afternoon. (*In this description of the Black Cat, George cried,
then pulled himself together, cried again, and laughed. Toward
the end, his tears and laughter seemed to become one strong
emotion.*) This was about 1952 or 1953, somewhere in there.
I found out that they had a satirical opera done in a comical
way on Sundays. They had an entertainer named José, and he
used to put on crazy women's hats and do *Carmen*—you
know, the opera *Carmen*—using these crazy outfits, and he
had a pianist who'd play. Like, Carmen would be in Union
Square, which is a main downtown park, and would be dancing around the park, you know, and obviously you knew
Carmen was . . . what he was saying was a guy was Carmen.
And then he would do Carmen with this crazy hat, dancing
around the stage trying to hide from the vice squad who were
in the bushes trying to capture Carmen. The best thing was
that he did it very deliberately, with a spirit of unity. There
used to be maybe two-hundred people would fill this bar, and
they would all cheer his satire, which was basically the beginning of gay liberation. The really exciting part was at the end
of each opera he would sort of informally joke with the audience, and in those comments was my beginning of my awareness of my rights as a gay person because . . . I get very
emotional about this . . . . It was the beginning of my awareness that I was not only a gay person but that I should come
out of my person and be in a broader sense aware of other
gay people and their rights too. Because José would say,
"Let's unite. . . ."

You must realize that the vice squad was there. At that time
they used to park their police cars outside of gay bars, and
they used to take down the names of people when they entered. They used to come in and stand around and just generally intimidate people and make them feel that they were less
than human. It was a frightening period. I am very stirred

by this, because at that time there was no place to go for your freedom, and you were very much aware that there was no freedom and that your freedom was in a gay bar, and when you got out on the streets you were Mr. Straight or Miss Straight.

But José would make these political comments about our rights as homosexuals, and at the end of them—at the end of every concert—he would have everybody in the room stand, and we would put our arms around each other and sing, "God Save Us Nelly Queens." I get very emotional about this, and it sounds silly, but if you lived at that time and had the oppression coming down from the police department and from society, there was nowhere to turn . . . and to be able to put your arms around other gay men and to be able to stand up and sing, "God Save Us Nelly Queens" . . . . We were really not saying, "God Save Us Nelly Queens." We were saying, "We have our rights too." José is still very much with us in the community here in San Francisco, and we treasure José to this day for making us aware in a lot of ways.

P: *It's ironic that someone basically in drag, who was in a lot of ways conforming to society's stereotype, was the one who really liberated a lot of people.*

G: Yeah. I wasn't really into men wearing women's clothes, I didn't really relate to that, but José could get away with it because we knew there was more to José than that—that the real José was not just making camp; he wasn't just silly. José was being silly with a purpose, and the purpose was to make us aware that we were worthy people and that society was wrong.

I have always thought that drag was great fun and entertaining, and I go to all the drag things. But I'm also very much aware that that kind of identity that a lot of people have is, to me, a way of saying that homosexuals are like women, because sexually they do some of the things that women traditionally do. So I think some homosexuals say, "Well, I am like a woman," and so they completely identify with that to the point of wearing dresses. I always thought this was bad—more so then than I do now. I was into the image, and at that time when the gay organizations had a demonstration, everybody wore a suit and tie, and the women would wear skirts. Everybody was to look middle-class and proper. If anybody had on an open shirt, or levis, they were shuffled to the side. They thought that was terrible for the image.

Today I have an entirely different attitude. I see now that cross-dressing and being yourself, regardless of who you are or what you wear, is very much the way things should be. I'm very much in favor of that. I think if back then I had worn a woman's hat and spoken in public, people would have been much more affronted than they are today. A lot of what's happening today is really exciting, you know—the women's movement, what happened in the Haight-Ashbury, the so-called hippie movement, the black rights movement, the Chicano movement—all these things have swept along at such a fast rate over the past ten years, and gay liberation has swept along with them. I think a lot of the credit we take for liberating ourselves is not entirely in proper perspective, because I think we're part of a general liberating attitude that came out of the black rights movement to begin with—and Martin Luther King and Birmingham. I think when the blacks refused to get on the buses in Birmingham because of segregation, that was the beginning of what we know as gay liberation today. I think that was the beginning of people saying, "NO MORE!"

So I think that when we were all together, like in the Black Cat, we felt that we were not oppressed, and we all played that game—and we understood that we played that game. But later on, some of us realized that we had to draw the line—that we were no longer really free at all and that we had been oppressed all that time. And what that does to you is at all times you feel that the world is moving for heterosexual people—that even in the schools everything is towards the family, towards raising children, towards things that are considered normal. This made you feel that you weren't normal, that

you were outside of society and couldn't be a contributing member, that you couldn't reveal your innermost things, that even on the job . . . For example, if you had been in a bank as a teller, you felt, "I really cannot advance because if I advance they may find out more about my life, and it will reveal that I am homosexual." So on jobs people actually accepted lesser work where they would not be exposed. And in personal life with other people—family, landlords, and straight people—they felt they had to play the constant game of not being themselves. We always had to remember that one closet door was there, and it was closed and couldn't be opened.

I think that most homosexuals pretty much thought that society was right, that we really were unworthy and something was really wrong with us, that we were sick or there was something depraved about us. I think a lot of homosexuals still think that. It comes out of this whole Judeo-Christian tradition that homosexuals are sick, and it comes out of the Church. I think it's logical that a lot of homosexuals would feel that they are screwed up somehow—that there is something wrong with them upstairs. I think that to this day there are a large number of homosexuals who haven't escaped from that period. Fortunately, some of us, such as myself, have got out of that.

P: *How did you?*

G: I think I developed in the Black Cat, and later on I began to develop a feeling that I was no longer a child, that I was an adult and a person and an individual—and that's not directly related to being homosexual—and that I had a right to lead my life. When I felt that, I think I just went out and did it.

P: *What gave you the strength to feel that way when most homosexuals didn't?*

G: Part of it related to my involvement with a gay organization. I'd been working at a factory for about five years (I work on an assembly line at American Can Company and have been there twenty-two years) when I had the opportunity to buy a house in Daly City. The former tenant subscribed to a gay magazine called *Vector* from the SIR organization in San Francisco. I started reading his copy, which still came to the house, and I got very upset politically with some of the things the organization seemed to be doing. I got mad and wrote a couple of letters to the editor, and finally I decided to go to one of their meetings. I was sort of frightened; I hadn't really come out as a gay person publicly—only with a few close friends. At that meeting I suddenly was very much surprised to find that I was on the floor speaking about this and speaking about that, and all of a sudden I found myself the membership chairman and then later a member of the board of directors. Within six months I was Mr. Gay Activist! For years, I gave my life to this organization. Literally. I would work full-time at American Can and then spend evenings and weekends down at the club. I finally burnt myself out. I got so exhausted and somewhat neurotic about things not going well that after about seven years I got out of it. But ever since I've been very up front.

P: *What do you do at American Can?*

G: It's very exciting in the sense that I am allowed the freedom to go in and do what is pretty much a rote mechanical job . . .

P: *You're not a supervisor?*

G: No, I work on an assembly line. I'm just like everybody else. I move levers that operate machinery and it's sort of a nonthinking job. It doesn't require a college education, which I have. The people I work with are interested in their cars and kids and sports and a lot of the things that I don't feel terribly related to, but I enjoy their company, and it's sort of like a constant education—a constant contact with the sort of world that I, in my personal life, am not that related to because I associate mostly with single men and women who are gay activists. I am not that involved with Middle America. Hundreds of people work in the factory, including a few gay people who I know of and others, I'm sure, that I don't know of, and we have sort of a camaraderie—a little bit of joking now and then. We don't all sit together but relate to everybody in the factory, and we all have our friends, mostly among nongay people.

P: *Do your co-workers know you are gay?*

G: Some of my co-workers know I'm gay. I have never made a secret of it. I have appeared on radio and television as a gay activist, and I have appeared in the newspapers with my name in relationship to gay organizations. I find that most people take it for granted that you're straight. If anybody asked, "Are you gay?" or implied that I was, I'd just say, "Sure." It's no big deal to me, and if they don't like it and want to reject me (which happens—there are maybe three or four cases in my factory where people reject me), I just say to hell with them. Who needs them? If they can't accept the total me, then I'm not going to bother with them.

P: *How about your personal life?*

G: I'm very involved with about six people whom I consider very close personal friends. One is a gay woman and the rest are gay males, but I separate my sex life from all that. Except for that once long ago, I've never had a steady lover. My sex life is pretty much occasional pick-ups, you might say.

P: *Do you think that's healthy?*

G: I've been told for twenty-five years that it's not a healthy thing to do what I've been doing for twenty-five years—and that is, I have been having sex with people without getting emotionally involved with them. I have been told time and again that I should get emotionally involved with someone and then have sex with them, or have sex and then get emotionally involved . . . I should have a lover . . . I should have a steady companion. And I say, "It's worked all right for me." I still enjoy sex very much. I still enjoy companions very much. Why should I judge my life on what society expects of me? On what a psychologist expects of me? I've got my life to lead. It's worked all right for me, and I'm not going to go bananas trying to satisfy everybody else. I'm pretty much happy with the way I am, and who I am, and I think the only times that I've had real trouble in my life are when other people tell me that I shouldn't be the way I am. (*laughs*) People are constantly telling me that I'm all screwed up, that I'm not leading the life I should be leading, that I ought to have a lover, that I ought to do this and I ought to do that,

that I ought to keep my apartment clean, and I just say the hell with all these people. It works all right for me, and I really don't give a damn whether people like it or not. Whenever I run across someone who is very judgmental about me, I just say that person must be screwed up or he wouldn't be so judgmental about me.

Happiness is a relative thing that you make for yourself, and I've made my happiness for myself. I feel like I'm a very well-adjusted person, but probably someone else stepping into my life with all their judgments would say that I'm a very screwed-up individual.

Tede

PETER: *Tell me about your childhood.*

TEDE: I was always told I walked like a girl, and I used to worry about that. We had a full-length mirror in the hallway, and I would walk away from it and look at myself and try to act like I had a steel pole rammed up my spine or something, and I'd try not to wiggle my butt. And I always felt that people knew I felt like a girl. Also, my pectoral muscles have always been very big—especially when I was fat, I had large breasts. I probably had the largest breasts of any child in school. I have pictures of me in swimsuits, holding my arms across my chest because I was afraid that because I felt like a girl inside that my body was starting to show it. I always loved it and hated it at the same time.

P: *What was your relationship to your parents?*

T: My mother was always my closest friend, growing up. What I identified with in my mother was her strength. She always told me that a housewife had a really busy job—you have to be a nurse, a cook, a gardener, a housekeeper—and all a man did was go out and get a job.

My father was mostly away when I was younger—doing some traveling job. He was always gentle—holding my hand, kissing me on the lips, being very affectionate. His energy, I feel, was very gay in a lot of ways, but he felt the contradictions of being in his father role. For the most part it was my brother who put male standards on me—he was into sports and was really a roughneck. He's eleven years older than me and used to terrorize me. He would try to make me count his push-ups, and he put a basketball ring up in the back yard which I would never use—I wanted to put a swing from it. My mother forbade me to have any toy guns, but one Christmas when I was five, I think, he bought me a gun. I went down to the corner and threw it in the sewer. When he found out what I did, he slapped me. He always used to beat me up a lot, and my mother would defend me. I remember once his saying, "He's going to grow up to be a faggot, but I'll make a man out of him," and my mother would say, "Well, he's what he is."

My brother and sister left home by the time I was seven, so it was like I was an only child, and I enjoyed the attention. I didn't relate to boys my own age because they were really competitive—I'd watch them beat each other up, try to knock each other off trees. I'd have much more fun climbing up a tree by myself than worrying about another little boy knocking me down. I played with two girls down the block. I would help bake cookies with them, and I remember the first time their mother looked at me and told me, "Boys should not do that."

Everything I was interested in was always placed aside for women—like music and art were always shown as being a woman's place, even though men were the ones to achieve in these areas. So I started thinking, maybe I'm not a boy . . . I was a mistake. I always felt I was a girl trapped in a boy's body.

P: *Do you still feel like that?*

T: No.

P: *Then what gave you that feeling?*

T: Well, there were two roles offered me. I grew up in the South—I'm sure it's the same everywhere. Well, actually, one role was offered me—the male role. And I didn't identify with that, and so the other role that was out for people to pick up on was the female role.

P: *Do you think you were lonely?*

T: Yeah. In all my isolation and not wanting to deal with the culture around me, I used to wear my mother's clothes a lot—when my parents were out. Occasionally I would stand at the front door and throw the screen door open and let it close real quickly. I'd flash out to the world!

P: *What was your experience like with homosexuals when you were growing up?*

T: When I was about fourteen in West Palm Beach, Florida, I'd walk around town and see these signs on the walls of the Greyhound bus station: "Meet me here for a blow job." And I was so naive I didn't know what "gay," "faggot," or "blow job" meant. They were always terms that little boys would use in jokes, but I wasn't close with boys, so I didn't know the terminology. One time in the ninth grade—if I couldn't get out of taking a shower, I'd always try to be the last person in, because the guys were always comparing size, and those of us who were fat were always getting shit from them . . . or those of us who didn't have as much hair or weren't as big as them—well, I went to take a shower and there was this guy who was on the football team. He had a hard-on, and he wanted me to give him a blow job. There was that word again! I still hadn't found out what it meant, but every time I would get to the point where I was about to find out, there would be a great traumatic experience. I freaked out and left. The next day a bunch of his friends—the athletes—threw me on the floor of the shower and started whipping me with their wet towels—calling me a faggot—and most of *them* had hard-ons.

P: *That guy in the shower came on to you, yet he accused you of coming on to him. What do you think that's about? Do you think he was gay, ultimately?*

T: I think almost everybody has homosexual feelings. But men who are more masculine have more to lose by acting out their homosexuality. To be homosexual means, in a lot of ways, to be treated like women have been treated—as inferior people. Athletes are always joking around in the locker room, and the context is always in a sort of rough way—there is this sort of violence like they are trying to push the other way, push that attraction away.

P: *What happened after high school?*

T: I went to junior college for about a term, and I started dressing up more—I started my Goodwill career then. That

was when the counter-culture was beginning to happen. At that time, people didn't know what a hippie was, so any man who chose to have long hair was a faggot. It made it a little easier for gays because people were more accepting of "freakdom" somehow. But my group of friends were all celibate in college—others were closet cases too.

At this time, my number came up for the lottery in the draft. I was in the peace movement and active at the Quaker and Unitarian churches. So I went to Boston and started working in a factory five to six days a week and living by myself and hiding from the draft. I felt really frustrated not being able to do anything politically, so when May Day came in 1971, I hitched up to Washington. This gay encampment in the Washington Monument Park was the first time that I had seen people selling the *Fag Rag*—openly gay people. I was really attracted to them, the way the men didn't have to relate to each other through women—they could be direct with each other. That's when I began to know I would be coming out; I had that feeling.

There was heavy action in the street and a lot of tear gas. A gay brother came into Dupont Circle, where I was, and he was gassed and crying. I took him to a Red Cross hospital and took care of him. It was the first time I ever felt free enough to put my arm around another man.

P: *Did you come out then?*

T: I went back to Boston, but I didn't come out for quite a while. I got into a men's liberation group. I told everyone I was asexual. There was only one gay man in a group of seven, and every week all these straight men would expect him to support them around their freak-outs with their women lovers. And then one week he had a freak-out. He had been busted in the bushes for having sex, and he started crying about being put into jail overnight and being attacked by these men. And the straight men in the group couldn't show him any compassion. And then me and this other closet case who was in the group went up to him and put our arms around him. This brought me closer and closer to being out. Then I worked at this radical bookstore in Cambridge, and a gay liberation group met there on one of the nights I worked. I started talking to gay men.

P: *How did you make the decision to come out?*

T: Well, everyone was telling me I was gay. I had some lesbian friends at the time, and I just eventually made the decision that it was crazy for me to cut myself off from my sexuality totally and say that I was asexual just because I didn't want to relate to women sexually.

And then my final big announcement! When I walked into my first gay liberation meeting, I got an ovation.

I was in a real privileged place in this country because I lived in a community where gay people already had a strong voice. So it was supportive of my coming out—I knew I could walk three blocks down the street and there would be a gay household; there were gay liberation meetings to go to and gay bookstores. This was a culture I could become part of, and it was political. Several gay men moved into my house, and it became a headquarters for a gay liberation collective. This was the most exciting period of my life. We used to go out together to concerts and dances and stuff like that after we went through the ritual of getting dressed and made up together. Before, it was something I just did on my own.

P: *The whole household went out in drag?*

T: Yeah, like female impersonation. It was flamboyant drag—lots of satin and rhinestone and glitter and gaudy make-up. It was costume. It was like a celebration.

P: *Why did you dress in drag?*

T: Because of my . . . identification with women.

P: *Aren't clothes a real superficial part of what a woman is?*

T: Femininity to me seems to say passivity and a real idea of where a man wants a woman to be—like a male identification of what a woman is. A lot of early drag feelings I had, and I think a lot of boys have, were around those passive female roles—and girls, I'm sure, act that way too. That's how society pushes a woman—through advertising, through TV. They're always helpless hanging on a cliff waiting for a man to get them. My wanting to wear women's clothes is representing something spiritual about me—that I'm female and male both at the same time.

Clothes on one level are very superficial because we're all born naked and everything anyone wears at any time is drag. And drag—what you wear—is how you want people to react to you, or how you want to react to yourself maybe too, because when you go out people are going to relate to you a certain way if you are dressed a certain way. Like most men dress in very drab, rigid clothes that are very utilitarian and make them look like they are doing something important—whether it's work clothes or business clothes. Most women are taught to wear makeup to appeal to a man, to wear clothes that are real restricting—like in the fifties, the spike heels and tight skirts. I don't see how a woman could ever escape a rapist.

A lot of clothes for women are bondage—girdles, brassieres, all those things that tie women down. So women are now starting to wear pants, starting to feel more comfortable in men's clothes, and men started reacting differently when women started dressing that way. It was a whole big thing when people started saying women are getting masculine. I know women who wear men's clothes don't go around trying to act like men. When I talk about growing up identifying with the female role, it's not so much identifying with the role as with what women were doing. A lot of that is playing the women's role, but I think women are much deeper than what a role is.

P: *Also, isn't there too little celebration in men's traditional clothes?*

T: Really! Men's clothes are so boring you have to be either a clown or an actor in an Arabian movie to dress exotic. I just don't like things that are strictly defined as women's clothes. When I was a kid, I loved Rudolph Valentino—I remember my mother talking about how she used to have a crush on him. I was always into movie stars of that period, or the ones who would play exotic parts, because I was always into how different the clothes looked and how I thought those people were able to express different things by what they were wearing—like being able to ride in a desert or go through a jungle. I wasn't really into the culture that showed dull American men doing dull American things.

Then I started getting more and more isolated from the people I lived with collectively, because they said I looked too much like a woman, and I thought that was a heavy pressure. What's the matter with looking like a woman, if that's the way I look? I should be able to look like I look and not have to grow a beard so I don't look like a woman. That was really ridiculous, and I couldn't understand it coming from somebody who was a gay liberationist.

Because of the pressure from the collective, I started living alone and got more and more shit and didn't have any support. Then I got more and more into passing as a woman in drag. And it started going back into the thing like before I came out—I thought I was a woman trapped in a man's body. So the more I got into drag, the more and more alienated I got from the rest of the gay community—except for the other queens.

P: *But if you went out into the streets in sort of a semi-drag and it was obvious you were a man, you got hassled?*

T: Yeah. I got stuff thrown at me and people yelling, "Faggot!" I lived in the ghetto. Just walking down the street, especially in warm weather when people were sitting out and drinking beer when they came home from work, people would take out all their frustrations on me. A woman or a gay man, I think, are the easiest people for straight men to take out their anger on—when I started passing more and more as a woman, they would treat me like a woman, so I was still treated like shit, but I felt more comfortable that way. I felt like at least I was having the freedom to live out some of my fantasy.

P: *Did you hustle?*

T: I couldn't get a job. I didn't have any skills. I was too scared to go into a factory for a job. Working-class people know that you're a drag queen even when you are out of drag. So I would hustle and didn't really like doing it.

P: *Do you think the men who picked you up actually thought you were a woman?*

T: I don't think it mattered really. I think some men thought I was a woman because a lot of them were naive. And some wanted to think I was a woman even though they knew I was a man. They just wanted to treat me like a piece of shit like they would want to treat a woman. Also I think a lot of them had homosexual feelings, and they wanted to know they were making it with a man even though they were seeing a woman. For some of them it was their homosexual outlet—they were married men and they took it as such.

About this time I started living with a lover and working in a factory. We both hustled at night. We were both heavy drinkers at that time. He had just gotten out of jail. He was a very macho butch, but he had a political consciousness. But it was your typical working-class marriage. We'd save all our anger and frustration from work, and we came home and gave it to each other. Since I was the "female," I got all the shit.

P: *Does that mean you were the "female" even in the kind of sex you had?*

T: No. It gets into an S-and-M, cat-and-mouse type thing where the mouse is leading the cat on too. And sexually he would want me to be the aggressor. I think maybe some of that was to placate his guilt feelings for the way he related to me.

I was with him for a year and a half. We started fighting, and he would get into beatings and stuff. We got into these real heavy fights, and I had never hit anybody before in my life—

especially somebody I loved—and it was very freaky. Then one night he was very drunk, and he knifed me with a cleaver, and I needed a lot of stitches.

I moved out to the West Coast, and he followed me out. It lasted for another year out here. But once I got out of that, I started teaching a male homosexuality course, I helped on the Vietnam street theater and with a street theater on Chile. Coming to San Francisco opened my eyes. It was like coming out again.

P: *How do you feel about children?*

T: Children are really important to me. I've done volunteer work at different day-care centers, and for a while I helped run one for lesbian mothers and other single women. I would like to adopt a child someday and help him or her grow up. It's really hard for gay people in this society to have control even of their own children. A lot of lesbian mothers lose their kids just because they are gay; I'm sure it's the same way with gay fathers. And so, at least now, there would never be an opportunity for someone like me to have a child legally.

But I know a lot of children who are between the ages of three to five, especially some children who are in the theater group I'm in—The Angels of Light. The children are very hip growing up around the counter-culture and the gay society. One time I was taking this one little girl to her day-care center. We got on the Divisadero bus, and there were about five boys in the back. They started making rude remarks like, "Look at the freak getting on the bus with that little girl," and they called me a drag queen. She turned around and said, "You know, you can shut up because I'm a drag queen too!" It was so amazing. She was really funny. And she says, "I always get pissed off at people like that." She's five.

During this same period, I was going to a dance class for a play. I had this Ken doll that a friend had given me. It was in a white-and-blue satin and tulle tutu with a Superman decal you could see on the chest sticking out of the tutu. These four little boys got on the bus, and I thought that they were

going to say something about the doll. It had a little pin on
its chest that said, "Make love, not war." They came up, and
they hit each other. Then one of them came over and said,
"Where did you get that doll?" and he was playing with it.
He said, "Why is he wearing that tutu?" and I said, "Well,
we're going to a dance class," and he says, "Where do you
get a doll like that? I want one." I was real surprised, and
everybody on the bus was silent and watching us, and I said,
"They don't come that way. You have to go to the toy store,
and the toy stores are sexist, so you have to buy the Ken doll
and then go over to Barbi's department and buy the tutu, but
don't worry, because they wear the same size." Usually I get a
lot of flack from kids, but every once in a while something
like that happens.

P: *How do women, especially the more militant feminists,
react to your drag?*

T: Generally women, especially those who haven't met a
drag queen with a feminist consciousness, are against drag on
men—for very understandable reasons. If a man is sexist and
in drag, he is usually more obnoxious playing what he thinks
is a woman's role. But historically, drag came out of a respect
for women—for the female principle, the goddess.

P: *Let's talk about how gay men oppress other gay men.*

T: Before I came out I thought, being gay, I would be able to express all my male and female characteristics—begin to balance myself out. And begin to bring forth all those things in me I felt were hidden. And so I come out and find that after the initial flurry of gay liberation, everything kind of settled back into this real masculine norm for gay men. Generally the gay men walking around on the street are either in complete leather masculine drag or they wear nylon air force jackets, and mostly they're in their short hair and mustaches. It isn't so much the way they look, it's their attitude. When I walk down the street or if I'm with any of my friends who are flashier, we always get attitudes. Like the other day my roommate was walking down Castro Street, and these gay men were making real rude remarks to him just like you would expect from a straight boy. It's real heartbreaking, especially to someone who's working in gay liberation and working for these people's liberation.

P: *How has your consciousness changed since Boston?*

T: When I was going through the period of being in full drag and hustling, I already had a feminist consciousness, but I would put up with more sexist bullshit—like that was my plight as a drag queen. Then I would rather be oppressed by somebody than be alone and depressed. Now I have more support—I'm around more gay men who have a feminist consciousness about roles and relationships. And we have a stronger sense of self-worth. That's something a lot of effeminate gay men suffer from—not feeling as worthy as masculine men because we are put down all the time.

P: *What do you see as the role of gay men and women in future political revolution?*

T: I think that this is one of the first revolutions—the one we are experiencing now in American society—where gay people are openly known as gay people. And gay people show that they can lead a revolutionary lifestyle and not be dependent on the nuclear family. We're working on our own personal liberation as much as on a mass level. And I feel that mass liberation is going to come about when people can no longer accept relationships of domination, whether it's a woman leaving her husband because she doesn't want to be dominated by him, or whether it's me leaving an oppressive relationship with a man. Once I start having the understanding of not wanting to be dominated by other people, I won't be able to put up with tyranny. Everything I do politically comes out of deep emotional needs. I can't stand rape in this country, and I can't stand it in Vietnam.

Nadine

VERONICA: *Let's talk about where and how you grew up.*

NADINE: I was born and raised here in Corrales. I lived in Albuquerque for about six years. In Albuquerque I didn't know anybody. I didn't even know my neighbors. Here, everybody knows me, and I know everybody. Everybody knows my business. The folks, you know, live right across the street.

V: *When did you discover you were gay?*

NA: When I was about eleven or twelve.

V: *Were there other gay people around? Did you talk about it with anyone? Was it talked about at home?*

NA: No. I never told the folks. They know. But they never asked me. My dad was always away working, and we never talked, really. There was twelve kids in the family—mostly older than me. I never really grew up with them.

V: *So your mother pretty much raised you by yourself? What did your dad do?*

NA: He worked out in California—during the war, you know. Maybe he'd come home every six months.

V: *So when did it all come out that you were gay?*

NA: Maybe I was about seventeen. There was a lot of gay kids in town, you know. We went to school together. I always felt a little thing around the girls. Little she-males, you know. Then a woman teacher told me about it. She used to take me out to play ball. We went to a party, and she got me kind of drunk—with a shot. Takes me a gallon now to get drunk! I remember her trying to touch me and feel me and kiss me, and I freaked out. I told my mom about it. She was real mad. So I stayed away from the gay crowd for a while. My mom more or less knew what was going on, and I think it hurt her a lot. If she would've asked me, we could've talked about it. But she never asked. She wanted me to talk to a priest. And

I said, "Why should I? There's nothing wrong with me. I feel normal." I started seeing women again when I moved out. I've lived with a lot of women—three, four, five years maybe. See? I'm an old turkey now.

V: You've always had what they call long-term relationships?

NA: Yes. I've always been with women. I always have a friend.

V: What made you move back to Corrales?

NA: Well, the woman I was living with just split the blanket. And I met Rosa, and at that time we didn't have a job or anything. We collected unemployment, and I knew about this little house in Corrales, and we've been here ever since—about four years now.

V: Would you say that you're openly gay now?

NA: Yes. Like, I feel free. Everybody knows I'm gay, and I guess they respect me. They don't treat me bad. They just talk behind my back, you know. I have all these women always over here, and the men ask them things—rude questions, nasty—you know men. It hurts me, but I don't pay attention to it. Like I said, they like me, but—what would you call them, hypocrites? In front, you know, they're beautiful people, but behind my back . . .

V: Do you have contact with people in town? Are you very isolated, would you say?

NA: Well, I have a lot of friends. A lot of people visit us. We don't go out much—like to the bars. We just stay here. Rosa studies, and I read or go for walks, go fishing sometimes, play with the dogs. Sometimes I go out and visit people; you know, straight friends. They're my age, married, with children.

V: And do you talk with them about your life?

NA: With the women I do, not the men. The wives, you know. They understand. They ask me questions.

V: *The wives ... do you feel different from them?*

NA: No, not at all.

V: *Do you feel luckier than them?*

NA: Yes, sure I do. Yes. All the way. For sure. In nearly everything—being free and doing what I want. I'm not tied down, you know. There's a lot of difference between straight and gay. I think it's beautiful to love women. You love each other; you care. You do little things for each other, and you always want to be together. It's not that I'm against men or anything. It's just, like, they don't care or something. One time, I went fishing with about ten men from here and my brother-in-law. I was the only woman around the fire. They were all talking man-talk, and I was in the middle. They thought I was just another guy, I guess.

V: *Did you learn something?*

NA: Yes, I learned that they're real nasty. All they think about is—you know what. They talk real, real nasty. Which women don't. I've been around women, you know. You can relax around women—and around men, you can't. You always feel something. They're always looking at you or something; you can't relax. You know what I mean? *Qué no,* Veronica? Maybe not . . . but, like, they don't come home from work and say, "Well, hello, sweetheart!" or something— "You look nice today!"—instead of "I'm hungry! I want supper!" I know because I've been around it—so I know. Fix 'em supper right now—"I'm hungry!" They fix it and wait— "I'm going to have a beer with the boys." Don't show up until twelve or later, and then they're mad when they get home.

V: *And supper's cold?*

NA: Yeah, and they don't like it. So they throw it.

V: *You don't have that with Rosa?*

NA: No, no. There's more love, more understanding. It's completely different. When I'm around my sisters, their husbands just take them for granted, you know—like, the women are here to do everything. They don't go to school. I go to school. They have the kids; they take care of them. The women are always doing everything for the men.

V: *Do you think that some of those observations provoked you to become gay?*

NA: Maybe. Maybe it doesn't have anything to do with it. But that's what I grew up around.

V: *Did you grow up in a very Spanish culture?*

NA: Yeah. We always spoke Spanish. But most of my lovers have been white—*gringas.*

V: *But you and Rosa are both Spanish. Have you felt a difference with her?*

NA: Yes, I have. I can relax around Rosa more than I ever have around my other lovers. I guess cause we're the same people. I can rap to her in Spanish. She knows what I'm telling her.

V: *Are you both Catholics?*

NA: Yes. We go to church. We go alone, though. Not every day; just when I feel like it. It makes me feel good. I just go to be real quiet and meditate. It's just a place where nobody will bother you.

V: *How do you think the Church feels about gay people?*

NA: I think I could talk to this priest and tell him about my life, and I think he would understand.

(Nancy joins the interview)

NANCY: *Do you find it difficult to talk about being gay?*

NA: No.

V: *Do you think there's anything that gay women can teach straight women?*

NA: Yeah, if you get real close and talk, you know. With the straight women friends that I visit . . . we have lots of fun. Once in a while they come up with a little wise remark—call me *jota* or something. But they like me. Sometimes they get real attracted to me. Like, there's this woman. She's married. We were both raised together here, and we got real close. One day she just came right out and asked me to have an affair or something. And I said no. I don't know . . . she's a married woman. She has children, and I respect them—and her husband.

N: *Did you ever feel like a man?*

NA: No, I never have. But older women—I guess they try to be . . . like men. I love being a woman.

N: *What do your older women friends think about you?*

NA: They sometimes make fun of me, cause I'm not unfeminine or something. But it's changing. You don't see, you know, young girls looking so dykey.

N: *Why all of a sudden has it changed?*

NA: Why? Cause I guess they think the way I think—that it's beautiful to be a woman, look like a woman, act like a woman. They're not afraid, I guess. I have this friend . . . I like her and everything, but I can't go places with her. She thinks she's a man. She looks like a man. She acts like a man. She walks, she talks like a man. She does everything like a man. But she hates men! Strange . . . And men just stare at her, you know. Every time we go out, she advertises it. It's not right . . . to hate anybody. I been hurt a lot by men. I mean, there's some that really hate you, like, they want to kill. I almost got raped three or four times. But I don't hate men.

N: *Do you ever talk to your friend about the way she acts?*

NA: No. I like her, but I can't. One day she was here and a cousin of mine was here, and she just says, "Well, didn't you know that Nadine dates women? She's queer." You know, I had never told him and, like, he didn't freak out or anything, but I didn't appreciate it at all. That's why I don't go places with her, because she tells everybody. I won't trust her to go with me to my aunt's, you know.

N: *But when people know because they've been told and it's not just felt, do you ever feel a sense of relief?*

NA: I did that day, I guess, when she told my cousin. And when he saw me the next day, he was just the same, like, he didn't care, you know.

N: *Did you feel better?*

NA: Yeah, I did. I guess I wish I could tell everybody around here—all these guys—who I am, but . . .

N: *How did you feel when you first came out?*

NA: Women, you know, were . . . just beautiful. But I felt, like, kind of guilty or something—like I did something real bad.

N: *Do you think you still feel that way sometimes?*

NA: No, I don't at all.

N: *When did you stop?*

NA: Oh, when I was about nineteen. I started feeling all right. See? I'm just me, you know.

N: *Do you have anything to say to young gay people who are just coming out? Suppose someone came to you and said, "I think I'm gay, and I'm afraid."*

NA: I'd say, "I went through it, and don't be afraid. It's something beautiful."

N: *Would you encourage them?*

NA: I think I would encourage. Like, my nieces . . . I'd like for my nieces to be gay, better than being abused like they are. I think it would be a lot easier for them to be with another woman. They wouldn't have all these problems, like I told you—fighting, slapping each other around, and being mean to each other, having babies every year.

N: *Do you think that, because of your experiences of being gay, you're stronger than other women?*

NA: Yeah, I feel stronger.

N: *I'd like to talk to both you and Rosa about how you met.*

(Rosa joins the interview)

ROSA: I met Nadine when I was a sophomore in college in Alamosa, Colorado, in 1969. I don't know how we got to be friends. Oh, we started working together, huh?

NA: Yeah, that's what happened.

N: *How did you become lovers?*

NA: We don't know to this day.

R: I ask her every once in a while.

N: *Was it providence?*

R: That's what it was, just destiny.

N: *Do you think it's important that you come from the same culture?*

R: When people get together, I think it's very important that they have something in common—common heritage, same faith, speak the same language, have the same kind of fire. Because for me it's too difficult to make it and stay together if you don't have something in common.

N: *Are you proud of your relationship?*

R: I'm very happy about it. I mean, "proud" is not the word I would use, but I'm very happy.

N: *How about you, Nadine?*

NA: Um-hum . . . real happy, for about four years now, *qué no?*

N: *Rosa, how do you find it living in the same town with Nadine's family across the street?*

R: Oh, I get along real well with her people—like, we're the same. I think her family knows, and I think they're happy for Nadine. She's healthy, she's happy, she doesn't cause them any heartache.

N: *All day today, people kept coming over. Do you think, in a way, that you're models for Nadine's nieces and nephews and all the young people around? Do they like you because you're different?*

R: Well, some people look at that difference as being too much, and others look at that difference as being far out. It all depends on where their heads are, cause we're good people. We treat everybody the same.

N: *But why do people come to your house so much?*

R: Because they're comfortable here.

NA: It gets heavy.

R: You see, people don't leave us alone. We're around straight people a lot—a lot of straight people—mostly cause we don't go out, and they choose to come to us. Mostly—and this is the thing that sometimes bothers me—people here and in Albuquerque and every place around come over all the time.

N: *What is it that you offer these people?*

R: I don't know. We don't even pay attention to them.

NA: Sometimes, the young girls, they just stop by and—"you want a joint?"

R: They bring us an earring or a little gift, a plant—something.

NA: Yeah. And they enjoy being around us.

R: I think they feel very safe with us. They don't have anything to worry about as long as they're with either of us— here, or at the bar, or at the store, or on the streets—cause I think that once you establish your identity and you know what you are, and don't have to be afraid of what you are, you emanate a lot of pleasant vibes.

N: *Do you think that your relationship has strengthened* *you individually? So that in a way, people come around so often because of the way you are together?*

R: I think so. I know so. It's a real heavy-duty world outside, and in our house it's real comfortable.

N: *Are you affectionate with each other when your friends are here?*

R: We're not. We're hardly affectionate with each other.

NA: Yes, we are.

R: Well, I mean not in front . . .

NA: No, no. Of course not in front of people!

N: *I've seen you snuggle up . . .*

NA: Well, not when we're around all those young people. I'm the old goat around here.

R: And I follow very close.

N: *Rosa, did Nadine, in some ways, influence your decision not to go to film school?*

R: No, she's never really influenced me in any decisions I've made. She's always left it up to me to do what's best for me. She's never told me one way or the other what I should do. I don't think I've ever told her what to do. We're very free people.

N: *You allow each other some space?*

R: Acres of space. . .

N: *Do you think that either one of you could have learned from a man what you've learned from each other?*

R: If it was the right person, I'm sure for me.

N: *You don't feel that there's anything particularly*

special about the lesbian relationship in terms of what you learn from the other person?

R: No, because love is a sexless thing, because you love a child and an animal and your lover and your brother . . .

N: *How would you describe what a lesbian relationship is?*

R: Well, to me, it's just exercising my own will, my choice, my preference. There's just so much freedom and closeness . . . women are very close.

N: *Have you had straight relationships in the past?*

R: Oh, little high school and college flames. But I was never comfortable. I always found the other gender somewhat rude and obnoxious. Not all, but most.

N: *Is there anything you would like to say to people who are just coming out or to the general public?*

R: For people who aren't sure, I would hope that they would find what is best for them and not be afraid. And for people who don't know or who don't want to accept it—well, they're just missing out on something. And for people who are gay, I think we're the best people around, because we're honest in what we feel and what we believe. Straight people would be losing much more than we would be losing by not accepting us.

Donald

ANDREW: *Where did you grow up?*

DONALD: I grew up in Dover, Delaware, until I was about eight. When I was nine, my parents separated, and I moved to Wilmington. I went to public school there until I was nineteen and then went into the military. My father raised all of his kids—all nine of them. But that's what he wanted to do.

A: *Do your parents know that you're gay?*

D: At this point, if they know, it's nothing that we talk about. If they would come to me and question me, then I would tell them. There's nothing for me to say to them about it, cause I feel that I have my own life to live. And I'm not doing anything to discredit them or the way they live. I live this way because it is the most comfortable for me. This is the way I want to live. My mind is satisfied.

A: *About what time in your life were you aware of other boys as physical beings, as people with sexuality?*

D: I think it came around junior high or high school. I can't remember the exact time. You really wasn't looking for anything. But you was aware of something.

A: *But you didn't know what exactly that something was?*

D: No. A lot of times when it first happens to you, you aren't aware of it. You pass it off as something else and keep on going. You don't know who you are at that point. You don't know how you are going to deal with it.

When I was in high school, I used to swing out with a buddy of mine and he was gay—much more so than I was.

A: *What do you mean by that?*

D: He was out—like, everybody knew. It was his actions mostly. And everybody knew where he was coming from, so a lot of people used to question me, you know, as to why I hung around with him. And I would rub it off with, "Well, he's a friend of mine."

My friend and I would discuss the fellows—our physical attractions towards them. We used to have our little rap sessions. But in junior high and high school, there really wasn't that much happening. Most of it was in conversation—like, if you saw a brother you could talk to him. But it wasn't to the point of trying to hook him or get down with him or anything.

A: *Were there other people you could talk to?*

D: No. Because like most of the guys in my neighborhood who I ran around with, they didn't know what was happening. It's not like you were trying to hide anything, but that your actions were different, or what you talked about was different.

A: *So you left Wilmington and went to Philadelphia?*

D: I went into the navy. I got to go halfway around the world and see a lot of different places. As far as the homosexual aspect of the military, I really didn't involve myself with that. I didn't look for it. My interest was to do my military time and to get out. I think the reason for going into the military was because I hadn't planned on going to college or anything. My father really didn't have the money. So I decided to get away. At that time most blacks were doing that.

A: *Were you active sexually?*

D: I was, but not with people in the military. My first two years I was stationed in San Francisco. And I was able to deal with a lot of people there as far as the gay community was concerned. I was able to go to a lot of gay bars and meet a lot of people.

A: *What did you do about the love relationships you had before going into the military?*

D: Love relationships? I didn't have any. Yeah, I dealt with people. I had people before I went into the military. I mean, it was just a hit and miss. It wasn't a case where you were going to fall in love. You weren't even looking for that.

A: *Did you have any relationships with women?*

D: Yes.

A: *At the time you knew you were gay and at the same time you were with women, what were you thinking about?*

D: Well, up until about age twenty-one, I knew that there was something. But I really hadn't said to myself, "Well, I'm gay." I really hadn't said it. I knew there was something; I kept knocking it, right? You know what I mean? So at that point if you was dealing with somebody, you really didn't feel that you were gay. It was just something that happened. I think I found out that there was more physical attraction with men. But I saw both men and women.

I didn't really make a decision until I had gotten out of the military. I had been married for the last two years. It suddenly dawned on me that I wasn't really satisfied with my married life. Building up to the separation was where I came to peace of mind, I guess. My wife and I had moved back to Philadelphia, and I had decided that—I guess maybe a year— I had really gotten my head together and decided, "Well, this is what I have to do because this is the way I feel." I had been fighting it before, and in fighting it, it was a head buster.

A: *I hear that!*

D: Yeah. You know, like you're just going against yourself, you know. And that's hard; it takes you out, you know.

A: *Did she know about your activity at the time?*

D: Uh, I don't know. I don't know if she knows now.

A: *I'm your wife. I find out that you're gay and you never told me, and I'm really pissed, dig it? Here you spend how many years with her and you didn't trust her enough to even tell her what was going on in your head?*

D: If I had told her, I don't know what her reaction would have been at that particular time. People's attitudes toward homosexuals were different then.

A: *How about with black people?*

D: Well, that's all I can be speaking about is the black people. But you see so much of it now. Like, it used to be that
you had to look gay in order for somebody to notice that
you was. That's not the point anymore. The person standing
next to you could be—and you would never know it. It's so
different now.

In 1969, you were only going to gay bars. And the majority
of people who were there were gay people. Now I find that
you can go to a gay bar, and you might find some straight
people in there. You can go to a straight bar, and you can get
into a rap with somebody, and it can lead to something else.

A: *You mean you might be able to get into a sexual situation? What kind of people are these? Are they known as
straight people?*

D: It happens all the time. They would probably consider
themselves straight. They probably don't deal all the time. In
the sixties if you said something to someone about relationships between two men, somebody might want to punch you
in the face. Now if you rap to a brother, if he's gonna deal,
he'll deal; if not, he will tell you nothing's happening.

A: *What do you do if you hear people make negative comments about gay people?*

D: That's no concern of mine if they make a negative
comment about gay people as a whole.

A: *Suppose someone was talking about black people and
said, "Oh, that nigger, they don't know what's going down."
What would your reaction be?*

D: It depends. If the comment was made directly to me, I
probably would respond to it. As a whole, there's no way
they can tell about all black people. So why should I get
involved in that? Cause it happens every day. A lot of times
you can go around knocking everybody in the head just because of their saying things.

A: *Here in Philadelphia, where most of the black gay men look straight, how do you know you are making contact with another gay person? Do you cruise other black people?*

D: You can usually tell. I guess everybody cruises in their own little way. Like eye contact—that's part of it. You make people aware that you are interested in them and in turn they do the same thing, you know . . .

A: *Do you have a relationship with a man now?*

D: Yes. I prefer a relationship with someone, but not as far as living with them. It goes back to being an individual and having your own privacy. I think people going together tend to be too close and try to start living like married people. As far as I'm concerned, two gay people should never try to live like married people.

A: *Do you still have relationships with women?*

D: As far as friends, I do. There are a lot of situations where—well, you should take a woman with you. It might be a party that straight people are giving. I would feel more comfortable.

A: *Why don't you take another man?*

D: Well, I guess you could do that too. But it might not be that kind of situation. It might be a scene where the rest of the people are married. Then you wouldn't want to come, you know, with another guy.

A: *The women that you take to these parties—are they straight, or are they gay?*

D: The majority of them would be straight. It's just that they know you are gay and that you are also a friend. But I know gay women too. I've gone to parties with gay women in the same type of situation.

A lot of times you go to a party, and, like, say it's a gay boys' party. There might be twenty or thirty guys there, and there's one woman, and she might have come with one of the guys or something. Like she's a fag hag. She goes to all of the functions that the boys are having. And, you know, she's just there, partying and dancing. I guess she's having a nice time. I don't see how she can, though. But she likes being with all the men. A lot of them might be straight women. Most of them are fashion conscious. Like, they would be dressed to kill and their face be put up, and they would really be looking good. Like, they would be looking like the front of *Vogue* magazine or something. Some guys carry fag hags with them. Why, I don't know. Some might feel comfortable around them. Or it might help their image out.

A: *Do you find that you are attracted only to black men?*

D: Myself, I am only attracted to black men. I don't deal with Caucasians as far as their homosexual aspect is concerned. Black is just beautiful to me. Brothers are fine.

A: *You found a lot of gay brothers who would date women, right? Do you eventually see them as having only male contact in the end? Do they like being with both women and men?*

D: I don't know. I find it this way as far as the black man is concerned. I find that women take the black men through such a hassle as far as dealing with them, you know what I mean, and I find that this is why the majority of them deal with men.

A: *Why do you think that the women give such a hassle?*

D: They do because it's, like, they want to be wined and dined, and they want to play a game.

A: *And what's the game?*

D: You know, as far as a sexual relationship is concerned, then they want to give you a big hassle about that. As far as, like, two men, if they're goin' to hook up, they just goin' ahead and hook up. They not goin' to go through all this— you know, the big hassle. Whatever the case may be, they goin' ahead and get down, you know, and get theirself together.

A: *So what you're saying is that they understand each other and what they want from each other. Right? Considering the way things are now, what would you say if a straight black woman approached you and said, "Say, brother, you are really jive. Blacks should be strong and be in love with their black women"?*

D: Well, the first thing I would tell her would be if she treated the black man different, she might not have that problem.

A: *What are your feelings about black "sissies"?*

D: Well, they have a place. I'm a firm believer that whatever you want to do, then do it. A lot have gotten out of the sissy bag and into a more discreet bag. They have found out in dealing in that sissy bag they really can't get what they want. Because straight males don't want to be bothered with them, but straight brothers will deal with someone who looks straight. As far as the straight black male is concerned, you could deal with him better coming to him from a brother aspect than out there being a flaming sissy. That flaming sissy bag—it's beyond me.

A: *What would you tell a young black gay person who was having trouble coming out and dealing?*

D: After they have come to the conclusion that this is it, as far as gay goes, they can deal with it as long as they are being themselves and doing what they want to do. I think that this is the most important thing—that they do what they want to do with their life. If they want to be a flaming sissy or if they want to be very conservative about it, then that's what they should do. If you aren't expressing those feelings that are within you, then you are knocking your head into a brick wall. You could never say that one is better than the other. To me, there's a place for everybody. Doing what you want to be doing will give you peace of mind.

Mark

PETER: *Would you describe yourself as pretty much always open—openly gay in the business world?*

MARK: Yes and no—I mean, I'd say yes. I've always been relatively open about being gay. Not that I advertise it particularly, but I don't make up stories either—you know, say I'm dating this one or that one, or tell stories about the lady who I went with last night. I never have, to clients or anybody else.

Part of it, I think, is that I came out very young. I never had the slightest inkling of guilt. I came from quite a liberal background. My parents were not conventional moralists in any sense of the word, and so I was never troubled by any feeling of guilt from day one. I never felt that I had any reason to think that I was less good or less acceptable than anybody else because I was gay. Never, from day one—even when I was a kid.

P: *Can you remember what your earliest gay feelings were?*

M: Yeah, it's really strange, I thought about it a lot. I came out when I was about fourteen. I was going with a girl at that time, and the guy who she had been going with before had been gay and had taken her down to the gay beach in Santa Monica, in Los Angeles, and so she thought it would be a hoot, and she took me down there one time.

P: *Little did she know . . .*

M: Well, that was it. I walked out on the beach. I was, I guess, a fairly hunky little teenager, and I walked out there, and the chicken hawks descended on me en masse. I got invited to parties and did things and met people, and people took me out. And I said, "Fantastic! This is for me!"

P: *Did you have fantasies about men before that?*

M: Ah, yes, indeed. I had played around with guys before. I had an affair with a guy when we were both fourteen in private school together. We came out and stayed together for six years. I have always tended toward long-term relationships, but at any rate I remember as early as six, seven years old, what I now recognize were really clearly homosexually oriented sorts of fantasies. And I understand the psychological reasons why—the particular dynamics of my own situation, the factors that led to my being gay.

P: *What do you mean?*

M: You can identify the causes in one person. I don't think you can come up with any blanket rules that are always true.

P: *Did your parents fit the stereotype?*

M: No, no, quite the opposite. I had a rather submissive—not submissive—a very, extremely pleasant, very feminine lady, who leaned on me a great deal and always treated me very much as an adult. And rather an extremely interesting and intelligent father—extremely cultured, wonderful man—who I saw very little of. Anyway, it gets very complicated. There were no horrible family scenes. Nothing of that kind of thing at all.

P: *Were there any homosexual models around for you?*

M: No, no homosexual models particularly. I had a relatively normal early, very early, teen life, dating and that sort of thing. Then at fourteen I was off and running. Yeah, I did have a good time too. Let me tell you!

P: *Did you have any fears about being queer?*

M: I just didn't think it was bad. I thought anything that was that good and that much fun and enabled you to have nice close relationships with people couldn't be negative.

P: *What was it like?*

M: I graduated from high school when I was sixteen, which was in the early fifties. It was very, very different then. In one way it was nicer. It was more naive, in Hollywood at any rate. You could always go down to Hollywood Boulevard on a Friday night at seven or eight o'clock, and there would always be a carload of people coming by—"Let's go to a party!"—and this kind of thing. It was very free.

P: *What about all of the oppression you hear about that went on in the fifties?*

M: There was oppression, but you didn't live in constant fear of it. At least I didn't. But then I don't take things that way. I tend to have a kind of positive attitude about most things. Of course, we weren't going to gay bars then, but the police would come in the coffee shops and roust everybody, make them move on—just general annoyance, that kind of thing.

In retrospect, it was awful behavior. I certainly would not put up with it today, and neither do the kids today put up with it. In those days we did.

P: *Why?*

M: It was before the whole spirit of rebelling and challenging which was born out of the late sixties. Gay liberation came out of that. You're talking about essentially revolutionary movements, social revolutionary movements.

I don't really identify with them to a tremendous extent. I find as I get older, that I am definitely becoming more conservative. As an ex-boss of mine who rose from communist to multimillionaire said, "There's nothing to make one conservative like having something to conserve." It makes good sense. You're more interested in preserving the status quo.

P: *Would you feel that your life has been at all affected by the sort of new gay consciousness?*

M: The whole corporate existence—you know, where your wife has to come along, and your wife is part of the thing, the entertaining—it's all part of that progression, and it's potentially dangerous, although I think less so today than has been true probably anytime—certainly than when I've been around. It's just that when you're gay and in that kind of structure, you can't take part in that. I feel that I have a vested interest in gay liberation. When I saw my first Christopher Street Gay Parade stretching for thirty-five or forty blocks up . . .

P: *Were you walking?*

M: I was marching. I watched at first, and I said, "What the hell! Join in . . ."

P: *Was it scary?*

M: A little bit. Actually, I was rather more . . . you know, my conservative side came through because I was looking at all these . . . these sorts of people who were, I thought . . . I was bourgeois enough that I didn't like some of the people in the parade who were being excessively . . .

P: *Excessively what?*

M: Well, you know, there were a lot of people who . . . ah, God!—I'm going to sound like a terrible rotten old conservative. I've never really been into this whole drag thing or femmy thing—you know, having models of giant cocks and people dressed in serious drag. I'm not knocking anybody's right to do that. That's fine, but at the same time when you're seeking public acceptance, the way to do it is to go along and make it more acceptable. At any rate, I was a little embarrassed by that kind of situation because I wanted to be gay and proud, and I was not proud of some of the people who were in the parade with me. But I stayed with it anyway. What the hell, it's certainly their right. They stir the pot and get things moving, and it filters down to people like me. It's just that extremes of anything, I think, bar or inhibit the broad acceptance necessary for change.

P: *Do you feel that there is a contradiction between*

working in the heart of the capitalist system and being a
part of a minority that's been left out of the system?

M: No. First of all we haven't been left out of the system. I don't see a contradiction between being gay and
working inside the system. Being gay and being a success
in a capitalist endeavor or capitalist society have nothing
to do with one another. We were never really inhibited as
long as we could cover it up, which doesn't exist with the
other minorities. With blacks and most minorities, and
women, there's no way they can disguise it.

P: *But nonetheless, you are sort of supporting a system*
that forced you to cover up who you were—or most people
to cover up who they were.

M: Oh, hell, it has nothing to do with capitalism. As a
matter of fact, a capitalist society is the only place I can
think of today where homosexuality is tolerated at all. It
certainly isn't in the Soviet Union. It certainly isn't in China.
Libertarian capitalism is the only kind of system where homosexuality can achieve identity. It's the only one that's sloppy
enough to allow it to happen.

There are a hell of a lot of us who have stable relationships,
who live well within the system, who are trying to achieve in
a quiet way—hopefully an orderly way—some degree of change
and some broader base of acceptance. I think that the radicals
are necessary, and I think that *we* are necessary. In terms of
coverage, we're less sensationalistic. I mean, who wants to see
Mr. Middle-of-the-Road? But, nevertheless, we are there, and
we're damned important in making the thing work. I just
want some people to know that there are lots and lots and
lots of us out here.

Another thing that's bothered me: people automatically
assume that gay people don't form close attachments of any
length or duration. And that's just not true.

P: *How long have you and your lover been together?*

M: Oh, Christ, since September 1962. That'll be fourteen years, I guess—something like that. Virtually all of my friends are in couples. Most of our friends have been together for ten years or more. They are people who live relatively normal kinds of lives, interesting lives too.

You give up some things being gay, but you get a lot too. You miss a certain kind of conventional family life. You miss the joy of children, that sort of family stability situation that occurs. There is a great deal of joy in that. I mean, I would really love to have children. It's one thing I miss a lot. You also give up, to a degree, the country club acceptance and that kind of situation. If that's important to you. It doesn't happen to be to me, but to some people that is important.

But you gain a lot. I think gay people have more fun than your average married guy in a home with two or three kids. You have more time and more money. You don't have the responsibilities. Like, for example, I can be "Uncle Mark" and lavish presents and things on my nephews and take them to the zoo and have a great old time. When they get tired and cranky, I take them back to mommy and dad who . . . you know, dad has just finished paying two hundred bucks for their teeth.

It's terrible for people who are still closeted. They suffer because of it. They don't have any friends—the ones who have a serious case of closet. I run across them sometimes—pathetic figures, people who are leading some kind of a double life because of family pressure, or because they're from small communities, or people right here in New York who lead that funny kind of life. They miss so damn much. And if they go out, those are the ones who generally are your market for hustling or for getting arrested in a john.

In my own case, I've been able to work for a company that's very understanding. They don't give a crap about my personal life as long as I perform well, but I better continue to perform! That's the way it should be. I like it. But you can get into structures in some companies where you have to go

along with the whole show, the whole moral kind of life, the corporate wife, and all that thing. It can be a real problem.

P: *Would it be fair to say that you've never felt oppressed at all as a gay man?*

M: I have never felt really oppressed as a gay man. That's not my character. I don't sit back and feel sorry for myself. If I don't like something, I get up and do something about it. I don't dwell on the negative; I accentuate the positive. I was born that way. I always believe that one largely creates one's own situation. Things are very much a function of how one presents them—handles them. In the early days, I used to join in the kind of camp behavior at parties or down Hollywood Boulevard, but I was never particularly effeminate or that sort of thing.

Part of being hopeful is wanting to see some kind of role models for closeted people to show them that the alternative of being out is not so horrible at all. It's very good. I mean, it's a damn good life. It's no different from any other—from a straight life, for that matter. You have friends, you go out, things go on. But those people don't know that. I guess they think that you ball and the rest of the time you suffer. Well, that's not true.

The point is that they're suffering now. If you're looking at it in terms of bottom-line sense, the risks in coming out are not that great. If you're talking about personal happiness, people in the closet aren't happy now. So what have they got to lose?

Linda

LINDA: I was a real go-getter sort of type in high school. I was everything: cheerleader, newspaper, president of the Honor Society, treasurer of the SEA, president of the SEA, and I had straight As—the whole bit. I was the American Dream Daughter, and I was miserable. I hated it. But I couldn't put together what was getting me down. Graduation was a complete trauma. I knew that people were watching me, my parents and friends, and I was supposed to be so proud of myself. Here I was, salutatorian, delivering the big speech. This was supposed to be a great moment, and I should have felt a great sense of accomplishment, but I gave my speech, then raced out, whipped off my gown, and took off. I hated it. My gut reaction was, "Let me out of here!"

LUCY: *Why didn't you buy it then?*

LM: It's really difficult for me to piece it together. I felt, "What's wrong with me?" I thought for a long time I had something drastically wrong with me to have gotten to the point in my high school career where I was on top and to feel such emptiness. I think I didn't feel emotionally fulfilled for a large part of my life. I never felt I was a real person. Throughout high school, people related to me as sort of a freak. Even though I was popular, it was hard for me to make people like me. There is a tendency in high school, if you're successful, to be singled out and be made a target for a lot of frustration and hate that other people feel. And I had such a bad concept of myself. I don't know what it was. There was a part of me that was driving me to do those activities because I had such a bad image of myself physically.

L: *How could that be? You're a beautiful woman.*

LM: I thought I was the ugliest creature that ever walked the face of the earth. I was not the Marilyn Monroe image. I would have given anything to wake up one morning and look like her because that's what the boys were into.

I always had a token boyfriend—you have to have that—somebody to escort you to proms and to homecoming dances. I wasn't particularly thrilled about any of them, but I figured that's the way it was—you have to have one of them around. I had to make myself into a lot of different people. If I was with men, I was one person; if I was with really good friends who were women, I was another person. With men, I wouldn't allow myself to be intellectual because that would put them off. I didn't think I had anything else to offer because I didn't think I was attractive physically, so I was putting myself out and trying to figure out what was wrong.

L: *What about your girl friends?*

LM: It was great! I had several friends when I was in high school. With one . . . we spent entire weekends together. I would go to her house and spend the entire weekend—and we had a wonderful time. I felt free. Those relationships, in spite of anything that went on outside, in spite of anything we had to do to fit, existed on another level. It was like with women, no matter what was going on externally, I could always get down to real life. I knew all this in high school; I just didn't know how to deal with it. There were very few men who I could talk to and wipe out the whole sexual thing. I've always known that when I really needed to relate to someone that I always could with a woman—it's always been a woman.

L: *Did you have any gay feelings at that point?*

LM: I didn't have *any* feelings at that point. I was like a robot. We weren't physical at all. I didn't even consider it with girls, and when I was physical with boys, it was nothing. God! I thought it was the worst. I literally never thought about gayness. My biggest feeling in high school was that here I was doing everything that I could possibly think of to make it, and I was miserable.

When I got to college, it was the same trip with the boys all over again, but I had changed a.lot. I began to look at myself very differently. I found out I wasn't the ugliest person on the face of the earth, so I got into the routine of spotting the best-looking boys on campus and going after them; it was total conquest. It was out of frustration. But that got to be really boring. By the time I hit sophomore year, I was happier to stay in the dorm with my friends and play around. I really enjoyed being with women.

L: *You got married in college. Did you feel happy about that, or did you feel it was expected?*

LM: I got married mid-semester my senior year during Christmas break. I had never sat around and thought, "When I get married, it's going to be wonderful." My husband and I dated for two and a half years, but it was never a steady sort of thing. He was in the navy most of the time. He came up one weekend and said, "Do you want to get married?" and I said, "Sure." I had never seriously thought about it up to that point. I think my parents were relieved at my getting married. They felt that deep down there was something of the person they had raised and that I was going to make it. I was going to turn around and be all right and be their ideal daughter.

We moved to North Carolina before I graduated. My husband was returning to school. The first two years we were together, I saw him one night a week—basically, he studied constantly, and I was supporting us totally. I had been really fired up to teach when I left school. I got down here and couldn't find a job teaching, so I ended up working as a receptionist in the medical school because it was the only thing I could find. That was a hard time for me. For the first time in my life I knew I could do a good job, and I was stuck in that position— which was probably the worst I'd ever been in. I would come home every night and cry. I would come home from work, and my husband would be studying, and I would cook dinner for both of us. He would eat and then go into his little cubby- hole and study. I'd wash the dishes and sit down. That was my day. I didn't know anybody. I would just cry, and after I got over crying I'd go to bed at 7:00 o'clock and sleep until it was time to go to work again the next morning.

L: *So when did your frustrations turn into . . . ?*

LM: Then I developed some really close friendships. I began to hang out with a woman at work. My husband was studying five and six nights a week, so I spent all the nights I wasn't with him with this friend, Sandy. It was wonderful. Of all the people I had met up to that time, she impressed me the most. I was more married to her than I was to my husband in terms of the amount of time spent and the emotional commitment. But we were not at all physical—not at all. It's strange looking back now, but it never entered my mind, and I don't think it entered hers.

L: *Did you come out while you were married?*

LM: Yes. I came out about three or four months before I left my husband. At this point, I had changed jobs and started working with a woman who I had sort of known or met or been acquainted with for two years—but not *really* known. She was a lesbian—the first one I had really gotten to know. I found myself asking a lot of questions every day; it was like a quiz show. I didn't really think about it. I was just curious. I think that what most attracted me initially to her was to see a woman who was so self-assured. She seemed to glow all the time. It was, like—oooowah!—electric! And because of where I was at that time, I knew that that's the way I wanted to be—not at that time relating it to lesbianism but just to the feeling of really being sure of myself—knowing that I was capable and knowing I could do something about it. Most people I had ever been around never allowed me really to go full tilt with myself—you know, to take it to the limits and see what I could do.

So things progressed, and we became really close friends. I raced to work at eight in the morning perfectly happy to work fifteen hours. This was the time when things between my husband and I were just starting to peak. I would get home at night and feel totally caged. I'd go to work and feel so good, so assured of myself—really strong—and then my husband was negating everything. My splitting up with my husband was not because of the other relationship, though maybe it propelled it.

L: *What was it like when you let yourself discover that you wanted to be physical, sexual, with a woman?*

LM: I was nervous, I was scared to death, and I couldn't believe it. Before the actual event—the last two weeks—the two of us were just berserk. We'd walk around—we couldn't even talk half the time. And I knew. I mean, I knew it was coming and just kept saying, "Oh, dear!" I mean, it was so insane—like a soap opera with the woman having an affair on the side. I never knew how I'd feel about that. I never thought I'd see myself in the position of having an affair in the first place, so to be having an affair with a woman was even more amazing. But I didn't feel bad about it.

L: *Did you make the first move?*

LM: Yes, which was even more surprising. I was really surprised. I ended up making the moves pretty much. We had come back to my house after a movie and my husband was out of town, and I just couldn't stand it—neither of us could. We both just sort of—waah-aah-aah—finally things came together and it was great. I was amazed. I was in heaven. I was just—yipee! I know now I could never go back. My coming out meant the years of being wiped out were over. Suddenly everything opened up and there I was, and this was where I was going after twenty-five years. And here I am—I've made it. It's incredible. I haven't totally tried to figure it out. I wasn't looking for lesbianism as a way out or as a way to make everything work. It wasn't like that. It made me aware of myself. It's the first time in my life I've been able to have a total relationship with someone who—instead of negating parts of myself—brought everything out. Everything I want to be I can be. Now I feel good. I feel beautiful. But it's not merely physical; it's just feeling so good there is no way you're not going to look good. It's wham, wham, wham—

every morning I just wake up and wonder, "What's it going to be like today?"

L: *This has to do with the fact that you're relating more with women?*

LM: I think so. Most definitely. Especially with my lover—she's my friend; I mean, she is everything. I was always split with men. There were certain things I had to do—especially with the way I looked physically—which got to be a real hang-up.

L: *Have you told your husband or your parents?*

LM: I reluctantly told my husband. But it's OK; I'm glad he knows. I don't want to have to skulk around town. In the last several months, I have really wanted to tell my parents. They have never really discussed my sexuality. My being a lesbian is not my entire personality; it's a part of it, and I feel good about it. It's going to be very hard for me to deal with their freaking out. I wish I could walk up to people and say, "I'm a lesbian. Oh, wow! it's great!" I just want people to share the good feeling; I don't want to have to try to explain it. I have never said anything in particular at work, but I know that everyone knows that I'm a lesbian, and it's no big deal. They really appreciate me as a person. I've never been able to relate to my lesbianism as something horrendous. It's so natural that it's difficult for me to discuss it with anyone who doesn't feel the same way.

I don't understand how I can approach my parents—they having known me for twenty-six years now. They could freak out. I don't want everything I have ever been to them to be erased and start all over again. It's just not like that. The things they have known about me in the past, or the basic person I am, hasn't changed. In a lot of ways, when I look back now, they have been a really large part of it—they may not be very happy about that. So I don't know what to do. I don't know when I'm going to approach them.

L: *Do you think gay women have something to offer straight women?*

LM: Strength. It's like my eyes have opened up. I have so much more feeling than I ever had. Whatever it was that had me tied down for so long has been removed. It has made me feel more sympathy for other women—more empathy. All women are women regardless of their sexual identity. I still have very close friends who are straight. I still appreciate them. I don't think the whole world is meant to be one way or the other. I don't think every woman is meant to be a lesbian.

L: *The whole way women are seen in the South is different from other parts of the country, or it is especially bad in the South. How do you feel about the way you were raised?*

LM: Role playing for women in the South is still very much alive. There are so few women in the South who really come to grips with themselves. My basic feeling about the way I was raised is that I was just popped into a little slot; you jump into that slot at birth, and you just keep moving until you die. There are certain things you have to do, certain ways you have to fit in. When you start at birth, you know, most people don't even question it. I don't know how most women can stand it, can stay alive.

L: *Do you see strengths there that are changing women in the South? Do you think there is something special about the power of feminism in the South?*

LM: I think so, yeah. I think it's finally taking hold. I think women in the South are beginning to look at themselves. They do it in different ways. It's hard to explain the southern woman. I don't know how to say this—she is like no other woman in the world. I think that probably more than any other women in the country, they have bought the whole package—and when they buy it, they stick with it, you know; they will fight to the end. They will do anything to support that way of life. There is so much strength in southern women.

It's just a matter of getting it directed into something else, into another lifestyle, into letting them see that they don't have to be this way; they don't always have to be wives; they don't have to make that their total life. They should be made to realize that they are capable, intelligent people, and that their lives don't have to be centered around men.

L: *What you were just saying relates to what I think about my mother and other southern women I know. For years, I've had to allow myself to pay more attention to myself. I think all women, but especially southern women, deny themselves.*

LM: That is a point which I think is really important. It's sort of what I was trying to get across before. Southern women—they've never been themselves. It's very seldom that I ever hear my mother speak for herself. She never talked to me as herself. She related to me as my mother. Her whole life, she was someone else; her whole life dealt with other people. That's fine. There has to be concern for other people. But in the South, it's to the point of excluding your own person. You don't exist as an individual. Women don't exist as people, they exist as roles. It depresses me to see so many women walking around looking like zombies—there is absolutely no life. You look into their eyes, and they are just like pits. I just want to reach out to them sometimes and say, "Wake up!"

L: *How does all this relate to being a lesbian?*

LM: For me, being a lesbian is being myself. Lesbianism has not just given me a chance, it has been a support, has helped me realize that I am a human being, that what I think is valid, that what I am as a person is valid. Never again am I gonna allow myself to be psyched in like that. I was such a non-person for so long.

L: *Has your involvement with TALF (Triangle Area Lesbian Feminists) helped you?*

LM: It's hard for me to imagine someone deciding to come out and having no one there, so in an indirect and direct way it's played a very important part in my life. It was incredible to suddenly say, "OK, I'm out here." I don't have the problems that most gay people have, you know; that wasn't my crisis at all. It wasn't weeks and years of sitting around my room crying and screaming, or the route I guess almost everybody goes through when they first come out. If I hadn't had those women behind me, supporting me and sharing my joy, it probably would have been a heavy experience. I've always felt that women somewhere deep down inside themselves really had it together and are the people who know what's going on. For me, I feel like it's starting all over. I've been given another chance to go at it again, and I'm going to do it right this time. I know what I'm moving into—and it's really exciting.

David

ROB: *What were your earliest gay feelings?*

DAVID: I remember being over at the beach, I think, with my cousin. I was about eight, and my cousin and I used to play strip poker and all sorts of neat things like that. Well, I did that same sort of thing for a long time with a lot of different friends from time to time until I was about twelve. It was very picturesque. I used to live out in the country in Connecticut, and there were a lot of hayfields around. It was nice mountainside, and the hay was high enough so that nobody in the surrounding houses could see anything. After the age of twelve, most of my friends started to become interested in girls, which I didn't, and I didn't know anybody that was still interested in going out in the hayfields and having a good time.

For most of my junior high school and high school, I really didn't have any sexual contacts at all. I had a girl friend through high school. We were very good friends; we're still good friends. I don't think she understood what was going on with me then.

R: *Did you?*

D: Yes and no. I thought I would change the way my friends had when they were thirteen and fourteen—but at that time I was seventeen or eighteen. I didn't think of myself as being gay; I wasn't homo or queer or anything like that. I mean, all I heard was the negative stuff, the negative and false stuff about what it was like to be gay. And while I knew that stuff had to be wrong, I didn't know what else it could be. I knew I wasn't interested in women sexually, and I was very attracted to a lot of my male friends, but I thought that would change. I just thought that I hadn't gone through the same stage that everyone else had gone through, that I was just a little bit late, but then things didn't change.

R: *Tell me more about what you were like in high school.*

D: I sort of acted out the role of a heterosexual—having a very public girlfriend, not fitting the stereotype. Limp wrists.

I don't know how limp the wrists have to be. Nobody suspected that I was gay; I had a good cover, but I was sort of in limbo in my mind. I thought I was probably gay, but at the same time, I didn't know anybody that was gay, and I had read very little about what it was like to be gay. I'd heard all too many of the stories about what queers and homos do. And I knew I wasn't one of them. I didn't want to be.

The first time I talked to anybody about homosexuality, I was shaking. I was literally shaking, because I was talking about so many feelings that had been bottled up in me for so long and that I had tried so hard to keep inside and not show anybody at all. I took a course called Silva Mind Control. A man in there in his late twenties who was gay somehow picked up on the fact that I was gay—I don't know how—and we talked. It was the first time I ever admitted to somebody else that I was probably gay. Before that, I had gone through periods when I was certain that I was, and then I would go through a period where I said, "Maybe, but things may change." I really did hope that things would change because I didn't really want to confront . . . I didn't want to go through what I'd have to go through as a gay person.

At first I couldn't get involved in the People's Gay Alliance because their office was so public. I could go to their dances because they were out in the boondocks; nobody was out there to see me walk into the dance. And when I first went to a dance, I saw people I knew—and some people I really admired. I saw somebody I knew who was a reporter who I had admired for a long time as a professional. I just had the greatest admiration for this guy. He was there, *and he was gay!* Nothing could have been better for me. I felt just great. There were one or two other people there who I knew, and from that moment on, I was out. It took me a while to get to the point where I really didn't care what people thought. People have all sorts of ideas about what gay people are. I realized after a while that people's own insecurities are operating when they react to gay people, and it's not something I should worry about.

R: *Do you mind talking about your first sexual experience?*

D: No. My first sexual experience wasn't that good. I went to a gay bar not far from the University of Massachusetts and met somebody from Amherst College. When I got back to his dorm room, I didn't know what to do. I'd never tried anything like that; there's nothing to learn actually, but I thought there might be something I should know about this before I got involved with it. So we went back to his room and had sex.

R: *What was that like?*

D: Well, I really didn't get off on it. I think I was too nervous, and it was hard for me just to flick a switch like that. Because I'd never—since I was ten—I had never had sex with another guy. And this was an actual bona fide gay experience, which the earlier ones at the age of ten weren't.

R: *So did you start having relationships with other men at that point?*

D: Soon after that, yeah. About a month after that I met somebody who I would call my first lover. He was standing next to a friend, and he started to walk away because he thought I was getting upset because he was staring at me so much. As he walked away, I asked him if he wanted to dance— even though I don't really like dancing, or I didn't then. So we danced, and talked after that—and we really hit it off talking too. He's somebody I really liked. We saw each other, I think, every day for the next week and a half, two weeks. And he was living in Springfield at the time, and I was living in Amherst. It was the middle of winter, and my car didn't have a heater. I was driving back and forth between Amherst and Springfield without a heater in my car, making all sorts of sacrifices—and I couldn't afford to drive from Springfield every single day, on top of that, but I managed. We saw a lot of each other, and it was really good. On top of that, we didn't have sex.

R: *All that time?*

D: All that time.

R: *What made it so fulfilling emotionally that sex wasn't even important?*

D: I really don't know.

R: *But it was?*

D: It was, very much. Very fulfilling. I was just crazy about Henry.

R: *Was this the first time you could love a man?*

D: Yeah. And that really thrilled me. I had almost forgotten about it, but when I was in high school, I thought I was one of those cold people who would never love anyone. Some people had the capacity, and I guess I thought I didn't; it just wasn't in me. And when I fell in love with this guy, it was just . . . it meant so much to me. It meant that I was a real person. I wasn't just a machine. I had really incredibly deep emotions. I didn't know that I could feel that strongly about anybody. I was just ecstatic. I really was.

R: *That's beautiful!*

D: It *was* beautiful. I'll never forget it. I was using a part of me—feeling a part of me—that I'd never felt before. And the best part too: my capacity to love somebody.

R: *Does your family know that you're gay?*

D: Well, my mother died a year and a half ago, so I don't have to go through it with her. But I knew I had to tell my father—for a lot of reasons. I was just too open to keep it a secret from one person and one person only. I think it's very hard to tell a parent that you're gay. Because parents tend to take responsibility for everything. I didn't want my father feeling guilty or upset or sad or anything like that.

R: *How did you tell him?*

D: I asked him if he was ready for a very heavy conversation. And he said, "Yeah, let me grab a cigarette." I told him to grab the whole pack! "This will be a very heavy conversation." So he brought the whole pack and sat down and was smoking a cigarette. I told him that it was very important for me to be open with people who are important in my life and that what I had to tell him, I was telling him because I wanted to be open; I didn't want my life to be secret. I wanted him to understand me and what I was doing. What I was telling him shouldn't upset him, even though it probably would. And I said, "There's something I've been meaning to tell you for months, but I've sort of been putting it off. I'm gay." And he didn't blink! He said, "Have you always been gay?" I said, "Always." And then—it really didn't seem to phase him—he asked some very logical questions. He asked me if there was an emotional part to my relationships with men, if it wasn't purely sexual. I told him that it—the emotional part—is, I think, the most important. And he asked me if I was gay because I'd had some traumatic experience with women, if I'd been shunned by some woman or had some awful experience that made me go to men to find happiness. And I said, "No. Nothing like that has ever happened to me." The one thing I told him that did upset him was that I was planning on doing this interview. He was kind of upset because he didn't want the family to get involved publicly. He thought that the family might be harassed or embarrassed or humiliated, or something like that.

R: *How did you feel about that?*

D: Well, it gave me some second thoughts about doing it. I really didn't want to bring that . . . despite the fact that I really think that . . . there's no way to avoid that. I'm an out-front gay. I'm not going to change my life to protect some other people in society who have warped ideas about gay people. I can't live that way.

R: *What are your professional plans?*

D: I graduated; I'm through with classes anyway. I'm working as a student in a radio station this fall. I'm working at a gas station now, and I think I'll actually have the job at the same time I'm working at the radio station.

R: *Do you feel oppressed as a gay man?*

D: No, not really. Well, you see, I really haven't been out in a place where I can lose my job because I'm gay, or where I'll get beat up because I'm gay. I've spent most of my time out at the University of Massachusetts, and I really haven't had to deal with trying to keep a job or living next to uptight neighbors.

R: *Do you think it's easier for you, having entered your adult life as an open gay person? Do you think it will be easier for you?*

D: I think it's going to be much easier for me having come out already than to be out there in the hard, cruel world and come out then. I don't know if the world is hard and cruel. I haven't been out there long enough, but, yeah, I think it's much easier now. First of all, it takes energy and time, and it's draining coming out sometimes. I would much rather have it all in the past.

Cynthia

LUCY: *Did you know you were gay when you were young—say in grade school, high school?*

CYNTHIA: It's funny, I had no idea at that point. First of all, I didn't even know what a lesbian was—well, no, that's not true. There were always queer days in high school and things like that, but I never thought about it in terms of myself. I can't remember thinking about it ever—except to wear the right color on the right day so that you wouldn't be considered a queer. On the other hand, I was really programmed to be heterosexual. But—I don't know—I don't think any more so than any other kids. On the other hand, when I thought about being a lesbian, my whole vision of it was just of the sleazy, gutter kind of depressing life, you know? I don't know where I got that! Cause I don't remember reading any books, or really hearing anything concrete. I don't remember anyone ever talking to me about it. So it had almost just seeped into my head, is all I could figure.

L: *When did you start thinking about it?*

C: Oh, much later, much later. The first I ever thought about it was about two or three years after I graduated from high school. I had several good friends who were men, but most all of my time I spent with my women friends. Most of them were going with guys—living with guys or sleeping with them or something—but I had never slept with a man. I mean, I'd dated men and stuff, but I didn't seem to be going in that direction.

A girl I had known in high school who had gone out to California came through town. She came over, and I started asking her about people we'd known, and she started telling me about all these people who were in California who were *bisexual*! I'd never even heard that term. I don't know where I'd been all my life, but I'd never even heard it. I just started thinking, "Oooh, weird. Weird." Like one guy who had been really very popular and good looking and all this stuff, and here he was supposed to be *bisexual*! That sort of started me thinking about myself and about how I didn't seem to get along that well with men—in terms of romantic, I mean, it just didn't seem to happen.

So I started thinking. Like, I had this one girlfriend—one of my best friends—who was a very, very physical person. Whenever she talked to people, she touched them. So from then on, whenever she'd touch me, I'd think, "Am I enjoying it? Am I enjoying it?" I was just very self-conscious and worrying about this a lot. The results of that one conversation were that for about a month or two I worried about this. And it was totally abstract. I mean, it wasn't like I had a crush on anyone or had felt any real inclinations or anything that I consciously . . . .

But, around the end of that time, I went out for coffee with these two women who were friends of mine. They were very, very tight friends. We were talking about just abstract things, and I started telling them about what had happened with my friend coming through, and had they ever known anyone who was bisexual or homosexual? I said that it sounded so creepy to me; I couldn't imagine doing it with someone of the same sex. It just seemed—I mean, how could anyone do it? And they sort of sat there quietly and smiled. Then when I had gone through giving this whole spiel, one of them looked at me and said, "It's not so bad. We do it." I was just totally thrown. I was so thrown that I didn't say another thing. I mean, I didn't ask them anything. I just buried it and decided to forget the whole deal. It was silly for me to worry about it; it was all abstract; whatever I was, I would be. Basically, I was just refusing to deal with it. I wasn't defining myself as a lesbian because that just freaked me out too much. I didn't want to be a lesbian.

L: *Were you relating with men sexually?*

C: No. I wasn't. When I was living in Boston, I had just about decided to become celibate. I was spending all my good time with women friends, and the people I was closest to were women. Then when I would sleep with these men, that just did nothing for me. I mean, it wasn't horrible or anything, but I just decided it was messing up my life too much. There was no need for it. I just sort of cut that off.

L: *So how did you start dealing with it?*

C: Well, a friend told me that she'd heard of this new political group she thought I might be interested in. We were kind of passing on the street, and she said, "I heard there's this new group. I think you might be interested in it. There's a meeting tonight at eight o'clock at such and such a place." So I said, "OK. What is it?" She said, "Oh, I don't know. Some political group." So I debated going to this thing, but finally curiosity got me, and I decided I would go to this meeting. So I went to where she had told me, and I walked into the room, and here I see this ring of women sitting around on the floor. I look around and there are—I could see one here and one here—these women, these well-known women, who I knew were Radical Lesbians. So I knew that must be where I was! I really freaked out! I sort of backed against the wall and felt like I was crawling around the edge of the room—sort of trying to sit in the back. And everyone kind of turned around and smiled at me. A lot of them knew me. Sort of like, "Ah ha!" And I thought, "No. No. Wait. You don't understand."

Well, it was this incredible night. Mainly the reason it was incredible didn't really have to do with lesbians; it had to do with the kind of conversations that I had with some of the women there. We broke into discussion groups, and we were talking about politics, and the conversation was so exciting—you know, intellectually or whatever. I mean, none of the kind of other, irrelevant stuff. So it was very exciting to me, and by the end of the evening, I wasn't afraid of these people anymore.

The other thing that happened was that I met this woman there who I just was immediately attracted to. I remember that her eyes were really beautiful. I just loved her eyes; they reminded me of my dog, Snooch's, eyes. And so I told her that night. I said, "You have the most amazing eyes. They remind me of my dog's." I guess she took it pretty well. She said, "Oh, well, thank you." Well, anyway, that began it; I proceeded to get this crush on her. I didn't know her very well; it was a lot physical, but also how she acted in these meetings.

L: *What happened then?*

C: I started going to these meetings. I still didn't consider myself a lesbian, but they were interesting, and the people there were interesting. Plus, there was this woman. The more I saw of her, the more I just felt that I *had* to have her. So finally, I think maybe a couple of weeks after that initial meeting, there was some party at her apartment, and all of these women who were in Radical Lesbians were there. I had decided that tonight was the night. So, one by one, these women left, and I just kind of kept hanging around and talking. I decided I just had to stick it out.

Finally they all left, and there I was in the apartment alone with her. And she said, "Well, you can either—you know, if you want, I can give you a ride home, or if you want to stay here the night, you can do that." I said, "Well, I'll stay here"— very casual, very cool. Then we got into bed, and I'm lying there—we're sort of lying on opposite sides of the bed, very straight. She mumbled something to me but I couldn't really hear her. Then it registered. She asked me if I needed a pillow. So I thought, "Aha!" I said, "Well, I mean, we could share one." That did it. We just—well, we just started. We made love, and it was really wonderful. I mean, I was just on cloud nine. Looking back, I don't know whether it was technically that successful or something, but it was just so wonderful! I just felt so comfortable, you know; I just did what I felt like doing.

L: *Was it different from ever before making love with anybody? Why was it?*

C: Oh, yeah. Yeah. Because, well, for one thing, she

obviously knew something about me, my makeup, what might make me feel good. She probably knew more about it than I did at that point. For another thing, somehow I didn't feel like I had to prove something to her like I'd felt with men. I guess with men I had felt like I could not admit that I didn't know what to do, or that I was inexperienced or whatever, because I felt like any admission like that would just put me at a disadvantage, and I'd be vulnerable. I don't know why I felt that; I can't think of any certain incident that made me feel that way. But with her, I just felt like it was cool if I didn't know what I was doing. We'd just sort of try things out to see if we liked them. If we didn't, we didn't. If we did, we did. As a result, everything was just much more loose and comfortable.

L: *Have you felt—since you are relating with women sexually or being in love with women—that there is something that is qualitatively closer than you had ever experienced with men?*

C: Oh, yeah. Without a doubt. There's no comparison. I mean, it's just so much better with women. Even at its worst with women, for me, it's just been so much better than with men. A lot of it is not just sexual; it's everything. It's who the person is that you're sleeping with. What I'm saying, I guess, is that it can be sexual, but sexual is affected by everything else. There's just a whole mentality that men have with women that makes everything more uncomfortable, more stilted. Plus I just like the way women feel. Men in my experience sexually always feel like they have to prove something. Whereas, I think women don't have that much ego at stake in proving that they can do this or that to you. With almost every woman I've ever slept with, I've just felt like she really wanted me to have a good time, and also really wanted herself to have a good time. That was maybe her primary concern—not proving to me that she could make me feel good. Do you see what I mean? From what I've seen, women are just a lot happier—whether with women or just without men. I've known a number of older women who aren't lesbians but who have not been married and have not lived with men, and they just always seem happier. I think all women would be happier as lesbians because women understand each other better than men understand women. Unless you enjoy being misunderstood or that kind of struggle as a lifetime proposition, then I think things are better with other women.

(Helaine joins Cynthia, and Nancy continues the interview)

NANCY: *Is it hard to have good friends that you are not sexually involved with?*

C: No. First of all, I think friends are very special, whoever you are. To have a friend who you can remain friends with for a number of years through all kinds of changes in your life and all—this is a very special thing. So, in that sense, I think it's hard—just because it doesn't happen with everybody. Helaine and I are very close, but we've never been lovers. We live together, and we work together; we have the company together, and we see each other every day. It's funny, but in some ways, I feel that Helaine and I can almost be closer in some sense than I can be with a lover. Maybe there's some element there that makes it possible for other elements to be there. I'm not sure what it is. It's just ways we can be together that are particular to Helaine and me. We've had a long history together, and we have senses of humor that fit together very well, and we have old jokes together.

N: *How do you two feel about each other?*

HELAINE: I'm tempted to say something like popsicles and candies . . .

C: Now, let's be nice.

H: I don't know. I never understood how to answer questions like that.

N: *You can try.*

H: I guess we love each other, and we've been friends for a really long time, and we've gone through a lot together, and our relationship has still lasted through everything. We've kind of weathered each other out.

C: It's not like there aren't any differences or problems or things like that, but I think the fact that we have them and still the relationship is important enough to hassle through them or to just yell at each other or whatever, that makes it all the more meaningful or something. I don't think that we store things up very much—resentments or whatever.

H: I don't think we can, because we work together, and we also live in the same house together, so if you hold things in, it means you can't function. You can't make dinner on time; you can't deal with your business.

N: *Tell me about your business together.*

C: We own and run Women in Distribution. We started it about two years ago. We've both worked a lot with various feminist and political organizations and projects, and several times along the way, we found that there were problems in putting out a magazine. The main problem came when you tried to get it out to people across the country.

H: A lot of feminists were putting out really good books, and really good newspapers, and records, and postcards, and things like that; but all their energy was going into producing these items. They weren't really putting any energy into or paying a lot of attention to getting them out to people.

C: It's not just like it's deodorant or something. Women, in general, are producing all these books and things to communicate with other women. For a lot of women—especially those who aren't in big cities—that's their primary means of finding out what's going on: by going to a library or a bookstore and picking up a book. If you can't get those things out to those women, then there's hardly any point in putting them out in the first place. So we started Women in Distribution. We did a lot of research to figure out the distribution business, which we really didn't know much about. In fact, we didn't know much about business. We learned a lot.

H: There's no other women's distribution company that I know of that deals with presses from all over the country and also sells to people all over the country.

N: *So why are you doing it?*

H: I would like to make some money.

C: Part of it also, why we got into having a woman's business, was that we were sick of working at jobs where we were working for men, getting fairly low wages, and never feeling like it was doing anything for us or other people. It wasn't that meaningful to us.

H: I also was really tired of being in different feminist projects where what I was doing wasn't going anywhere. It really was affecting a very small number of women, and I wanted . . . I would like some woman in Paraland, Texas, to be able to walk into her Safeway and to see a lesbian book there. I don't know if that will ever happen, but it's what needs to be done.

N: *The two of you are, you know, such good friends and work well together. Why is it that you're not lovers?*

C: Why is it that we're not lovers?

H: I think the reason we first became friends was because we were attracted to each other, but . . . are you attracted to me?

C: Oh. That puts a whole new light on it.

H: No. I used to go over to her house in the afternoon and eat oranges, but it was like pure chance that we didn't become lovers. I think because I was more interested in someone else at the time. I don't know what your situation was, but I'm glad. I'm kind of glad it happened that way because I think we make better friends than we would have lovers.

N: *Why?*

C: *(giggles and covers her face with her hand)* I feel like saying, lovers are a dime a dozen, but a good friend is hard to find. That's kind of it, but not it. It's just that when you have a lover relationship with someone, lots of times it ends.

H: Well, it's just there are a lot more things that are, in some ways, more complicated. It's much harder a lot of times to be totally honest with each other, and there are different emotional things that get involved because of the sexual . . .

N: *How do you keep from getting turned on to each other?*

C: I don't know. It's just when you've been around some-one for such a long time—well, I don't know. It's also like there are a number of women that I think are really attrac-tive that in some . . .

N: *. . . as attractive as Helaine?*

C: *(laughs)* No. None as attractive as Helaine.

H: It's like that was then; that was part of our history. Like, we went past that or into the outer zones or something. I think once you become really good friends with someone, and you've been that way for a long time, you are not attracted to her. It's because you know so much about her. There's no mystery there. You know that she's attractive, but it's just a different kind of relationship.

Michael

ROB: *Why don't you start telling me about your child-hood—your family situation.*

MICHAEL: I grew up in a gang situation in a West Philly ghetto. I really didn't seem to fit in. I was quiet and enjoyed my school work. My teachers loved me, and I sort of fell into that teachers' pet syndrome where the other kids don't really approve of you, and they begin to take it out on you. My mother always wanted me to fight. I was called a sissy because I didn't like to fight. To be called a sissy was something I didn't like, because I knew "sissy" meant girl. So they were calling me out of my sex. The area was . . . the gang situation was bad.

My mother saw my not wanting to fight as a kind of weakness. *Boys* were supposed to fight. I remember several times when she virtually forced me to fight. Once a guy was picking on me, I refused to fight, and ran into the house. She took me right down the block and made me fight the kid. My response to aggression was to cry. The kid was a bit bigger than I was. There was a piece of wood on the ground in clear view. I saw it. My mother was watching. I wasn't going to pick it up and hit the kid with it. When the fight was over, my mother sort of pulled me aside and yanked me back up the street, saying to me, "You saw that piece of wood. Why didn't you use it?" But that just wasn't me, you know. Later she apologized.

I'm sure it was very important for a kid to learn to defend himself, and it was something I had to learn. But I still have a very negative response to those memories of being forced to fight. Somehow I think my mother was not so much teaching me how to fight but trying to make a "man" out of me. Because even though I was good in school, I was soft; because I wasn't really "out there" getting into fights, getting girl friends. Kids used to ride up to my door and yell sissy. I was constantly on the run because I was always vulnerable.

I read books, liked to play the organ, and I spent a lot of time by myself. But I think most of my life I have been a loner. Maybe that was fostered by having bad luck relating to people when I was young. I was close to my cousins and locked into my family where I could get support. My grandmother was the real metal of the family. She pulled us together when my father left. I was raised by my mother, grandmother, and aunt—the only male in a group of women. When other six-year-olds were out in the street playing, I would go up to my grandmother's room and lay on the bed beside her, and we would discuss things.

R: *What about your education? What kind of school did you go to?*

M: I started going to Episcopal Academy when I was in the sixth grade. I was on a full scholarship—one of those programs where they recruited kids in underdeveloped areas. Going to Episcopal was the most important move in my life. It's largely responsible for what I am today.

R: *You got in on an academic scholarship? Is that why they sought you out?*

M: Right. The academic standards were incredibly high. And nobody called me a sissy there, even though I was not an athlete compared to most kids in the program. The only thing I could do was run—I had plenty of practice at that! But what I immediately noticed was that a lot of the kids there had been alienated in the same ways that I was—because they were good students. By comparison, I ended up being one of the stronger types.

R: *Do you think that had to do with your background?*

M: Sure. They were afraid of me. Because I was black, they automatically assumed that I could fight better than they could. And that sort of put me in a situation where I commanded instant respect. I was in a situation I had never been in before. Right off the bat, kids my own age respected me. And I didn't have to fight. I really bloomed in a lot of ways. I got academic food; I got into tremendous debates with my teachers. It was an incredible incubator for anyone who wanted to learn.

When I got back home each day, I would have to put on my protective armor. My life was quite schizophrenic. That has a lot to do with the way I handle my family situation now. One of the worst things about the program was the "Catch-22" element—they took you out of your neighborhood and put you in this academic heaven, which then alienated you from the kids in the neighborhood. There was also a strong schism between my family and me. I had become somewhat critical of my home situation; my mother and aunt responded in a very defensive way. You see, when I would leave Episcopal, I didn't quite want to take off the Episcopal Academy blazer. When I went home, I became Michael instead of Mr. Mintz. Eventually I began to bring Episcopal home, and I started to take potshots at my home situation. It wasn't a resentment of my family. It was a resentment of my social condition. I couldn't understand why there was so much to be had and why I had so little. In the cruelty of youth, I made criticisms of my family. And this culminated in a conversation where my mother and my aunt called me a "honkie." I immediately burst into tears. That hurt. And there was the "Catch-22." You lose touch with your family.

R: *Were you adopting white attitudes? Did you notice a difference in your language?*

M: That's something that changes even now. I read a lot when I was young. I took very quickly to English and writing. When I got to Episcopal, my vocabulary expanded incredibly. And in comparison to my family . . . I mean, none of my family had ever graduated from high school. Even now, when I'm about to go home, my voice changes; my grammar goes down a few pegs. When I think of family, I think of the drawl.

R: *How did you develop when you had all this freedom?*

M: At home I was never athletically inclined, before I went to Episcopal. When I went to Episcopal, I discovered that I could run, wrestle, play football, play soccer. I discovered, "Hey, you know, I'm an athlete!" I always related athlete with macho, and macho with male, and male with men, of course, and so I was beginning to make the connection between myself as a man and becoming very proud of myself as a *man*.

R: *You mean you found a way to do it without . . . ?*

M: Without fighting. I mean, I had ribbons and medals to bring home, you know, which just sort of added to it, and I began to feel a lot better. I still didn't meet the social requirements as my mother saw them, because I was still kind of quiet. But athletically, there was no way anyone could say I wasn't a man, because I was a jock. And a lot of people got off my back.

I still didn't like to fight. But there was one guy—he wasn't even the person who picked on me most; it just happened that he picked on me on the wrong day—he called me sissy. Now, I had been wrestling for two years. This guy called me a sissy and went home to get his sisters. They were all going to beat me up! So I walked home and told my mother, "I'm going to have a fight." I could see the grin on her face already. We walked over to where the guy was and I dumped all over him. You know, I pounded him into the dirt.

R: *How did you feel after you beat this guy up?*

M: Somewhat proud because I had done it. I also cried, as usual. But I think that was a point of pride for my entire family: Michael had fought and beaten somebody. I think that the fact that I had beaten somebody up was more important than the fact that I had defended myself.

R: *Were you a high school hero? Sounds like you had a complete reversal from the sissy who was picked on by everybody in the streets . . .*

M: That's pretty much true. I was one of the best hurdlers in my area, I was captain of my wrestling team. Wrestling was very important to me because through it I developed an acceptance of discipline. I was a good speaker and won several public speaking prizes. I also held pretty much every office in the student body.

R: *Play football?*

M: Yes. I was a running back. But I really didn't get along well with it. It took away my individuality. I liked to do things myself. I didn't like team sports because someone else could lose for you. But on the mat, it was me and the other guy. And if I lost, *I* lost, and couldn't blame it on anyone else. And if I won, it was *my* victory.

A character change occurred in me. I basically withdrew into myself. Some of my friends called me a "soldier." They said I walked like a soldier. This was very much my intention. I was there to win. From ninth to eleventh grade, I went through this machine routine, and I called it "control." I controlled my emotions by simply trying my best not to have any—at least not having any when anyone was around. My wrestling style—the whole idea of discipline—very much describes the way that I treated my life in general. The way to get over in this society, as a man, is to be unemotional, is to be ruthless, is to have no other goal—to think of no one else but yourself. I mean, this is cutthroat, and this is what I'm thinking . . .

R: *Is that the way you saw yourself?*

M: That's the way I saw myself. I saw myself as being as much of an asshole as I had to. I couldn't relate to people on a friendship level. I didn't touch.

R: *In some ways, it sounds like you found your own means of achieving a male role. Did you have any gay feelings then?*

M: I was always attracted to men as long as I can remember, but I wasn't sexually active until I got to Princeton. I bottled up *all* my feelings. I had done a lot of crying, and the decision to close off my emotions was to keep me from crying any more. I didn't understand or deal with my sexuality at all. I mean, I liked girls, but I just didn't want to go to bed with them. It was pretty difficult for me to have relations with anyone at that point. I had friendships with women because it was the social thing to do. The big man on campus had to have a girl, so I got a girl. I had impressive statistics. I was president of my senior class. The first girl that I was very close to was also president of her senior class. We sort of matched socially.

R: *Why did you choose to go to Princeton?*

M: Princeton was sort of a life-long dream. At Episcopal, it was *the* school to attend. It's a very cloistered place. I was sheltered at home, the gates around Episcopal certainly sheltered me, and Princeton is just as much a shelter. Then I got into a relationship with Earl which somehow shielded me.

R: *Did you come to Princeton knowing what you wanted sexually?*

M: I came to Princeton with the intention of letting the cards fall where they might. If I met a girl who I really liked and cared for—well, all right, there would be no closed emotions. But if I met a man, I was going to care just as much, and it wouldn't matter.

I really didn't discover what the word "gay" meant until the end of my first year with Earl. Then when he was away during my second year, alone, with only myself, I began to develop a very strong gay political consciousness. I guess I had always been naive about the way people are, simply because I had spent my earlier life ignoring people, but I began to feel rejected by black people for my gayness. I funneled my anger into the Gay Alliance. I injected my own political perspective into it. I really needed it. Short of going into the closet and locking the door, the Alliance was the only place I could find support.

R: *What kind of activities were you involved in with the Alliance?*

M: In addition to planning dances and social activities, we became more visible in the school newspaper. Then there was the hanging of the banner—a huge orange and black banner that said "Gay Alliance of Princeton." We marched in the gay parade in New York with it; it stood as a symbol of pride. We hung it from the window of our dorm room. I had told Doug, my roommate, "You know, we are coming out in a very half-assed manner." So hanging the banner was really making a big statement.

R: *What kind of reaction did you get?*

M: There were screams of "faggot"—you know, the old "fairy" type of thing. Doug and I looked at this as sort of a triumph. The idea of the banner was to bring the whole issue to a level where people on campus would have to deal with it consciously. Eventually it got violent. Someone smoke-bombed our room, heaved rocks through the window three stories up . . . must have been a jock!

R: *Were there any black people doing this?*

M: There was one. I was so shocked to see him out there. I opened the window and said, "You, of all people?" It was quite clear that he was gay. He was hiding. I guess he still is.

The final incident was when eight jock-type characters burst through the door while Doug was sleeping and ransacked the room and smashed up things. They took the banner and left. We never expected this type of violent reaction. We were in an academic community, where people supposedly consider things rationally and are loathe to resort to physical violence. But that proved not to be the case.

Every major group on campus took a stand against the violence. The blacks said nothing. It was amazing. I mean, here's a situation where active oppression of the same type has been happening to black people for centuries. Black people just didn't make this connection. Really, at this point, it shouldn't matter what minority is attacked. I mean, you have to eliminate oppression against *all* people, or nobody is safe. But apparently, the black people on this campus lacked the political perspective to see that.

R: *Do you think they were afraid of aligning themselves with a gay group?*

M: It's a possibility, but I think that the oppression of gays and the oppression of blacks is a connection that the black population on this campus is unequipped to make.

For a while, I felt betrayed by black people because they didn't come to my defense when I needed them. I was no longer part of them because I was gay or not fit to be protected. I certainly developed some strong resentments for gay people because an awful lot of them don't want to do anything. It's a "You're gay. So what? Suffer with us" kind of attitude. Having a consciousness of one seemed to demand that I lose the other.

I used to say that I was a black gay, with the emphasis being on *gay,* especially when I was feeling alienated from the black community. I turn it around now. I've decided that, given the political situation and temper of the society, by far the most important label that I have to defend is "blackness."

R: *No matter what?*

M: No matter what, ultimately. If it came down to a war, my blackness is going to stand out. I look at the gay movement as one which will, hopefully, self-destruct. I would like to see the movement bring social alienation and discrimination to an end; then we can go on being what we are. The major response I had to all the violence of the banner incident was that my sexuality had gotten completely out of hand with the rest of my life. It's really just one portion of my personality. And it's just another facet in my blackness. I changed the phrase around. I'm no longer a black *gay;* I'm a gay *black* man.

R: *What is your reaction when you are rejected by black people?*

M: That says I have to do more work. I can't help but believe that black people in America have very few social perspectives that we've developed ourselves. I can't be too hard on black people because they are victims of the same faulty socialization that whites are.

A black man here on campus walked up to me and asked me if I thought there would be homosexuality after the revolution. My response was, "There should be freedom after the revolution."

R: *After the banner incident, did anyone approach you about it?*

M: I was pretty devastated and sort of lost faith in people. Given that I don't like to fight, what I really wanted to do was hit somebody! Once I was approached by two black guys. They were talking about "the faggot." As they got closer, the conversation got louder. One of them, a big football player type, stopped right in front of me, somewhat drunk, and I just stood there. Finally he asked me what I was going to do. I just looked at him. He pushed me, and I just went off on him. He went down . . . bloody nose. I was very upset. I went back to my room and cried and called my mother.

R: *In some ways, you were working toward the same ends that your mother wanted you to—to conform to a role?*

M: I wasn't working to conform. I was working to succeed, to be unemotional, which is to be ruthless and cutthroat. I think it's simply a sad coincidence that meeting my mother's macho standards for me just happened to coincide directly with my perception of how to get over in the society. In retrospect, I wonder how anybody ever got along with me. I was respected, but with a lot of dislike.

R: *Were you hoping that this new image of yourself would make you heterosexual?*

M: I think you really have to understand that clearly I was one of the most anti-social and consequently asexual people that I've ever met. I mean, I couldn't relate to people on a friendship level. I couldn't touch. I was too wrapped up in myself.

R: *Why?*

M: Because of hurt. I didn't belong. The temporary success of athletics and high school politics fell apart. I was just left alone with me and my ego. And now since I've gotten to Princeton, everything's changed.

(Earl joins Michael, and Peter continues the interview)

PETER: *I'd like to hear the story of your meeting Earl from both your and Earl's point of view. Who noticed whom first?*

M: I did. I got to Princeton on September 3 and met Earl on September 6. The first time I saw him, my tongue hit the floor. He was standing on the balcony of the pub on campus. I walked in and looked at him, and he just politely nodded back.

P: *Did you think of yourself as gay, Earl?*

EARL: I was engaged to be married for a couple of years. During the summer before I met Michael, I broke up with my fiancée. I was sort of checking out my new-found freedom. Most of my relationships had been with men. But I considered myself as enlightened; I don't like the term "bisexual" because I think it's a cop-out. I simply relate to whoever I feel like. I'd never considered myself gay. I had never had a really emotional relationship with a man. Michael was the first one to show me that I could really care for a man.

P: *So you walked into this pub, and he cruised you more or less, huh, Michael?*

M: Yeah. I mean, he was just gorgeous, with his red hair in the light. After that, I think it was a day or so before I saw him again. That was on the basketball court. There was an interesting kind of nonverbal communication going on between us. I would take a shot and miss, and he would take the ball and give it to me anyway. I really couldn't shoot.

P: *Were you cruising him, Earl?*

E: Definitely. In the pub, I actually thought he was someone else. It's my nature to be aggressive, but I had a very soft approach with him because I figured I might scare him away. We were talking in between basketball, and I asked him to come over and watch television. When I saw him cringe, I sort of jumped and thought, "I've gone too far."

M: I was really nervous about having any kind of relationship with a man.

P: *Did you get sexual vibes at that point?*

M: Definitely. But I was really impressed by him. He was so self-assured—sort of into the same kind of game that I had played myself. But it wasn't really a game for him. It came naturally to him. That night was when we got to know each other, and we decided to become friends. There was no sex yet. I left feeling more safe with him. That was something very important to me. I didn't want to be hurt emotionally.

P: *Were the two of you fantasizing at that point about what could happen?*

M: I definitely was.

E: I think I took it for granted. I have a lot of faith in myself and in situations. I found that in spite of his caution, Michael was very willing. And it was simply a case of getting through the self-imposed barriers. I'm very good at that . . .

M: He is also modest!

We met again, on the basketball court. I was looking for him. He invited me to his room again. I just assumed something was going to happen. That night, we discussed the most important parts of our lives. I really left no possibility of a one-night stand and no possibility that there was going to be sex and run, or sex and hurt me. I was attracted to him, and I didn't want to go to bed with him and smile—and that's it.

E: We didn't discuss anything about our sexuality, really. By the time anything happened, we had committed ourselves to a long-term relationship and never mentioned a thing about sex.

P: *There doesn't seem to have been a lot of nervousness about the fact that maybe the two of you were faggots, or that maybe one of you wasn't? Being gay wasn't an issue?*

E: It's never been with me. I simply chose a man. Like, I am definitely gay and proud of it, but I didn't have any bad images to go on.

P: *Michael, you must have picked up on Earl's confidence?*

M: I just didn't feel very self-conscious about what people thought of me. I never thought anything bad about myself. At that time "faggot" would have meant "bad."

P: *The whole love story sounds very much like heterosexual love. I mean that in the good sense. The fact that you were two men didn't enter into it?*

E: Michael is very much an idealist. He couldn't see anything negative about himself in that light. It was simply him expressing more of what he already was. I'm very realistic, in that I tend to see the complications—the reactions of other people. But I didn't see anything morally negative about it. I was a senior, and I was going to be leaving soon, so I figured nothing could hurt me.

P: *How was the sex initiated?*

M: Earl looked at the clock and said something to the effect that it was late, "There's a couch over there, or the bed's big enough for two." So he took off his clothes and got in bed and purposefully told me, "Don't watch me"—because he didn't want to make me feel embarrassed.

P: *I'll bet you wanted to watch him?*

E: You have to sacrifice certain immediate things for long-range goals . . .

P: *Was it different than other times you had had sex with men or women?*

M: My sexual life very much began with Earl. I didn't have much experience except some necking to relate to.

E: For me, it becomes better with someone I care for. It was better than it had been with virtually anybody.

P: *Did you tell anyone at home about your relationship?*

M: During that summer after the first year, I told my mother and my grandmother. I came home and said, "Grandma, I'm in love." And she said, "Oh, really?" She knew exactly what I was talking about. I said, "I'm in love with a man." And she didn't flinch too much.

P: *That summer was the first time you were away from each other?*

M: It was very painful. The phone bills! When we could be together, we were trying to make up for lost time, trying to make sure that nothing had changed. When we saw each other, it was pure, unadulterated heaven. Later, I was becoming more and more involved politically with the Alliance. Earl had not come out in any kind of political way. We spent more time crying about not being able to be with each other and not sharing than in actually enjoying the time that we had together.

P: Earl, were you threatened by Michael's gay activism?

E: Yes, definitely. I was very unliberated politically. I was trying to create a career for myself in law. And the problem was simply that I was paranoid. What it came down to was that I was denying us, and Mike saw it that way in no uncertain terms.

P: How did you feel, Michael?

M: It made me angry. I guess it scared me more. I was frightened that it was going to be a definite point of separation between us. But if I was going to be political and become more open, I needed Earl, and I needed his support.

P: Were you friends with any of the macho Third World blacks? Did that get you in trouble?

E: I was such a good athlete that they had to think about it for a while.

P: Did they accept your being gay because of that?

E: No.

M: What he is saying is that he could match macho with them. When we play football together, we are pretty good. I mean, it's the whole macho mystique. They have to accept us, or they have to question themselves. If two faggots can go out and beat them at an athletic game which is supposed to be the hallmark of masculinity . . .

P: Earl, wasn't your being a jock and also being openly gay more threatening to straight jocks than if you had been more effeminate?

E: Definitely. At the same time, I'm the type of person who doesn't let someone get away with sniping at me behind my back. I don't tolerate disrespect from people.

P: *Do they think of one of you as a man and the other as a woman?*

M: That's very difficult because we are both jocks. They find it difficult to assign masculine and feminine roles. The best they can say is that I'm quieter and Earl is more bois- terous, but that's the only thing they can get a handle on.

P: *Do you expect to be together forever?*

M: Pretty much. Yeah.

E: We both believe that we will be together, in light of how we feel about each other. We have had problems in terms of being apart, but there's no question—our love for each other doesn't change.

P: *How long have you been together?*

E: Two years. And it's been good.

Freddy

ROB: *How did you come to realize that the straight life wasn't for you?*

FREDDY: I guess I really didn't recognize it for a long while, but when it hit me, I realized that I was just more attracted to men than to women sexually.

R: *Did you know before you got married that you were attracted to men?*

F: I really didn't. It was always sort of shuffled under the carpet. Because I was attracted to women, it just didn't occur to me what my actual feelings were. But I always felt that I was kind of acting. I didn't feel that it was me, even though I enjoyed doing what I was doing—being a husband and a father. But it just didn't feel quite right somehow.

R: *How did you tell your wife?*

F: We weren't relating very well for a period of time—six months or so—and it became very painful for both of us. Neither of us would approach it, you know. Kind of in desperation, I went to a shrink in Boston—the first time I'd ever been to one. He kept questioning me about my fantasies, so to speak, and how I related sexually. I was really getting freaked out and trying not to show it. I finally admitted that I was just as attracted to men as to women and he said, "Well, in this day and age, this seems to be the thing, doesn't it?" He didn't really say he approved of it. Suddenly like a light-bulb in the middle of the room, I realized I was gay and that I really was more attracted to men than to women. Immediately I got this sense that it would come out of me eventually. I'd have to wait for it to see what would happen, although I was very freaked over what I was going to say to my wife. When I went back home, it was very difficult telling her. I thought she'd feel rejected. My palms were sweating and my heart was beating and I was getting real nervous. But she didn't freak out. She just sort of took it, like, "Well, I've lived with you and I don't think you seem all that gay to me." It was really what she felt.

And so we lived together quite a bit longer. Things sort of relaxed for a while. I felt better once I'd told her. When we actually split up, we were coming to a point where we really wanted to be independent anyway.

R: *What finally brought about the split?*

F: For a while we sort of assumed I was bisexual. When it came right down to it, I fell in love with the conga drummer in the band I was playing in. One Christmas—it was like a terrific weight lifting off, because I hadn't slept with anyone else in the seven years that I'd been married.

R: *How has your life changed?*

F: Really a lot. I mean just coming out was the beginning of it. It opened me up to things like playing music. Before, I didn't feel I was being honest and up front, and in order for me to stand up and perform, I had to be saying, "This is me."

R: *Can you describe what's special about a gay band?*

F: There are the usual hassles as in any band, but it's a tight feeling. By the time I left the last band I was in, I was the only gay person in it. It was just very weird—easy to fall into a kind of posturing, or whatever.

Being in a gay band makes things looser—loose in the way of being able to feel free and perform and not feel restricted all the time.

R: *Is your group pretty much musical or is it also in its own way a kind of support group?*

F: Any gay group of people who spend time together are very mutually supportive, I think. Just being a minority makes it something kind of special.

R: *How has coming out affected your relationship to women?*

F: I still like women a lot, but I don't want to give them

the wrong impression. I don't want to mislead anyone into thinking I'm something I'm not. I mean, "I like you" doesn't necessarily mean that "I want to sleep with you." Though I still do sleep with women, I haven't for a long while. I prefer sleeping with men.

R: *How is it different?*

F: There are different things that you do with a man because of anatomical differences. Sometimes I think it's the abstraction of it—that we're not making babies, just relating.

R: *Has this sexual difference made you see things differently?*

F: It really has. It's given me much more of a conviction of my own feelings about the world and how people relate to each other. I think that knowing what you like and being able to go on doing it is very important. Otherwise you can't really take seriously anything you do.

R: *What about your life now?*

F: I live with my lover Andrew. He happens to be black. In a place like San Francisco, it's a regular salad of people, you know.

R: *Is it significant at all that you live with a black lover? You didn't marry a black woman.*

F: I think that white people come in much more contact with black men than they do with women. You just don't run into black women at all. It's frowned upon by the black community for a black woman to go out with a white man. Actually, before I met Andrew, I was going with a black woman. We'd go places and get so much attitude from everybody. The reason she went with mostly gay white men was because they treated her as a person.

R: *Freddy, how do you feel about being a father?*

F: It's great. I'm really glad. I don't regret any of being married. It was a really happy seven years, and being a father or a mother is an experience that obviously most gay people don't have. They miss the good part of straight life, so to speak. I remember when we were going to have Harriet, somebody said babies smell bad and they were a lot of trouble, but I think they're really worth it. I took care of Harriet a lot while she was growing up—my wife was working or going to school. We're still very close.

R: *Is your fatherhood something you can share with the people around you?*

F: I found that gay people in general really like seeing children—love having them around. My friends always love it when Harriet comes over. They look forward to it because they don't see children very much. Andrew was a schoolteacher, so he knows quite a bit about kids. There's no problem there.

R: *How about the fact of having a daughter rather than a son?*

F: When she was born, I was with Ruth, my wife, until almost the very end of her labor. The doctor came in and told me I had a daughter. I got this instantaneous disappointment—it was a reflex action. But it was just for a split second. Having a child, period, is so amazing . . .

R: *Does she know you're gay?*

F: I've always been very open with her as far as who I felt
affectionate toward. I mean, I am the same in front of her
as I would be in front of anyone. I actually brought it up; we
had a little discussion about it. I got the sense that she knew
the way things were—not only how they were in relation to
her, but how society felt about them. She understood that
some people don't feel especially sympathetic to gay people.

She has two friends, two little girls, and there are some gay
women who live down the street. Ruth, my wife, told me
about a time when the girls were getting into a car and one of
the gay women was also getting into a car down the street.
The two kissed each other, and the two little girls sort of
giggled and made some derogatory comment about dykes or
something like that. So Harriet's aware that it is not necessarily the most popular thing in the world . . .

(Andrew joins Freddy)

R: *Maybe you can tell me something about your life
together.*

ANDREW: We met in 1975, and it's been eternal bliss ever
since.

R: *And for you too, Freddy?*

F: Yeah, absolutely.

R: *Do you talk together about being gay?*

A: I think we talk together about how to work out the
relationship more than about being gay. I think gay relationships are different from straight ones.

R: *How do you think they're different?*

A: Ego, to begin with. You know, who's going to win.
We're in an equal position, and so it makes it harder when
you're arguing.

F: It's really easy to get into wanting to concede to the other person—doing what you feel would be pleasant. You get both people doing that, and you're nowhere at all.

R: *By current gay styles, you both would be considered pretty butch. Is it something you're conscious of?*

A: It's something I'm conscious of, but I think I grew up in a very butch society and I guess, in a way, I'm mimicking it. But in other ways, I've learned to express my feminine side.

F: Right. I find I've really gotten back after going through some changes about my feminine side. I've kind of settled into what's comfortable for me. But I get off seeing really imaginative drag queens walking up and down the street as much as I do someone butch. The whole national style has become really butch. Like, there was sort of a unisex thing for a while, with fashion and the magazines pushing it.

A: I've thought about wearing women's shoes, but I wear size 12! Somebody said that you find out what the other side of the coin is like when you try to dress up differently.

R: *How do you work out your relationship? Do you see other people besides each other?*

A: Yeah, we both see other people. I think you have to.

F: You just never bring anybody home. That's a very important rule.

A: I think we both have needs that have to be fulfilled separately. For about the first five or six months of the relationship, we spent a lot of time together.

I think the whole monogamy thing is changing for everybody—for straight people and gay people. It's not the thing to stay at home with a lot of kids anymore, or even to have a lot of kids in the first place. So that sort of starts a new move away from the family.

F: You know, what I've learned is that we, indeed, do create our reality. We can do whatever we want in this country—as long as you know where you're going.

Ann

NANCY: *Have you always known you were a homosexual?*

ANN: I met one homosexual when I was about twenty-three years old—an old man who happened to be at a party. He was the only gay person I'd ever met until I met the woman who I fell in love with and came out with. Until I was twenty-five, I lived a very straight life. I had a lot of experiences with men and several long-term relationships with men; I lived with men and came very close to marriage. None of my relationships were bad, but when I was a senior in veterinary school, I began to realize the pressures that a heterosexual relationship placed on me. It happened that the man I was engaged to was also a veterinary student, and I found myself embarrassed when I did better than he did. I noticed that I would be submissive at times when I shouldn't be, that I was hesitant to express myself sexually. I realized it was very wrong and very stifling to me as an individual. So I ended up not getting married. Also, at that point, I had pretty much made a decision that I would never get married, and I even discussed this with my parents. This was before I'd even considered homosexuality as a lifestyle.

N: *Do you feel that if the roles had been less rigidly defined, you might have gotten married?*

A: Yes, I probably could have gotten married and been fairly happy. But now that I'm a lesbian, I have doubts that I could ever do that. I think a lot of my coming out was sort of fate. I just happened to meet the right person, a person I was not afraid of.

When I was in veterinary school, I was very close to six other women in my class. Sexually, I was not involved with any of them, but at that point, my true feelings about women and feminism and sisterhood really began. For four years, I was definitely in a male-dominated area, but all of us—the women I was emotionally close with—shared a lot of ideas and gave each other a lot of support. Also I became more aware of the strengths of the women in my family. I noticed how my mother and my aunts functioned in their roles. Even though I wasn't out marching, I considered myself—and was considered—a feminist. I think the closeness I shared with the six women in my class gave me a solid background in the strength that women can give each other—the sharing that can't be gained in a heterosexual relationship.

N: *Did it ever occur to you to have a sexual relationship with a woman at that time?*

A: No. I was very repressed. I think I had not any permission at all to even consider it—permission from society, permission from myself. I never considered it as an alternative. I grew up in a fairly small town in West Virginia—in the country. I didn't know any gay people. I'd no experience—nothing to base any feelings on, really. I did have feelings about women when I was younger, but I didn't relate to them as sexual feelings . . . not until I met a lesbian and talked to her about her feelings. Then I realized who I was. It didn't take long!

N: *When were you first aware of homosexuality?*

A: I remember my parents talking about one of our distant relatives who had been married and had gone off to the war. When he came back, something had happened, and he was a different person. It was insinuated that he had turned queer because of the stress of being away from home. Then, when I was in veterinary school, we went to this state mental institution to test their cows—all the state institutions had farms and cattle that the patients tended.

Anyway, we worked in the morning testing the cattle for TB, and at lunch time the supervisor was telling us what went on and where different wings were, and he said, "That wing over there is for people who are rapists; and that wing is for people who have committed murder; and that wing over there is for people who are homosexuals." On the way back to school, we all rode in this big van, talking, and I said I couldn't believe that a whole wing was homosexuals, that just because of their sexual preference they were there. Well, they had probably committed other crimes, but they were signified as being homosexual.

When I look back, for some reason, I had a very positive feeling about gayness and homosexuality. I thought it was so unreal that people would be classified in a mental institution that way. I didn't think it was particularly sick to be a homosexual. Maybe because I'd led such an isolated life. I hadn't had a lot of influences to make me have negative feelings toward gay people.

N: *How did you come out?*

A: I had been working for a year, and I moved down here—not knowing anybody. I led a pretty lonely life. I was busy with my work and didn't have much of a chance to get to know anyone. The main contact I had was with people I worked with. I met a woman who was a lab technician at Duke, and I was involved in some of her research. We became good friends and started doing things together. She was living with another woman who was also a professional person at Duke. When I went to visit them at their house, I noticed there was only one bedroom, with only one bed in it. I put one and one together and started thinking, "Could they possibly be gay?" And I thought, "No, they're both just nice people and beautiful women." I don't know exactly the picture of lesbianism that I painted in my mind. I'd never met a lesbian before and never had any pictures. I knew Ann had some secret about her life she wasn't telling me. She'd talked about how she had almost lost a job one time, but when I asked her why, she avoided the question. I tried to think of the worst thing. "Well," I thought, "she's into drugs." And then I thought, "No, that's not bad enough." It didn't seem logical. We were sitting in my living room one night and I said, "What is this terrible thing? I'm really an open person and I can handle it." And she said, "I really don't want to tell you about this." And I said, "It's to the point where I know there's something, and you might as well tell me." And she said, "I'm gay. Did you know?" So I said, "I'd thought about it some." I remained very cool and assured her it wouldn't matter.

After she left, I went through all kinds of freak-outs, at first thinking it'd be a strain on our friendship. But I thought it over; I was able to overcome my fears. I said to myself, "Well, she can be my friend, and I can probably learn a lot from her about this type of lifestyle." Which was sure true. It also gave me permission to start thinking about myself. The more I was around Ann and the woman whom she lived with, the more I saw what a strong relationship they had, and I felt that it was really good. I wasn't freaked out about their sexuality with each other.

As time went on, I was being very turned on when I was around Ann. I had had a lot of experience sexually, so I knew that's what it was. I had to go through a long process of thinking whether it was worth it to me to take the risks as far as a job goes, and to make the sacrifices as far as society goes. When I finally made the big decision, it was all a very calculated thing. I went to the beach with a man over a long weekend and knew that I didn't want to be there, that I wanted to be back with those women. And I came back from that weekend accepting that I was gay, wanting to have a relationship with Ann but not knowing what that would involve with regard to the other woman, not wanting Ann to lose that relationship. It was really a radical change.

N: *Why did you say you were gay as opposed to bisexual? Didn't you feel that you might simply be attracted to this particular woman and that maybe it was a phase?*

A: Because I had a lot of experience with men. I knew that I could do very well without them, that if I could have a relationship with a woman, it would be much more fulfilling.

When I came back from the beach with this great decision in my mind, I was really the first one to make the move with Ann. One day when we were alone, I reached over and took her hand, and that was an indication that I was willing to be physical with her. I had not only decided that I was gay but also that I was very much in love with her. Talking about it was not as significant as the actual physical touch. I mean, never having had an experience with a woman, for some reason it was just more important to indicate with a touch that said, "Hey, I'm in love with you. What are we going to do about it?"

It was sort of a gradual thing until I actually had a sexual experience. And there was also the involvement with the other woman Ann was living with. We worked things out among the three of us.

N: *How did you feel after your first sexual relationship with a woman?*

A: Well, it was a wonderful feeling. Aside from being so much in love, it was definitely a different life for me. It was a whole . . . just like opening a new door into a new life. It would be impossible to really describe my feelings that whole summer. It was very different. I was able to be more expressive—more aggressive, possibly. Sex seemed more gentle—not that I had particularly rough lovers before, but women are softer. Talking about sex with women was somehow different.

N: *How were you able to live with Ann and the other woman?*

A: Originally it was the three of us together. Then I felt the need to have relationships with other people. I think a lot of it was because I was pretty new in the gay scene and had a lot of questions that I wanted to answer. For several years, we had a lot of problems just dealing with each other's jealousies. We have been in group therapy together—and it's working, in that we can be open with each other and say how we feel. Even when we go through terrible stresses and get upset at times, we are still able to sense the great strength that we all have and how much we can give each other. We have had different types of relationships, and they keep on changing.

As far as the future of the farm, we all want to keep it together. We like living in the country, and we all enjoy each other. We make each other aware; we educate each other.

N: *Do you feel that one reason you have the living arrangement that you do is that, in some ways, you lose closeness with your family because you're gay? Is the farm an alternative family?*

A: Well, I'm still very close to my parents, but it's a matter of establishing your own place, establishing your own family—just the way heterosexual couples do. It's your own identity, really. And we function basically as a family as far as making decisions and sharing money.

N: *Does your family know that you are gay?*

A: My parents don't know. I think they sense that I'm gay and that I'm very happy—happier than I've ever been. And I'm sure they can sense that I'm stronger and more independent. They recognize my friends here at the farm in lots of different ways. Like at Christmas, they give everyone a gift. My mother said, "I know the chance of you getting married . . . I don't even think about it anymore—even grandchildren." She said that as long as my friends at the farm came to visit, she would be satisfied. And she just came out with that. We weren't having any deep discussion or anything. It was just something she wanted to tell me.

N: *How do you feel when your friends go home to their families or when their families come to visit here, and there's all that recognition of familiness and love, and you have to restrain yourselves?*

A: It's very frustrating. For one thing, I would like very much to share with my family my happiness. I can see the heterosexual people in my family bringing their spouses or their boyfriends or girlfriends home, and it puts me in a very strained position because I can't do that openly. I'm the only adult who isn't married, and they tend to feel sorry for me and try not to talk about things that would upset me. Whether you are with your lover or without your lover, she is as much a part of your life as your immediate family is. If you are with your lover, you can't really express yourself, even if you're lucky enough to be able to sleep in the same room, because you're afraid somebody will walk in or overhear something. It's far from being what I would say is a really good situation.

N: *Why don't you tell them? What is it in your sense of yourself that doesn't allow you to be open with them?*

A: I think I'm really afraid of hurting them, in giving them a situation they won't know how to deal with. That sounds like I don't have much confidence in them, but I have had no indication up to this point that there would be acceptance of me. I hope that someday I'll be able to tell them that it's a good thing, that there's nothing they should blame themselves for. Really, I give them credit for giving me the character that I have—to be open to make these decisions about myself. I think the time is pretty close and I will talk to them.

I've talked to my brother. He was feeling very different from the family and thought he was getting a little distant and I said, "You think *you* feel different! I am gay." And he has been very supportive. He was the first person I told. It was important that a member of my family know, because my family is a big part of my life.

I think my parents would be very afraid of homosexuality, just because they don't have any experience with it. I might be rejected temporarily. I have no doubts that they will still love me. They have strong feelings about me because I am a doctor. But I don't want them to think they have failed for some reason. One thing I'm worried about in doing this movie is that, not my father, but members of his company may see the film and then have some negative feelings about him. And I know that's possible. But one of the reasons—I think possibly subconsciously—I wanted to be in the film is that it may force me into talking to my parents about myself before they find out another way.

One of the big things to know is that there are other people who have this problem of how to tell their parents. There aren't a whole lot of alternatives other than getting up and saying, "I'm gay, and I don't care what other people think." I am trying to deal with it in a more acceptable way—sort of ease them into it. I want them to know me and love me and know what I'm doing is good for me before I just tell them and have them make a lot of hasty decisions about it.

N: *What are your priorities?*

A: A woman first, then a lesbian, then a veterinarian. The one I place the most value on, the one I cherish the most, is the fact that I am a woman. I enjoy other women whether they are straight or gay. The next most important thing in my life is my lesbianism. It's more a way of life than a sexuality for me. The last thing I place priority on is my profession. I don't put it before my womanhood or my lesbianism; if I had to give up any of the three things, my profession would be the first to go. Just by being in this film, I am willing to take the chance professionally. I suppose it has to do with more confidence in my sense of myself and my lesbianism. I find myself expressing my anger more, taking more chances than I would have several years ago. There are just so many

things to be angry with, from the standpoint of a gay person—
like not being able to freely walk down the street with a lover,
like filling out your income tax and having to deal with "your
wife's name," filling out surveys that ask whether you're
single or married. I participated in a survey on women veteri-
narians that was done by some students at Cornell. One of
the questions asked about marital status, with boxes to check
that read, "married, divorced, single, or widowed." When I
filled out the questionnaire, I realized that none of these definitions applied to me. So I drew in my own little box and put
"lesbian, with own responsibilities." I wish I could have
been there when they opened all these questionnaires and
started reading them. Until we do things like that and make
people aware that there are a lot of gay people who aren't
able to say who they are because there's no chance to say it,
no one will be aware of us. When I drew the box and checked
it, that was an expression of my anger and frustration. I'm
not the type of person who screams and yells and throws
things.

N: *Is being a feminist an expression of your anger?*

A: Definitely.

N: *How do you feel knowing that you are one of the few
professionals who was willing to be filmed?*

A: One of the reasons that I wanted to do the film is that
I think it's a real sad situation that more professional people—
men and women—don't feel that they can be open about
their homosexuality and aren't able to express it even with
other professional people who are homosexual. I know that
there are many gay people who are in positions they are
afraid to risk, but the public isn't going to be aware of gay
people in professional positions unless gay people are willing
to speak out.

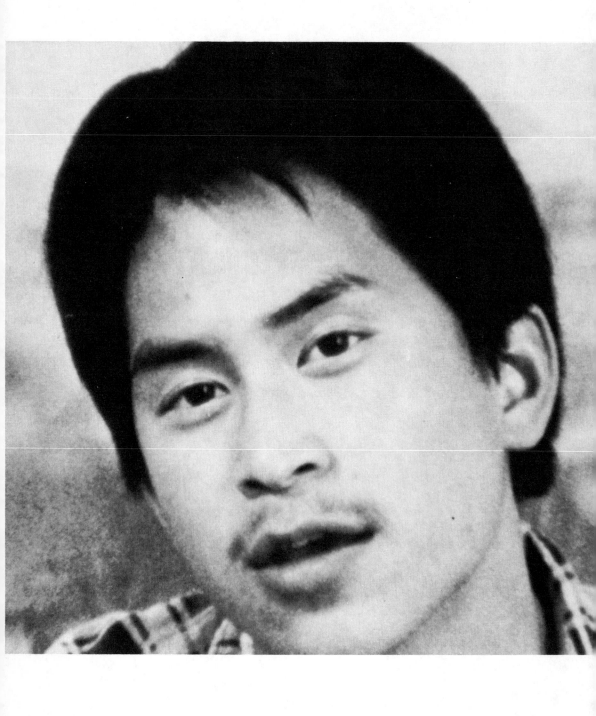

Dennis

ROB: *Tell me about yourself—like, are you out of the closet?*

DENNIS: In a sense, I'm in many closets. When you've been a long time not yourself, it is really hard to creep out. I'm in a closet as to my being neither gay nor straight in the accepted senses of the words—I sure could do without those labels. I think they're really dangerous. It's so easy for a gay Asian coming out to say, "OK. There's a gay counter-culture; let me start going to gay movies, gay bars, pick up gay literature, become interested in gay liberation." I think that's fine, but also there's a point where you have to establish your own individual boundaries. One has to be careful to remember that one is oneself and that one cannot rely on these individual labels for support.

If you're a minority within a minority, it really requires—at least for me—sticking up for myself in a lot of ways. I don't belong to the 80 percent Caucasian, straight majority. I don't have those allegiances. So you feel kind of marginal in that you're neither white nor black, and if you don't fit into the gay mold, then you're not exactly gay either. It's a matter of living up to people's expectations. No matter how hard I worked, I would never come up to my expectations of what a gay person or an Asian person was like. I don't fit into either of those slots.

More and more, it's true that I don't need white images to prop me up. But, to some extent, I really feel deficient physically and in terms of my cultural background. Like, I'm still trying for new images; it's the process of image-making which is really important.

R: *Why is that? What is that process?*

D: I think, in the beginning, it involves forming mental images of the people you would like to be, and it doesn't stop until you've found an image of yourself which makes all those other images much less important. When you're a kid, you have John Wayne, you have Steve McQueen, and if you're a slant-eyed Chinese kid, and if you happen to be slightly effeminate—really, it drives knives into your stomach! It's really scary standing in isolation from everybody else— and that's what I feared most of my life: the fact that I wasn't part of a group. I think far too often I carry a mask. There's part of me that wants to be the stoic man, buddy-buddy type thing. And there's a part of me which is really very gentle.

R: *Which part is easier for you to accept?*

D: I think they're both equally uncomfortable. It's easier for me to be a robot, I think. That's one way out—to carry a mask every day. It's partially a defense mechanism because I see the world through eyes of anger. It's really hard to tell yourself: it's really OK to be confused, it's really OK to feel that you want to be masculine if it doesn't make you uncomfortable, it's OK to act feminine, to let it out. But the idea of flowing, of being graceful, of yielding is really pretty terrifying—yielding in the sense of expressing feelings of comfort, of warmth, of desire, of sensuality. Sensual man is probably a faggot, according to a lot of images that I have in my mind.

Basically, I'm a sensual person. Part of me is very movement-orientated, physical. I feel I have so much to explore in terms of my body feelings, but I think that in the present society it's considered unmanly to be concerned about subtle physical responses—just any kind of physicality. Dance, for instance— dance is something that I know a lot of men that I've met felt very uncomfortable about because you don't see Al Pacino or Robert De Niro really concerned about feeling comfortable about their bodies. It's considered obsessive to live your day with the maximum concern for the way your body feels. But that's not really too positive. I think it behooves me to really consider what it is I feel good about—and that can be a very simple thing: how my body feels when I stretch or something, little things that tell you your body is unique, and nobody can take that away from you. I mean, you're secure in your own body, and it doesn't matter what other people say.

R: *Let's talk now about when you were first aware of sex—*
your family informing you about sex and what kinds of things
they told you, or what the whole feeling about sex in your
family was.

D: My parents never talked about sex. It had to do, I
think, with sex being something aggressive. There's a kind of
anti-social thing about sex which I think really influenced
me. In a sense, the body was not supposed to elicit pleasure
or anything like that. My parents never, for the life of me,
mentioned sex, but there were unconscious things. I think
sex is something that's like a great feeder for a lot of other
feelings, and I think that my sexual feelings were partly pro-
jections of my own anger and discontent with my parents.
It was sort of a rebellion against all of their taboos. It was the
ultimate challenge to their authority to be sexually aware,
because in their whole world there was no place for sex.

R: *So when did you have your first sexual experience?*
Can you tell me about it?

D: I was aware of sex at a very early age. I had sexual feelings. I had penile erections at a very early age looking at illus-
trations of powerfully built men—probably because I wanted
to be one myself, and the only way that I could do that was
to have these sexual fantasies. I masturbated—ever since the
fourth grade or something. There was this book I was taking
a look at, and, all of a sudden, I connected that with all these
other feelings I had when I looked at photographs of men in
swimming trunks or something. I felt rather guilty about it. I
guess part of the feeling was that my body was always the
body of a boy, and the body of a man is something that I
kind of feel my parents never wanted me to feel comfortable
with.

R: *What was your first gay experience?*

D: I was sitting in this auditorium for a screening of Part
Three of Kenneth Clark's *Civilization* series, and it was all

very innocent. It was in the dark, and somebody sat down right next to me. It was really outrageous. He put his knee, you know, really close to mine, and I don't know how it happened, but our legs just . . . just crossed over, and his leg was really, really warm. It was electric, and I responded spontaneously. I was, as the expression goes, turned on. It was my first turn-on—probably the first and last of its kind too—the first time I ever had physical contact with another man. I went back to see, like, Parts Four and Five!

R: *How about your first sexual experience with a man? Was that good or bad?*

D: My first sexual experience was a bummer. I can't beat around the bush on that account. It was with a guy who was really rather uptight about sex. He was married, and he had children, and he was, like, ten, fifteen years older than I was. I think he was really discontented with his life. He wasn't a person I was really interested in getting to know. That makes a big difference. We got off onto the wrong track. You kind of suppose that every sexual encounter is going to be the same way—a quickie-type thing—when, in fact, I think I was really looking for a long-lasting relationship. It was very frustrating. All my fantasies were about having a long-term, physical, sexual, and emotional relationship with another guy closer to my own age—a kind of older-brother-type image, somebody I could idealize, idolize. He wasn't that at all. It lacked the romantic, basically. That is an important thing for me.

R: *Let's talk a little bit about gay Asians, and how you feel—what you have to deal with in this country being a gay Asian.*

D: It really makes me feel much better to say that I'm neither straight nor gay. When you go out into the "world," it's basically yourself. You put yourself on the line; you don't sell your gayness, or you don't sell your Chineseness. It's the doing of the day-to-day activities which makes me myself—

my own idiosyncrasies, my own patterns of the way I react to things. Now I feel some comfort in knowing myself, in knowing my own true feelings, not having to keep clothes in every closet. For one, I don't feel comfortable with a lot of the gay counter-culture. It only evokes in me a kind of phony "Well, let's act gay" kind of thing. I recognize that it's so easy for me to act gay in a conventional sense—which is not me.

That's not where my head is at. I think people really have to discover—not where their genitals are at, but where their hearts are at. I think people are really afraid of giving their hearts away. You have to be willing to go through a lot of hurt. I have tended to shy away from experiencing a lot of pain, but I can survive a certain amount of fear; things are not going to totally overwhelm me if it looks like my environment is indifferent or hostile or repressive. Really, when I started to say, "I'm going to be myself. I'm not going to come out and also put on a mask," then I really got a sort of . . . dignity for myself.

I think a lot of gay people put a high premium on looks. It's a movie-star type of feeling. It's like—what are those birds called?—mockingbirds. All they do is imitate the chatter of other birds. That's why I feel uncomfortable with a lot of gay people. I know it's so easy for me to go around doing limp imitations of reality, of those things which are really real. I sense a lack of genuine feeling. A lot of gay people mirror back in the same arrangement what we call straight values. I think there's a lot of emphasis on the plastic, on the materialistic, on the shiny, the harsh.

R: *Does that include gay Asians?*

D: That includes Asians particularly, because I think there's such a societal instinct to try to act white, to act straight, or to act gay. And it's really infuriating to see people settling for second best. Gay Asians tend to mimic a whole lot of white gay values which I think are really detrimental to the emergence of selves which are free to create. I think there are a lot of gay images that emphasize the whiteness, the blue-eyedness, the blondness. I'm angry about that. I think the only way not to be second best is to start gaining support from being one's self—no matter how tacky, no matter how unfamiliar one finds oneself. I'm never going to gain an inch by trying to imitate other people. Dishonesty hurts more than the truth ever would.

I think it's a whole social consciousness. It starts with individuals saying, "Yeah. I'm gay, but how do I feel about being gay?" That question, in itself, makes you appear more human to yourself. In terms of coming out for gay Asians, I think that one can come out when one can come out as an Asian. And I think that if Asian parents accept themselves as having yellow faces, they can truly accept their children as having different sexual inclinations. I think that's the gist of it. That's one thing that gay Asians have in favor of themselves that white gay people don't: every Asian knows deep down somewhere that it is rough to be an Asian.

It's a hard point. I think gay Chinese people have to deal with the fact that they are of a different color. It doesn't separate people forever, but it's something that they have to come to terms with. Being white gives you a kind of security in a sense that I don't have. I cannot fall back on white impersonations. At a certain point, people start throwing all these labels on you. You start to realize, "Yes, I do have a brown or a yellow face, and the way I act is characteristically feminine or masculine, and it's wrong to do these things." For me, it's a question of somehow getting through this whole thicket of confusion: "You should be this way; you shouldn't be that way." I know a lot of Asians disregard this whole thing and say, "I feel like an American. My yellowness doesn't have anything to do with my relating to other white people." But where I'm coming from is the fact that I do feel unique. I do feel different things. Maybe it's an indication that beneath the yellow skin, I really do have different spatial, logical patterns from white people, but I've been afraid to show these. A lot of Asians are just too damn passive. I mean, it's like they try to act like white people. Nothing turns me off more than a Chinese person who tries to act like an American.

R: *How about a gay person trying to act straight?*

D: A lot of straight behavior is what I term "normal behavior." A lot of gay behavior is not normal. It's a perversion of some sort. A lot of what I see is something I'm thoroughly disgusted with.

R: *Well, what is positive behavior? What is normal?*

D: Normal is happy. I think you have to have an inner strength and peace—that kind of thing. I think to really be yourself—no matter what that might be—is an asset. Just believing enough in myself to be what I can be. I think that if you can relate to one other person—gay, straight, male, female, white, black, yellow—you know that's where it really starts to count. In that sense, I'm really afraid of limiting my

experience to people of one kind. I think I have a lot to learn, really, and I think a lot of it has to do with giving up the fact that growing up was really painful for me.

You go through a lot of hurt when someone calls you a "Chinaman." And so, in one sense, you're more able to deal with someone calling you a "fag." And you can spring back more easily and say, "I'm a person. I am me."

Nick

VERONICA: *Talk about the first times you felt sexual—straight or gay.*

NICK: I can remember when I was in around the fourth or fifth grade having one or two friends who I would always wrestle with in the schoolyard, and it wasn't at all heavy, in a sense, because you were just wrestling. You were at a time before puberty. It was a time when everything was all right; boys were still boys. There wasn't this feeling of territory and all the sorts of myths that came in puberty— a certain sense of isolation which guys had to have from one another. It didn't exist at that age. I just remember, really, this sort of sublime feeling and sort of an afterglow, like, wrestling with friends—just the feeling that I got out of it.

V: *What was your contact with girls at the time?*

N: There was one girlfriend I had—around third grade, fourth grade, fifth grade—whom I liked very, very much. Somehow, there was no shyness between us; we were very natural together. It didn't feel like a role. It felt like male/female, but it didn't feel like male/female in the extreme sense. It seemed as if we were equals; when she would go up to sharpen her pencil, I would go up to sharpen my pencil, and we used to go out on dates and go ice-skating. She ice-skated well. She was a good athlete, and I never felt with her that I was playing any games; it felt very natural.

During this same period, I can remember being very, very fascinated with boys. It was still prepubic—a time when everything is just starting to wake up and feel good—but everything is still very nonspecific. I remember around fifth grade, there was a boy in the sixth grade—I remember really liking the way his rear end looked. I guess the way his pants fit was probably pretty good. I remember really liking it. Then I also remember during a Boy Scout campout, a jamboree, we would try to seduce other boys who were camping out. This is still prepubic, considering I hadn't come yet. We'd take off our pants, and we'd lie together and neck in a sort of way and certainly rub our crotches together and stuff. And I was really into it. But it wasn't unusual at that time; everyone was sort of into it. I think at that age everything was just happening. It was just sexual; you didn't think of it. There weren't any stigmas yet.

In seventh grade—I was coming at this point—I remember we used to have these parties about every two weeks down in someone's cellar—with 45s, and coke, and potato chips. One party turned into a queer party. All of a sudden, these two gals just started to French-kiss one another—I guess we were around thirteen. They were just kissing and kissing. So we put on these slow records, and all of the boys were dancing together to these real slow fifties' rock-and-roll records, and all the gals were sitting over on the couch French-kissing. And I really loved it! I liked dancing with boys more than dancing with girls—probably because, at that point, girls were so crinoline covered. Everyone had just layers of crinoline, so you didn't feel you could be openly sexual with the gals. I remember that the thing about dancing with the guys is that it immediately became erotic. The girls seemed less like real people and stuff. The feelings at that time were: the guys wanted it; the gals prevented it. I remember actually being shocked in my very late teens by actually hearing a girl say that she desired a guy.

V: So your relationships with girls were just as friends. Then when the crinolines came in, it changed into a relationship with the boys. Could you talk about that?

N: I remember being so hot! I had sort of mixed feelings about it. I remember telling a good friend of mine, "You know, sometimes I really want to blow somebody, and sometimes I don't want to do it at all." It's like you're so concerned with your concern that you're paranoid. You attempt to figure out what's going on and how to play it. I felt ill at ease—but it wasn't consciously because I felt I was gay. I had the same kind of consciousness that any adolescent has—very paranoid about my nose and stuff like that. I don't think I could really separate my gay feelings from my insecurities.

My answer to my ill-at-easedness was union with other boys. Sexual intimacy. But going to bed with a guy involved really giving up something, in a way, and there are not too many people who are willing to do that. That was pretty much unrequited, so it became obsessive—like anything that you don't get enough of in a clean way. You begin to have a real big secret. I would stand in urinals and wait for other kids to pee and check out their cock size. I would have fantasies. In a certain way, I realize now that part of that obsession was, for some reason, I wasn't willing to accept myself as a male. I guess I had very little sense of myself. Therefore, you sort of get out of balance; you're looking for that male everywhere around you. There was very little else I could think about. I was an only child—I didn't have any brothers—so I became extremely fascinated with what other boys were. Here was this amazing thing that I was experiencing, and I was just fascinated with what other boys were doing, what they were experiencing.

One thing I remember that's interesting—right as the male/ female-type dating started. The girl I'd been friendly with up until this point was very pretty, in retrospect. But, at least in terms of the conversation among the guys, she wasn't considered a real "catch." Because my relationship with her was so friendly, it was outside of what you were supposed to get—which was a girlfriend. It seemed to me that because we enjoyed each other so much—and we'd go skating together and stuff like that, and shared a mutual sense of humor—that somehow that was considered outside the area of romance— of sex, in a way. Actually, I remember complaining to my parents that I didn't like the girls as much as the guys. Many of the girls at that period were extremely poised and a little artificial. There wasn't a kind of interaction that I'd see with the boys. There were interests I could share with the boys, but the gals seemed to be in such a different place, in such a different world. I didn't feel comfortable with the whole thing.

V: *Can you talk about what you liked in men, in boys?*

N: There was something warmer and less mannered with the boys than with the girls. Like I said, there were a few girls whom I felt really friendly with, but I think I was really afraid somehow that that wasn't romance or something. Then when I got older, in junior high school, it was the first period when you realized that in order to be a guy, all of a sudden you had to be a little less friendly—in a very subtle way—to other guys. That edge began to enter into it, where you all of a sudden realized you couldn't display that interest. You began to sacrifice part of your heart in a sense.

I think that's maybe true of all boys at that period. During high school years, it wasn't that unusual for guys to have some sort of sex or another with one another. But starting around the ninth, tenth grade, it first started to become frowned on. It's sort of like, "We're over this sort of discovery period; we're more like guys, and we're generally interested in gals." But I found myself still equally interested in guys. Partly, there were a lot of unrequited feelings. I became so fascinated with other guys! I got myself into a position where I admired other guys so much, thought they were so beautiful, so perfect. They were all that I wanted. I got into a state of mind where I, in a sense, lost any sense that I was also a guy. It wasn't extreme. I mean, I played sports, I took out gals, and so forth, but way down deep inside, I was getting so completely preoccupied with other boys that I began to lose the sense that I myself was also a boy. The whole syndrome became more and more intense as we went up through teen-age years to the point where I had just an absolute fascination for other boys. And more and more, I forgot about what possibilities I myself had. It seems kind of odd in retrospect, but it became a very intense reality for me. At that point, going out with gals and so forth became more and more difficult because I almost went down this tunnel of feeling more and more inferior in a way.

V: *. . . to the other men?*

N: Yes. It was a double thing. I didn't really feel inferior to the other guys, but I had such a yearning and a longing to have intimacy with other boys, and there was so little room to express that in any kind of wholehearted, open-hearted way, that it almost began to enter into the realm of a fetish. I would be almost hypnotized by the qualities, the physical qualities, that other boys had—and never would take a look at myself in any positive way and say, "Hey, I'm this way too." I can even say why I was attracted to the guys.

V: *I'd like to hear that. Do you think you felt that because you were gay, you felt inferior to the other guys and wanted them?*

N: I liked the other guys. For me, being attracted to them had nothing to do with being a fairy or being effeminate or anything like that. It had to do with the fact I liked their maleness, and, in a sense, I wanted that. For whatever reasons, I prohibited myself from simply saying, "I've got those qualities." In a strange way, it's sort of like you deny yourself in order to get something. I'm not sure why I thought I didn't have it, and why I thought everyone else had it. I don't know. Part of it is that actually I found the boys very attractive, and that feeling was so misplaced in the society at the time.

V: *Do you think that your attraction to men is purely physiological? Is it the difference in anatomy?*

N: Well, I don't know. I can't separate anatomy from male psyche or whatever—what a male is and what a female is. What I like about men, what the really beautiful thing is about men— or can be about men—is a very clean sense of maleness. There's a real beautiful quality in male energy, which I found was most beautiful when it had its feminine part equally woven into it—which is why it became so intense. The boys had the maleness, the strength, a sort of strength and directness mixed in with a sort of floatiness, a sense of prettiness.

V: *. . . whereas the women had it beat out of them? It's not clear to me how much of who the men were and who the*

*women were was because of who they were allowed to be,
and how much of it was because of inherent difference. See
what I'm getting into? Maybe there is no basic difference?*

N: I think that each person has to find that which balances
him off the most. I feel that I have a very good balance of
male and female qualities. I really enjoy both of them tre-
mendously. I find that the women that I get along with, who
are my good friends, share that kind of balance in male- and
femaleness. In a sense, we're both really sharing the same
kind of friendship, sharing the same kind of balance within
ourselves.

V: *Straight women?*

N: I would say modern women. Whether they're gay
women or straight women, or gay men or straight men, the
people I enjoy the most seem to feel really comfortable with
the balance. The men and women I know, especially gay men
and women, are really finding out about their "male" quality—
which is really terrific. Not in any cartoon sense of being
butch, but that kind of directness that I feel is the real heart,
the real beauty, of being male. Many guys are being less paranoid and cartoony about their softness. There's so little para-
noia, so little territory, that, in a way, it's a return to the kind
of friendship that I talked about earlier. It's the kind of thing
I feel very comfortable with myself.

V: *Do you feel that your feelings about homosexuality
have changed in the last few years?*

N: I'm thirty-four now, and, in an odd way—to be perfectly
honest—I'm finding that a lot of the real strong homosexual
feelings I have are—at this point—almost nostalgic. I'm almost
nostalgic for that hunger, that intense sort of circle that I was
a part of all during adolescence. Essentially, I was almost like
a junkie: "I'm looking for a guy. Oh, if I could be that guy,"
or "Maybe that guy'll be around the corner; maybe the guy'll

be here; maybe the guy'll be in the grocery store; maybe the guy'll be in the class I'm taking."

Over the last few years, I've gone through a change where—I don't know if it's natural maturation or what—I realize that I *am* that guy. I *am* the guy. That, in a way, is disorienting. There is an incredible sense of relief and simplicity—to come to the realization that I am it, that it's not outside me some-place. At the same time, to give up all that pain is hard in a way. It was my identity. It was also like alcoholism in a sense. I didn't have to deal with other things because all I had to do was get into this thing that I'm looking for myself, and I could become so self-absorbed in that that I didn't have to worry about anything else. Now there's a lot more freedom; I don't feel like I'm a slave, that I'm being led by the nose anymore. But there's also something about giving up something that intense.

It might sound from what I'm saying that my homosexual feelings are just something from adolescence that are sort of going away. I don't think that's it. I think really what it is, in a sense, is that I'm becoming a more mature human being in that I'm free; I feel a freedom just to be sexual. I don't think my psyche can notch into this thing of being straight, gay, bi-sexual—like on a dial from one arrow to the other. I imagine it would be different things at different times in my life, and I also feel that I want different balances. The one thing I think I have now is the freedom to love *people.* I have the freedom to love someone—I have the freedom to be human, in a sense, rather than just the object of some kind of hysteria—which probably came out of just trying to keep something a secret for so long.

Betty

VERONICA: *You asked whether you were going to be the only black lesbian in the film. Could you elaborate on that question?*

BETTY: What I was trying to say when I asked you if I would be the only black lesbian in the film is: do you know we come in all shapes and colors and directions to our lives? And are you capturing that on the film? As a black lesbian-feminist involved in the movement, so often people try to put me in the position of speaking for all black lesbians. I happen to be *a* black lesbian among many, and I wouldn't want to be seen as "this is how all black lesbians are." There are so many of us black lesbians who live out lives in so many different kinds of ways that I was hoping the film would be able to give a broader spectrum of a black lesbian than just me.

There are few blacks in the gay movement, in that there is a polarity in the general society. And so I find myself very much alone in many instances. One of the heaviest questions I have to deal with is "Are you black first, or are you lesbian first?" I'm obviously black always and forever. And I am committed to feminism as a lesbian. It's an increasing process of working within all that I am, without trying to co-opt or rationalize. I don't see these identities as separate, though in reality one would say that there are things that I do not do in the black community because I know that I would feel the hassle of rejection if I present myself fully as I am. At the same time, I have a binding relationship with black feminists—women who have a sense of themselves as somewhat eccentric, on the outside of the black community.

I find I have conflicts about working in the gay movement with its priorities of sexuality and sexual preferences when I consider, as a black person, the racism, the suffering, the poverty of the black community. At the same time, I have to look at where I come from. I think that so much of the oppression of women is a key, is central to the other craziness like racism. I have a feeling that if we can get at really changing power relationships and power understandings around the oppression of women, that's where it has to be right now. And I'm not saying that everybody should give top priority to that, in the same way that I don't want people to say that every black person has to make top priority dealing with the oppression of blacks. They all come together, and they all have different places.

V: *Have you always been gay?*

B: No, I was straight most of my life. I got married in 1965, when I was twenty-five. I was just beginning to have a black consciousness—not in terms of the whole concept of "black is beautiful"—and there was not a feminist consciousness at all. There was something simplistic about the marriage. We thought it was what we were put on this earth for, you know. We were just sort of following the rules. You know, he'd get a good job and we'd just progress in our careers and have a couple of kids and buy a house and make our parents proud grandparents; that our kids would be better educated. They would have more opportunities, whether it was to be in Little League or in all-American, apple-pie kinds of dreams. While we really loved each other and had respect for each other, in a sense our souls were not totally in it—our souls that were yet to evolve. We were happy in a simple kind of way. I used to date white fellas. Most of my friends in New York were from college; it was a very white world that I moved in. I just never had much contact with the black community. And at one point in my life I remember getting very frightened and thinking, "Oh God!—I'm never going to meet somebody to marry—you know, cause I couldn't deal with marrying a white person. It just wouldn't work in this culture. So when Bill came along, I think we were both enamored to find each other. We were both Catholic, college-educated, with the dream that was very real—to be what our parents wanted us to be, to be freer, have more of a chance at creating the nuclear family and staying together because we wouldn't have the economic oppression that our parents and their parents had to face. And we struggled very hard to be the perfect young black couple.

V: *What happened?*

B: What happened? My husband told me he was gay. I think he went through the classic process that many gay males go through, when you're viewing homosexuality as a sickness—thinking that marriage would cure it.

V: *Which is how the Catholic church views it?*

B: Right. I think it's just being brought up with so much consciousness of sin and guilt and how you're supposed to erase sin and repent for it.

V: *How did you react?*

B: I was devastated, because as much as I had a sense, as an educated person has, of what homosexuality was, it was as if it were an unknown to me. But it wasn't unknown. I think I knew more about it than I would let myself know . . .

V: *How do you mean that?*

B: Ah, it's hard. I had a relationship with a woman before I was married. It was a sexual relationship, but I never knew the word "lesbian." Part of that relationship was a whole emotional support and going to school together through our master's degrees and going out on dates together. It's very hard to talk about this because it was such an uncanny thing that I completely dismissed it from my mind and got married. I guess a lot of people have what would be homosexual relationships, but they're either short-lived or a once-in-a-lifetime kind of thing where you tend to discount them as if they really didn't happen—especially if you couldn't put a label on it. The fact that I had gone on to get married and build the dreams . . . there was just no way I could understand how Bill could possibly be this. Like, it wasn't supposed to happen.

I felt betrayed. I was supposed to have this perfect life, and here you're fucking it up. I mean, I'm laughing now, but it was that kind of devastating thing that took a year to get over. I thought I was going to die. It was the end of the world, and I had disappointed everyone—my parents. You have to understand—it was so important when you're black and educated and things are supposed to work—because for so long our families haven't worked in the way of the American dream of what a family should be like.

V: *Was he very devastated too, or did he feel liberated?*

B: I think, in a sense, that he felt liberated—that he had concluded that the attempt to right the wrong simply did not work. At first he wanted to try to hold on to the marriage and work through the homosexuality by going to a psychiatrist—which, when I think of it today, is what I'm fighting now as a lesbian: that lesbians and gay men think of themselves as needing psychiatric services because it's somehow a sickness that can be cured. At the time, I absolutely agreed with Bill.

V: *It didn't make you insecure about your femininity?*

B: I guess it did, yes. I hadn't thought about that—I guess on some level it did.

But what happened after Bill and I broke up was that I really had to think for the first time—I was about twenty-eight—like, I had to live an adult life on my own, and I gained a lot of strength from that. I lived a very super-heterosexual life. I got involved with a lot of men—the kind of cliché at the time. I was growing professionally. I had quit teaching French and was working with the black art gallery and teaching at a community college part-time. I was exploring my interests and also my own sexuality. My paying job was with the Human Resources Administration as an educational coordinator. I helped high school dropouts get into equivalency programs, and I negotiated with colleges to take these students—this was before full open admissions in New York—kids from ghetto areas in Brooklyn. After a year, I started teaching at Brooklyn College in the school of education, where I now wear a couple of different hats. I teach general language theory and methodology and also team-teach a foundations course, with a focus on urban sociology. I'm working on my doctorate in urban education.

In the area of my personal development, I was trying to act out a sense of relating to someone as a whole person and looking for that in the other person too—mainly in men—but also my friendships became more substantive. For a period of three years, as much as I could say that almost all the relationships I had with men were positive, there was something of substance that was lacking. I didn't go trying to look for it or anything. During that time I reconnected with an old acquaintance—my present lover, Virginia, who was also teaching at Brooklyn College. We became friends over a period of three years—began to see each other for lunch, for dinner, went over to each other's homes. I was getting into somewhat of a feminist head, a feminist understanding—like, not letting men displace one or the other of us. If we had a date with each other, you know, and some fellow called one of us up, we wouldn't cancel our date just to go out with the man. I was seeing men at the same time but with some consciousness that she was very important to me.

V: *It's amazing. Nobody ever talks about that in their adult life—that they would cancel dates with women . . .*

B: Yeah, it's not so much that it necessarily happened, but that we were aware that it *could* happen. You have to check that out, you know—what are you saying about your friends in terms of value?

Anyway, I was beginning to get increasingly as excited or more about going out with my friend Virginia as I would be about going out with a man. I became aware that the emotions were stronger than just friendship. I started fantasizing, but I still didn't have a language for it.

V: *What was the nature of your fantasy?*

B: For example, when we'd see each other, there was a kind of hugging that wasn't satisfactory. It didn't match the intensity of the feelings, so that I would extend that through fantasy, even to fantasizing about her during lovemaking with men. It came to the point that I had a sense that everything I was feeling was love—a word I reserved for feelings between men and women. I didn't know anything other than the feelings I had for her; they were very real, and I didn't want to deny them at all, but I had to keep denying them over a period of time because to come out and say "I love you" to another woman was like—you didn't do that. You just didn't do that. And you certainly didn't act on that. It went along to a point where I ran up against a line that you just did not cross. I had crossed the various levels of intensity, but the one line was any physical acting out of that love. It was a very visible line. In my heterosexual head, I had to keep denying those feelings until, finally, I had to just tell her what I felt because the feelings were getting . . . I was unable to contain them. The dialogue that ensued between us told me a lot about what I had been missing in my love relationships with men: intimacy—the kind that is ongoing and understood. I mean, now, as a lesbian, after five years, I know that I would just never find it with a man. The same time that my emotional life seemed to do this flip-flop, I had a sense of not only choosing to be in love with a woman and to act on it, but that for the first time in my life, I felt I was choosing, myself, where I wanted to go for the deepest levels of fulfillment. I felt, "At last!" And not having sought it in a direct kind of way but having come to it, it seemed to me a very natural flow of events.

As I began to turn my life around and share it with this woman, and then the two of us deciding that we wanted to share a lifetime together and therefore to live together, and so forth, there was never a point at which I was questioning how I was feeling, the rightness of it. It was always right with me from the moment that I chose it. Obviously, I realized that it wasn't as innocent, as naive or whatever as I felt. The reality was that you love another woman, and the world calls that "lesbian," and the world doesn't like lesbians.

V: *Did you declare it to everyone?*

B: Not to everyone, but to those people who were close to me. I knew I couldn't live my life tiptoeing around them—like, my brother, my mother, a couple of close friends, people with whom I work closely. That was the kind of "out" that went on for a couple of years. We moved into this house together very easily, without raised eyebrows. Two women living together is OK in this culture. It stamps you as spinsters. So we had a very good shield. The hiding was obviously realizing that "I am a lesbian." I was aware that it could cause me pain to have to deal with people who would look at it as something negative, but the reality for me—which was living our lives together—was very positive. But as my feminism grew, my sense of myself as a lesbian grew. I joined the Gay Academic Union and quickly went through all kinds of consciousness-raising about the oppression of gay people.

V: *Did you ever feel a strain on your relationship when you couldn't be public about it?*

B: In the very beginning, Ginny was very adamant. We'd be riding along in the car and holding hands, and a truck driver would drive up and I would pull my hand away. And Ginny would grab my hand and say, "Ya know, that's the public. You're afraid of this truck driver?" And sometimes I'd get mad that we couldn't hold hands. But things are balancing out and we're kind of saying, "To hell with the world . . . ."

V: *Did you grow up in New York?*

B: No. I was born in Miami, lived there until I was eleven. My parents separated, and I went to live with my father, who was a career army person. That meant traveling around the United States. We lived in Germany for a while. My two older brothers stayed with my mother. My lifestyle and exposure was much more middle class. My mother was a maid. She knew that letting me go would give me opportunities I couldn't have in Florida.

So in my adolescent and young adult years, I was in a kind of painless, integrated military setting. I think the pattern that was begun from eighth grade was one that has helped me in relating to white persons. Somehow, by sheer chance, I guess I have been spared a lot of the ugly human experiences that many blacks have had to go through.

In my senior year of high school, I went back to Florida and right back into a black community and an all-black school. I had converted to Catholicism while I was living with my father. My family is heavy Southern Methodist. I was an impressionable, dreamy kid, got into some Catholic literature, thought I'd found the answer. So I wanted to go to a Catholic college, got a scholarship to St. Catherine's in St. Paul, Minnesota, while most of my friends were going to black colleges.

V: *You chose to be different?*

B: Yeah.

V: *You even chose to leave your mother and travel with your father, and you chose to become Catholic . . . .*

B: Yeah, I feel that this is part of my choosing my lesbianism—that I think I've been making conscious choices that were leaps from my background. Like the time I was eight years old and had gone to California one summer—when I came back to Florida, I announced to all the kids in the neighborhood that I was no longer gonna talk with a southern accent. Now I see that was a part of my black oppression— I thought there was a "right" way to talk—but it was a pretty big thing for an eight-year-old to do.

V: *What did your father think when you came out?*

B: I didn't tell my father. I have not told him yet. I feel, somehow, that he would not understand, but he would accept. And I don't know if I'm waiting to feel that he'll be able to understand it or what. It would be like going through molasses to try to explain it to him. Somehow I want my father to understand that the lifestyle has value and is deeply meaningful to me and has meaning for large numbers of people. And I know he's not going to be able to understand it on the societal level as well as on the personal level with regards to me.

V: *What was your mother's reaction?*

B: At first she accepted it and accepted me but was not able to understand what lesbianism meant. What she understood was totally negative. A lot of it had to do with her deeply religious values. She perceives life in such a way that there is no room for homosexuality. At the time, when she was rejecting it, I felt totally abandoned, like an orphan for the first time in my life—like to be into this thing is to really be alone.

V: *Did it ever make you doubt yourself?*

B: No, actually it didn't. I was sort of living with the illusion that I would never have the real deep pain that a lot of other people talk about when telling their parents. But after a period of time, my mother just sort of worked her way back to communicating with me. She's one of the few people in this world who really practice that Christian ethic and love. She accepts Ginny, you know, to an extent.

She knows that my father doesn't know. Her thinking is, "You can tell me, but don't tell anyone else. Why flaunt it?" Telling my father would be like a betrayal of my mother.

V: *You have constant contact with the straight world. You don't live a kind of lesbian ghetto life, do you?*

B: Well, it's probably getting increasingly more lesbian-oriented, relating to women in more and more exclusive kinds of ways. We have straight friends, but there's so much time taken up being with women that it does begin to be sort of the center of our lives. It's also a preference. I much prefer

being with women than being with men. I have difficulty looking at heterosexual interaction because it's very hard to watch. I find it so oppressive—it's just a built-in part of the heterosexual structure, even when the wife is a feminist and the husband helps with the house and the kids and the whole thing.

V: *Do you think that gay people have something to offer?*

B: Definitely. If you take away the negative perceptions that the straight world has of gay people and deal with the majority of us who are aware, who are activist, who come out of a feminist consciousness, there is an awful lot to offer in terms of dropping the roles. The heavy accentuation on role-defined relationships is something the heterosexual world needs very much to look at—which it *is* looking at through its own feminist movement. I think the gay people offer the straight world the breakdown of the Puritan ethic, in its most negative sense. As a lesbian in the movement, I'm involved in redefining human ability for expression and freedom, the real freedom to *be,* where the ecstasy of life is not killed by having life defined for you and imposed on you from the outside. I think what the gay world has to offer the straight world is a definition of self which comes from the inside, a definition for which you are responsible yourself.

V: *Would you encourage coming out?*

B: Yeah, because it's the only way to turn the society around in terms of its values. As we become more visible, it gives lie to the judgment that we are horrible monsters with two heads and horns, and so on.

And the coming-out process is not something that's simple. It isn't something that you do once and it's over. You are constantly coming out. It becomes the work of your life, in a sense. But the more of us that do it, the more support the next person who's going to come out has.

V: *What are some of the problems that you find related to your lesbianism?*

B: I have to grapple with the fact that I'm once more removed from the black community, because as a feminist, it's bad enough . . . . The black community has such difficulty viewing a black woman feminist in any way other than as a castrator. And in terms of the family, feminism seems to be talking about the dissolution and breakup of the black nuclear family just as it's beginning to see itself more and more. And that's difficult. I will not deny my lesbianism either, even though it removes me yet one step further from the black community. The hassles of being with a white lover come more from my head trips, from the guilt-tripping. Actually the racial conflicts between us are very, very minimal.

V: *What are your plans for the future?*

B: To do whatever I can to project the positive aspects of being other than the norm. I do that increasingly; I do things that are very political. I'm co-chairperson of the Board of Directors of the National Gay Task Force, which is the civil-rights arm of the gay movement.

I'm getting fed up with academia; it just doesn't bend to new efforts. Anything that speaks to real change in how we educate people is a kind of subversion because schools educate people to function in a capitalistic, racist society. The system lets you go only so far with innovative programs. There's not total commitment to the kind of change we want.

I hope to be able to write and reach wider and wider audiences. The writing will be feminist as well as lesbian-feminist and will project to the world that we're not talking about a handful of people but that this is indeed a world-wide movement, that women are on the move in this world, that people whose sexual and affectional preferences are different are on the move in this world, and they are moving toward fuller and fuller recognition—moving toward something that, in the end, will be to the benefit of not just women, and not just lesbians and gay males, but of the entire human race. There's a lot that we have to offer to the world culture in terms of restructuring it in a more positive way.

Roger

PETER: *Let's start with your childhood. Where did you grow up?*

ROGER: What's interesting about my childhood? Everything to me, nothing to you! I grew up on a farm. I have an older brother. He was the only playmate I had until I was, like, five years old. It was a very idyllic childhood. My first gay experience was with my brother, whom I absolutely love dearly. It was just like kids playing at first, but then it got more into the real thing because we had nobody else, right? The outside world was represented by a town of one hundred people.

I was a sissy right from the start. On a farm the male and female roles were very clearly defined. Outside, it was hot, and you had to work like a bastard; you had to get all the hay in, working out in the heat with the dust and bees and the ants and the things that get down you, and you're filthy. I didn't want that, you know. The alternative was to make busy work in the house and to relate to your mother—cool, comfortable, nothing to do, no sweat, you could read books. So I opted for that. Unconsciously my behavior became what would, back then, have been construed as feminine, effeminate, sissy. It still is to this day, in a way, but I love it. I'm really not into physical hard work. You know, I feel guilty, even now, telling you this. Do you think that's still a thread of the Puritan ethic? the "males work hard" thing? You're supposed to *like* to go out and do that stuff. Well, I didn't. It was easier, it seemed to make me happier, to do the things that, back then, looked like I was assuming a female role. I remember Sam Levenson used to have a joke when I watched him on TV. He was talking about his inability to excel at sports, and he said, "I was the kind of a guy they used to say: 'You take a girl, and we'll take Sam.'" That used to happen to me in grade school, junior high, high school—all that trip.

P: *Do you think your gayness was a result of your upbringing?*

RH: Well, what are we? We're just the products of what's gone in our eyes and our ears and our senses, right? Who am I? I'm Tallulah Bankhead; I'm Mae West; I'm Gloria Swanson; I'm my mother; I'm Jean Harlow. I'm a lot of the archetypical female images from that particular era. But I'm also me, you know. I'm male and I love it. It's really fine. I wonder why I made the choice to model myself on those archetypical female figures? They were head and shoulders above the crowd. They totally chose their own personalities—larger than life. Then they brandished them like shields in the face of mediocrity. They were female humans using the equipment to make a statement; they were artists. They highlighted the things that women were supposed to have in order to have equal footing—even a rapport—with men. What happened was that they looked so God-damned brave that they still stand out today. They took whatever was available, and by the strength of their personalities, by making incredible choices, said, "I want to be myself, and these are things I'm going to put up with, but inside, I'm myself."

Why did that make such a strong impression on all of us queens? They did all the weird things that women used to do in order to fulfill whatever role they let themselves get suckered into, or what men gave them. Faggots took those things—textbooks say that they were doing it out of hatred of women, but perhaps they adapted those characteristics because they saw them as being the weapons that women used against males to even things out a little bit. I think I relate to straight men very much like a woman would do if she was smart. I think I'm an interesting fossil, in a way, of what a together woman might have been like in the late fifties.

P: *What was so different then?*

RH: I think perhaps faggotry in the late fifties required you to think a great deal more than anybody wanted you to think in the late fifties. That was Eisenhower, that was after they had fought World War II, and they set this joint up, and they said, "This is what we defended; now fit into it." And then they got old. And the kids are there trying to be . . . like, khakis and everything. It didn't take much thought, and it didn't allow for thinking; it didn't allow for the thinking that comes out of frustrated emotion. You just frustrated your emotions; you didn't say, "Why am I being frustrated?" It was hard being a faggot back then because you realized more clearly then than you do now—on this other side of 1968—what it was like to be an outsider, to be different.

P: *Were you attracted to girls or to little boys?*

RH: To little girls. I thought they were fabulous. But at the age when the reproductive urge came to me, I thought the male body was more interesting. Its engineering appealed to me, and it was more readily available to me. The Catholic upbringing made it impossible to even think about touching a female body. I was terrifically interested in females when I was, like, in the beginning of sex's manifestation. I was omni-sexual. The choice to be with men is because both genders have had a rough row to hoe just having to live a role all the while, but it's easier for me to relate to males because I happen to be a male, and we're absolutely different from women—I always feel for the poor bastards. I mean, I just like men. That's why I was gay. The reason I exhibit—by choice—the behavioral characteristics which could be called a "screaming queen" is because—God!—we've got hands; we've got a voice that can cover two octaves. It's so damn foolish not to use them.

It became harder to relate to little girls because they weren't little girls anymore. They were girls on the way to being teen-agers with all that meant in the 1950s. A Bob and Ray routine that I heard about 1951 stuck in my mind as a wonderful analogy for compressing what the pressures were in the fifties. They did a great long commercial: you could send in five dollars and your name and address and they would send you a cardboard Cadillac cover that fit right over your Chevrolet or whatever you had. That's the image I keep using. Like, there was a cardboard Cadillac cover that you had to put over your real self back then to protect yourself, and to get what you wanted in the world, and you probably had to lie to yourself about what the hell you really wanted. Not only did you have to assume a disguise and maintain it, but there was a spectrum of things that you could allow yourself to think that you wanted. There really was.

People would laugh at you. People would call you a sissy. Liberace was on television then and, like, he was the epitome of a sissy. I don't know how in the name of Christ the man got on TV in the 1950s. He had that enormous smile and the whole trip, and I had a real enormous smile, so they teased me, and I acted everything, and I smiled and was nice to people, so my nickname became Liberace—and crammed into that was all the disapprobation all the little males felt. Even at the same time that they scared me, and I felt somehow that I was wrong, I said, "Listen, it can't be all that bad if I can relate to them one to one. They're probably just as scared as I am, and their trip must be that they get into groups and agree on what they're going to be like."

P: *Did you assume a disguise? Like, when you were in high school?*

RH: Sure, to a point. Only to a point. I discovered—in spite of all the traumas and the pain of trying to fit into the molds (and I really did try)—that I had a sense of humor. Sure I role-played, but my saving grace was having a sense of humor.

Laughing is a bark. I swear, laughing is barking left over, and we do it when we're surprised by the truth. And I discovered that I could do that, for some reason, probably because I was so further outside than they were, so I did have a better picture of what was going on, though I was not conscious then that I had a picture. I could just see things from a different point of view.

And from a farm family and a farm town—to want to be an actor! The pressures made me realize that this was an out. It had something to do with stepping back from relating. It had something to do with being able to regulate your behavior, which it seemed that I could do already. It also had something to do with "There's another world full of glamor and acceptance," so I was propelled out by all of the mental pressures that I probably did not . . . I mean, I can't . . . I can only talk about them now, as a thirty-five-year-old. I must have been subject to enormous pressures. I wasn't happy. I had pimples of death, for Christ's sake. But just knowing instinctively that in a year, in a hundred years, nothing is going to make any difference at all—humor is having a long view.

P: *Did you have a sense of yourself being gay or homosexual?*

RH: Homosexual. It's hard, by the way, as a homosexual, to use any of the words such as "homosexual" without being conscious of the weight. Every time I say "sissy," every time I say "faggot," every time I say "homosexual," it's weighted with all that I'm talking about. Isn't that odd—that you should even have to think about it at all? It's a pain in the ass.

The first person I related to was my brother because we had nobody else. First of all it was just like touchie, feelie, examinie—you know, measuring up and all those sorts of child things that kids do. But it got to be like a really pleasurable experience to me because it was honest—being naked and being assured that nobody was going to hurt you or pass judgments on you. I can only say this in retrospect, but I got into it because it was like a rare chance to let down your hair; it was one of the few times that you could be honest about your body, honest about seeking a release, honest about being curious about somebody else's body, touching somebody else's body, you know. When I started, I didn't know it was considered bad. It just felt good, and it was fun. I think that's why it was prolonged past what I guess might be considered the youthful experimenting stage—that, and the fact that there was no other sexual outlet, just the pressures, the biological pressures. It was simply impossible to find a suitable female person to experiment with, to do anything with, because we went to school on buses, came back to the farm, and there was no female within five miles. There was just no opportunity. And we were Catholics; we couldn't fuck girls. Anyway, I found out about it being a mortal sin. All of a sudden my brother started to get second thoughts about what we were doing.

P: *Did he start to perceive it as wrong?*

RH: Yeah—and I would be fascinated to know how the idea got planted in his head. One day he said, "You know, we shouldn't be doing this. People might think that it's queer." I had never thought about it one way or another. I never connected it up, like, with my effeminate behavioral manifestations. I never thought of myself as queer until he said that. This is when I started to get fucked up as a person, I think. Because I was still deeply religious. I used to pray to be God's little actor, you know—to be a tool of God. But I just wanted somebody else's body beside my own, and dying because of this instilled guilt from Mother Church. That, I think, was about the only real pain that I had. I could deal with the pain of people better than I could deal with the pain of losing my place in the cosmos. I didn't want that, and that's what I got fucked up over for a while. But I got over it. One day I just didn't go to church anymore. I said, "It can't be real. Nothing in life should be that painful for such a long time. You have a choice." So I just forgot about it.

(Rob joins the interview)

ROB: *So you wanted to be an actor. Was that your association with your gayness?*

RH: I had a very peculiar idea of what an actor was then. My knowledge was only gleaned second-hand. I wanted to put on makeup because I had pimples. I wanted to cover them up and see what I would look like with a smooth skin. I thought I'd be prettier if I had thicker eyelashes and bigger eyes and stuff like that. I used to sneak up and put on my

mother's makeup when she wasn't looking. Sometimes I'd come down in it. God bless their sweet hearts, it didn't freak them out that much. In retrospect, I guess the reason I love my parents so dearly was that to the best of their lights they loved me and accepted me and let me grow the best way they could. They sincerely loved me and cared about me and would have sacrificed their lives in order to have my life continue.

So I wanted to be an artist in some half-assed fashion back then. I wanted to be an actor for ego-fulfillment reasons, to go away and pretend that I was somebody else, to get up in front of people and look gorgeous and have fabulous clothes and have adventures with no threat, no fuss, no muss, no cuss, make a lot of money for it, be adored and glorified for it, maybe get all the sex I wanted at last, right? There we all were—pimply, fucked up, sad, hopeful, confused—on the brink of the 1960s. You know, if I knew I was going to be seventeen again—I swear to God!—I would kill myself. What are we talking about? My point, my point?

R: *We were talking about your being an actor.*

RH: When it came time for me to go out in the world and be responsible for myself and my own survival, I made the choice that I was very sexual. But that was just a way of feeling good. Separate from that, I had some kind of a half-assed notion that I wanted to be what I consider now an artist. You look around and you see the things that are wrong, that keep you and other people from having that together feeling with yourself and with the world around you as much as you want it, and you realize somehow the way all the information coming in affects you, and you want to do something about it. The wonderful people in this world are the people who all the while deal with the truth as best they can. In a way, they are the artists of life, and that's great.

And then there are people who want to be artists and hang something up in front of people in some way—as an actor, as a painter, as a sculptor, as a filmmaker, as anything. Artists are people who see that things are wrong, and, using themselves, try to suggest alternatives by presenting something that—like a sense of humor—takes all the lies, compresses them, and makes you see the truth for an instant. You go away changed if the actors and artists are working right. A work of art is taking some of the fucking chaos that's around us, selecting elements of it, putting it together in a new way, and saying, "Look at this." And it hangs there in space and time for a minute, and then it's gone. But making all the other little apes look at it makes the dumber ones get their act together. That's what works of art can do—make human life possible, force you to be honest. And behavior such as I manifest when I'm feeling comfortable and brave could be interpreted by an insensitive person as being archetypically faggoty.

So I came along, and I'm sitting in the box office of *Cuckoo's Nest,* and the guys who are directing it and producing it are there. I'm selling tickets to the show—I'd never seen it cause I suspected it was a melodrama clumsily done, as indeed it probably is, and was. So I auditioned for it—a cold reading, which means you come in, and they're sittin' there, and you're up there, and I took the script . . . I guess I knew by that time that he was a tormented faggot. I hate it when I say that, in a way—all you tormented faggots out there—cause it's judgmental, and it makes it sound like . . . what *does* it make it sound like? It makes it sound like there's something wrong with it. And there isn't anything wrong with being a tormented faggot. But it's wrong going along with the gag and not letting the people who create that world, and let you fit into it . . . it's wrong once in a while not to let them know that you know that they know that you know. You know what I mean? You know? I feel a responsibility to the other weird people of the world to be a representative intelligent weird person so that the people who are made uncomfortable by the presence of us weird people, or who can't deal with us at all, will—not come to love us—but will know that it might be easier to relax and be a weird person, and only have an occasional brush with the powers that be . . . as opposed to living through the hell of being a weird person underneath, like we all are . . .

R: *I find that it's often true with gay people, especially gay people who were pronouncedly so, like you were, that they are sort of aware that the macho behavior is sort of learned by the other boys . . .*

RH: I think it came to me way later. I don't think I realized that macho behavior was as much a conditioned behavior as my faggot behavior until I got to college. Somehow, I was always able to use my schmarts, my ability to make people laugh, my charm discreetly applied—intelligently applied cowardice—so that most of the time, I could be myself. I discovered what was probably my entertainer's instinct. I got to be the class clown—but aware of what I was doing—because we were such a small group. There were only eleven of us in my graduating class, and we'd come from the first grade together. We were very familial in a way, and they accepted me just as I was.

R: *As an actor, being conscious of your own nelly image, can you pass? If you don't care about passing for straight, why don't you care?*

RH: Why don't I care? Cause I can't lie all the while. My craft is understanding and recreating human behavior. If I had to pass for a role, I would. Technically, it would mean listening to straight people. I've listened to them all my life. They don't use the fucking vocal instrument they've got to the fullest extent. I'd have to cut my hair. I'd have to cut my beard. I'd have to uglify myself a tad and not look quite so exotic. I'd have to find, you know, my lowest register—"Hi! This is Ted Cliché speaking"—that whole trip. But for who? Who do you want to please?

R: *But there nonetheless must have been a lot of pressures when you were young?*

RH: Yeah, there were so many things that I realize, only in retrospect, were pressures. There were just so many alternatives in that town. You could quit school at thirteen and go to work in a garage, you could get married and work on the farm, or you could go to a trade school and work in some kind of a factory. There was not enough to keep the mind alive.

R: *So, in a way, being gay sort of almost saved you from that . . .*

RH: You bet your ass, kid. Absolutely. Sure. I'm *so* glad I'm gay.

R: *Do you think that there's anything inherently different between gay people and straight people? Do you think that gay men are different in any way other than that they just happen to like other men sexually?*

RH: Yeah, because the straight man is motivated by fear—which is the thing that makes you rigid. A straight man who doesn't think about being a straight man has not thought about all the alternatives and made the choice to be straight and gone with it—a straight man who is a straight man because anything else is just not done. I mean, think of the pressures on a straight guy, for Christ's sake! We don't have the same kind of fears. There's just no comparison. They're afraid of not fulfilling a role. They are trying to live life according to models. They're trying to hang on. That's the great sin of life. That's death to art. They spend their whole lives trying to live up to a model. The thing that being gay gave me, I now realize, was freedom from that. It's so hard to be a straight man, harder than to be a faggot, because the rewards are so stupid—the rewards that you are told you can have. Whereas if you're a faggot, I guess you can make up your own rewards, or you don't even have to think about rewards. It seems like it would be harder to be straight—you must feel yourself playing roles; you must feel yourself closing off parts of your mind that you can't allow to be open because it might make you feel something that you're not supposed to feel. It's more fun to be a faggot because nobody expects anything of us.

That's why I'm grateful I'm gay. I had to think about relating to people because I wanted to belong. But just wanting to belong means that you have to think about what you want to do to belong, means you have to think about what you want to belong to, about the people you want to belong with. It forces you to make decisions. That's why I'm grateful that, whatever happened astrologically, I wound up being gay at the time that I was. It makes you come to grips with a moment-by-moment reality of life, as opposed to trying to fill a pattern and feeling vaguely miserable and never giving yourself the benefit of thinking. But I wasn't able to put it together then. I'm still not able to put it together, obviously. But I have a good time trying.

For a straight man to let another man kiss him, hug him, touch his sexual organs requires letting down every defense. It's giving in to the heart demands of another man, experiencing it with him, probably liking it, probably realizing that it's part of life. He'd trusted somebody, you know.

This spring I had this experience of attempting to trust my body with a woman, which is like the opposite of what is close to me in terms of the physical-heart-mind connection. I've been trying to think about love. I haven't got a clue what love is anymore. I've decided it's a combination of lust and trust—which is kind of nice. It's trust, really. I mean, we're walking through a miracle every day, right? Everything that is around us is a miracle, and part of the human sin is doubt. Somehow we do not believe that all of this can be happening around us, and we don't trust that it's going to last. The same thing is true with love and the ability to trust yourself in the hands of another person.

Harry and John

PETER: *Why don't you start talking about the early days, when you were a child?*

HARRY: When I was growing up, there were no words for us. In the late 1920s, there was a wonderful cartoon in the *Literary Digest,* I think, that portrayed a bunch of women with their hair tied up in curlers and bandanas; they're hanging out clothes on the back line and talking to each other over a fence. Farther down, you can see what is obviously not a woman, also with his hair done up and a little bandana, and he's also putting out clothes. And one woman says to another, "You know, I hear there's another one in Chicago." I must have been fifteen before I first heard the word "homosexual." And in those days, looking it up in the dictionary didn't help very much!

P: *Have you always thought of yourself as gay?*

H: Well, I probably first began to sense the difference when I was about eight or nine years old. I was seduced by a guy who was about twelve or thirteen. He said that all the other boys look at pictures of girls and go jack off behind the fence, but we'd go even farther and do something real fancy. He introduced me to 69, and it was great stuff, though he was more avid because of his age.

I liked older girls when I was about eight. There was one girl who used to sing soprano in the choir, and I thought she was just wonderful. The boys all called me "sissy" because I always wanted to walk home with her instead of walking home with the fellows. All the fellows were walking together, you know, say between seven and ten, seven and eleven. And I was about eight or nine, and I wanted to walk with the girls. Later on, when they started walking with the girls, this was when I decided I wanted to walk with the boys.

P: *Do you think this was out of some sort of perverse nature?*

H: I think that gay people develop at a different rhythm than other people.

JOHN: . . . Curious. In my case, when I was about twelve, I had a big romance with an eighteen-year-old woman. She was still in the eighth grade. She wasn't very bright, but she seemed like the Great Mother to me. When I entered puberty, I came into full realization of sexual attraction for people of my own sex.

P: *Did you act on it right away?*

J: No, I didn't. I had attempted to find a gay society when I was in my late teens and encountered a few of what you call "screaming queens." They did not coincide with my idea of how I should live my life, and since I had no access to other gay life, I was put off. I took the course of marriage in my twenties, and I didn't come out until I was forty-seven.

P: *My God! What did you do for those twenty years?*

J: Well, they weren't bad years. I had the company of men, from the time I'd joined the navy and gone into engineering and so on. And I enjoyed a very nice relationship with the woman I married. She was in many ways ideal for a homosexual husband, because she was a person of sturdy independence, was rather boyish in her manner, and was a good companion. And we had a satisfactory, although unexciting, sexual experience.

It continued for a decade or two, but then as I came into my forties, I began to despair. This was false to my nature, as I had known all along. It was at that point that I decided to face the fork in the road. And I took the fork toward my own true nature.

P: *Why did it take you that long?*

J: Because once I married, I felt I was entering a heterosexual world, and I stayed away from homosexual haunts and kept myself in isolation by choice. You see, I wasn't the sort to prefer a boy on the side. It was all or none.

H: Well, I was very attracted to boys by the time I was twelve. In those junior high and high school annuals, they'd have pictures of all the different boys. And I used to have one-star, two-star, and three-star people that particularly excited me. I was information gathering. But at fifteen, I suddenly wanted to be like all the others. And so I figured out what I had to do—I had to do what you do in acting classes; I was taking drama in high school by this time. I realized I had to act in such a way so that Betsy would respond to me in exactly the same way as Mary was responding to Bob, because if Betsy acted differently with me than Mary did with Bob, other people would notice that there was something strange there, so that it was not a proper relationship.

P: *Do you think Bob was doing the same thing? In other words, did he learn his behavior as carefully as you?*

H: Well, Bob was one of these people who took everything for granted. Bob did, and Ed did, and Pete did, and Al did, and all the other guys who were in the gang were . . . these were the sort of people who swaggered around taking things for granted. I had to learn it, and I had to learn it hard.

Later on in life when I was with the Hollywood Repertory Theatre during the Depression, I got a job as the understudy for about eight actors. I could step in and play one after another. Having done this kind of observation with people at an early age, I found that I had to imitate them. You see, in a repertory theater, people are so accustomed to playing with each other that they really don't respond on cue; they respond on count. If I were to give an inflection differently than what Arthur Treacher gave—he was one of the people I was understudying—the whole cast would be flubbed. Consequently, I had to play the part exactly as he played it, or as any of the other men played their parts.

In the height of the thirties, the heterosexual world was very, very straight, very uptight, very macho, very unemotional. The epitome in the movies was the untalking, slightly unmoving Gary Cooper, or the very heterosexual, emotional-only-under-great-duress Clark Gable. In this period, we had the lilies and the pansies, and all the queens would have chiffon four miles long—all slightly lavender. It wasn't a question of a limp wrist; everything was limp. I could play the strutting macho if I wanted to, and I could drop my wrists if I felt like it. Consequently . . .

P: *It was a role you consciously played, whichever you chose?*

H: Yes.

P: *John, would it be unfair to describe your life when you were married as closeted?*

J: Well, no. But there were two sides to it. Unlike Harry, I never found any reason to act straight. I always acted exactly as I felt. I didn't feel I had to imitate the men with whom I worked. I just simply had my own manner—much as the manner I have now.

P: *Do you think you were singled out as effeminate for that reason?*

J: Yes. And there were a number of times when traps were laid which were perfectly obvious to me—trying to catch me out, you know. But I simply walked by them. Then people who had set the traps were contrite about it. One time a couple of young engineers placed themselves where I would be passing by. They started to go on with a lot of sexual talk about how they were in the navy and how they slept with each other and how so-and-so was a good lay, and so on. And I just walked by and said, "Hi," and continued, you see, not picking up the cue. So I was left alone.

But certainly I was in the closet in the sense that I didn't tell anybody that I was homosexual, except in the case of the World War II draft. I thought I ought to be honest there. I had been in the navy, but anyway, when I told them, they gave me a 4-F.

P: *What influenced you to come out, John?*

J: After twenty years of marriage, I felt it had gone on long enough. I had to break with my former existence and find gay people.

I was living in Hollywood at the time. I began to go to bars. About a year after I made that choice, I met Harry at One, Inc., the homosexual educational institute in Los Angeles, where I had been taking courses on aspects of gay life. Here I found an approach that made sense to me and a larger sector of gay people than I had first encountered before I was married. I waited until things were just right according to the terms I would accept. But I've had no experience, you know, coming out in the gay ghetto. When Harry and I found each other, we saw immediately that we were right for one another. So we set up as a couple. We recognized each other. You have to remember also that we were people now nearly fifty, so we had a lifetime of experience to draw upon.

P: *You had experience in the gay ghetto, Harry?*

H: Oh, boy. Well, you see, I lived back in the times before it was a ghetto. I can't really say that I lacked any sexual experience; I got plenty. But I was aware that I was always looking for a lover. I wasn't looking for sex. And I was pretty lucky in that regard too. Before I met John, I had been involved with a man nineteen years younger than I was. I had come to the end of it and recognized that it was time to go back to the banquet table and find a relationship with a contemporary. I tried a number of different relationships in the course of three or four months, but they weren't working. I was fifty-one, and I decided that probably I'd muffed my chances. I wanted to work out a program with One, Inc., that would make it possible for young people to find each other and not make the mistakes that I had made. I was organizing a gay square dance group called the '49ers—as in the mining days of the Mother Lode. In the meantime, I would renounce completely any idea of companionship for myself . . . I would put full time into this project. One afternoon, John was in the office when I was describing the square dance group, and I heard him laugh. And I knew I'd found the right guy.

P: *Were you as sure as quickly, John?*

J: Oh, yes, of course. I'd been out a year and had found no one at all. So when Harry proposed that we should, as he put it, "Let us walk together hand in hand," this was to me a tremendous thing. Harry's a beautiful person, a man of most distinction. And we found that when we came together, we certainly did need each other. There was a tremendous physical attraction. Electric current seemed to flow; it still does. Now these were old men, but we were bringing together five decades of thinking. So that when we sat down to dinner Friday night, it seemed as though we were still sitting there Monday morning at breakfast, talking and comparing our ideas and our experiences.

And that particular dialogue has continued ever since, on all these great subjects and questions of who are we? what are we for? what does it all mean? We made conquest after conquest of understanding, and this is an ongoing work between us still. To this day, our motto has always been that we made no pledges to one another. We said that every moment we decide whether to continue together or not. And so every moment of the last thirteen years we have made the same decision, and we're closer than ever before. You see, in those days, so little was known—in fact, little is known now—about older gays. We said to each other, "Well, here we are, around fifty, each of us, so what is this supposed to be?" We said, "Let's find out, and whatever it is, make the best of it." And we found to our immense surprise and joy that we had never known ecstasies and passions equivalent to the depth of our experience together.

Of course, we've gone through all the struggles that couples do. But we modeled ourselves on the idea of being companions rather than lovers.

P: *Do you see gay love as different from heterosexual love?*

H: We are talking about a way of seeing that heteros don't have. In our type of loving, we see each other as subjects, as equals. This is something that heteros don't. The hetero boy is always talking about a girl as though she were an object. This is a very important difference. We are struggling with an objective language to talk about a subjective experience in ourselves. And it won't work. This is one of the reasons we keep coming apart and waving our hands around—we are upset by competition. Competition is not common to us. We were not competitive as kids; we don't like it. It's a role we play, but it's a hetero role, and we learn it because we don't want to be left out. But it isn't natural to us. The fact that we see subjectively instead of objectively is the reason why we go into artistic things, because art is a subject-to-subject relationship.

P: *It could be argued that among heterosexuals, it's simply socialization. But you think that gay love inherently is different than heterosexual love? Even in an ideal heterosexual society . . . ?*

H: I don't think there is such a thing as an ideal heterosexual society. I think they wish there were. You see, we are not looking for an object that we can manipulate—which, when you realize it, falling in love is your projecting on somebody else what you wish that other person to be. But the love between equals is something that can't be manipulated, because that other is a power equal to yourself.

I'm talking about what I believe to be inherently possible and part of gay consciousness. I have seen it among gay men and women.

P: *And you haven't among heterosexuals?*

H: Well, yes, I think I have, but very rarely. But you know, it's a good thing to let heterosexuals speak for themselves—isn't it?—because it would be silly for us to start comparing. When you compare things, you have to reduce them to what they have in common—whereas, what we're interested in is everything other than what we have in common. We're interested in what it is to be gay.

P: *What about domination and submission in gay love?*

H: I think we see domination and submission in gay relationships which ape the heterosexual. In a loving relationship between equals and between companions, I don't think you see domination and submission.

J: Certainly not in my case. I was very definitely not going to put up with any imitation of a hetero love affair. I think it's our role as gays to be free of that, because perhaps it's easier for us to find truly nonpossessive love. We don't start with the convention of domination and submission.

P: *What you say reminds me of the kinds of things that women talk about in terms of straight men . . .*

H: Well, you see, some gay men have been able to relate to certain types of straight women because they see them as sisters, as subjects. And women love to be seen as subjects, so they oftentimes can talk to gay men in a way that they would never talk to a straight man.

P: *Do you see gay consciousness as reflective of matriarchal values as opposed to patriarchal?*

H: No. It's too bad people use those terms. Patriarchal is really the wrong word; there should be a little more digging. What we mean is an androcratic culture—"androcratic" refers to men, not necessarily the father. After all, the only society in western culture that was patriarchal was the Jewish. But the type of culture found in Germanic society, for example, is not patriarchal, not concerned with passing power from father to son necessarily, but more, man to man. This is androcratic. Most of Greek and Roman literature is concerned with androcratic relationships. I think that women are struggling to find themselves in what is obviously a male-derived, male-oriented world.

You know, I've been involved in radical circles for years. I knew many women in the late forties who were struggling with what was known as the "woman question." In the first Mattachine Society, we had quite a lot of women who were equally active along with the men.

P: *What was the Mattachine Society?*

H: Well, to give you some background, I had been involved in many of the so-called progressive organizations during World War II. And I had been involved in trade union organizing, organizing for the NAACP [National Association for the Advancement of Colored People], organizing voting activities in the barrios of East Los Angeles. Any one of these activities was enough to brand you as a communist after the war.

P: *So you were a troublemaker from the beginning?*

H: Naturally. I learned a lot from the heteros. By 1948,
the security drives began in the State Department, and homosexuals were being driven out. I suddenly got the feeling that
there was a huge fascist movement toward totalitarianism.
After all, in Germany just before the end of the war, homosexuals were wiped out. The scapegoating was coming on in a
big way. One hundred fifty homosexuals were dismissed
from the State Department during the McCarthy era. As we
began to move into the cold war, it looked like the forces of
big government were going to try to split and divide and
finally conquer. They wouldn't use the blacks, because blacks
were now organized in the trade unions—and were actually
on the move. They wouldn't use the Jews, because Jews
already had the sympathy of the world for their sufferings
during the war. So the new scapegoat might very likely
be gays.

Not only had scapegoating begun in a big way toward gays,
but people were being dismissed from government jobs because they knew homosexuals—guilt by association, suspi-
cions, fears running around creating havoc. There wasn't a

single voice from any liberal quarter which said, "You shouldn't be so hard on homosexuals."

It was high time that gay people finally drew together. I knew that even before the fifties. In 1948, I was at a party where many of us were gay supporters of Henry Wallace, who was running on an independent third-party ticket. We were sort of full of what the Wallace party might be able to do. I had the idea of organizing a sort of faction which we would call Bachelors for Wallace, of writing up a platform attacking this guilt-by-association problem. I finally wound up doing the writing of a prospectus which included how we could help each other legally, and so on. I knew a lot of liberals, especially ministers and lawyers, and I talked to a lot of gays who thought it was a good idea. The liberal ministers were enthusiastic but wouldn't endorse the prospectus until I had a group together. And the prestigious gay people whom I knew liked the idea but wouldn't join a group until the prominent ministers and educators and doctors lent their names to the prospectus. This went on for two years until I met a guy who said, "Yeah. I know half a dozen people who'd be interested." So we went out recruiting.

By the spring of 1952, we had a sphere of influence of about five thousand people in the state of California alone. We had groups in San Francisco, in Monterey, in Bakersfield, in San Diego. A news journal was started by some of the original members of the group as an independent endeavor but sponsored by the Society. Later on in the fifties, classes were set up in gay history, gay sociology.

P: *What happened to the Mattachine Society eventually?*

H: Well, in that initial two years, we had grown too fast. The type of vision with which the Society was founded was not shared by most of the people we attracted. They were attracted to the idea, to the excitement, but they were not attracted to the fact that the only attorneys we could get to work with us were labor radicals or "pinks." These were the only people who had the courage of their own convictions to stand up for us—and they could take a fifth-amendment position on anything. But the majority of people who joined the organization wanted respectability.

Finally the original group dissolved as an organization. We persuaded ourselves that our purposes were finished. But we felt that the name belonged to gay people, whoever they were. So we dissolved. But that sphere of influence of five thousand people dropped to six hundred in six months, because the dream was gone. The people who remained were interested in being middle class. They were all going to rush up to Sacramento and pound on the doors and tell the legislature to change the law—but otherwise be respectable. So the moment they became as good as the middle class, the dream was gone, and the movement died. And nothing was reborn until the late sixties.

P: *Can you tell me something more about the early activities of the Mattachine Society?*

H: Well, before there was any gay consciousness, before there was any voice speaking for us, we spoke for each other. In 1951, we had our first semi-public dance. People who didn't even know about our discussion groups came to the dance. One guy came up to me in the course of the evening and said, "Man, you don't know what it means to be able to hold another man in your arms and dance and all of a sudden walk outside and stand under the stars and breathe." Well, we had a number of dances, with people who until then maybe knew four or five others within their small circle who danced together. But these dances would draw maybe three hundred guys together. This was something very beautiful and liberating for those who'd never gone through it.

J: When the first homophile movements began, a homosexual was placed in three categories: to the doctor you were sick; to the lawyer you were a criminal; to the minister you were wicked. These were quite contradictory categories, of course, because the minister implied that you had chosen your state by your freedom of will, while the doctor implied that you had caught it from somebody. I think that the founding of the Society was the first step we all took in getting rid of these three categories.

P: *Do you feel that we're born homosexual?*

J: I like the modern view that we are products of our genetic heritage and our cultural heritage. And that the development of a gay person comes about when the homoerotic genetic strain is there and when the culture provides support for that person to have a gay consciousness. When I speak of gay consciousness, I mean that creative possibility to disengage oneself from the fixed roles of humanity and move into new possibilities. The gay consciousness values the right of choice. The hetero says, "How is it done? I want to do it how it's done." The gay person says, "Well, how am I to do it?"

P: *John, don't you think there's a danger in trying to differentiate between homosexuals and heterosexuals? Isn't that a ploy that heterosexuals use in trying to say that we're so different from them?*

J: Look, I'm not really interested in comparing heterosexuals and homosexuals. I'm interested in looking at each of them for purposes of clarity. I have never thought that I was feminine or masculine. My understanding of the gay person is that . . . there are a tremendous number of qualities people can have. It's the heteros who label them masculine or feminine. They draw a little box around little dots here and little dots there and call that one masculine and this one feminine and then legislate themselves into these boxes, you see. To be gay is to be out of those boxes. And so, if you're out of the box, then you're no longer comparing.

What we're studying now are the particular powers and strengths that come from the common experiences that gay people have, given that we face the difficulties we do. You know, quite a number of studies used to show that gays were neurotic because of what they've suffered. It turns out not so. We're no more neurotic than the rest of the population, yet we've lived under this pressure. So doesn't that imply that we either came originally equipped with or have acquired certain powers to react to all this pressure and survive it? Now these are interesting questions—what are the powers? how do they show up? Information like this can help explain why gay people are remarkably innovative, inventive in their own lifestyles and their relationships with each other . . .

P: *Doesn't that sort of reek of supremacy?*

J: Well, look. If you're gay, it means that life, and nature, has pointed you in a direction toward consciousness and given you a good swift kick in that direction. We start from the fundamental recognition that we, nearly all of us, have a set of experiences which are remarkably similar. For example, we, nearly all of us, have discovered that we are different, and we think we are the only one in the world who is like us. Then we, nearly all of us, find later on that this is not so, that the terrible rejections that are put down on us are local in nature—they are our family, our home, our church— and that the world does belong to us after all. So we make a return in our own minds, then, to belonging to life and to feeling that the traditions, the great things of the human race, are ours as much as anyone's.

P: *There's a sort of force in a lot of the gay movement to say that gay people are like everyone else, that we are different only in that we have different choices about with whom we want to go to bed . . .*

H: At this point, I'll stick my neck way out and say that in my estimation what you have described is what I call homosexual. Those people who are exactly like heteros except that they have a slight difference in their sexual and affectional preferences. But gay people are people who, maybe from birth, have known that they have a multidimensional quality which separates them from other people. And in this respect, you might say that gay people are almost opposite from everybody else, except in bed. Because after all, since

the sexual revolution, everybody does everything to everybody. We are different from everybody else, except in bed,
I think.

J: One of the things that Harry and I came to recognize
in our dialogue with each other was that the word "homosexual" completely misrepresents us, that to be gay is to be
of a certain undefined, but very strong kind of temperament.
And that homosexual preference is just simply included in it.
Instead of putting the sex first, you see, we put it as part of
being gay. And that from the earliest . . . for instance, the
common rejection of the homosexual son by the father,
which takes place as early as age three. We find that, as Harry
likes to put it, we don't smell right to our fathers.

P: *You're saying that we didn't become homosexuals
because our fathers rejected us, but that our fathers rejected
us because we're homosexuals?*

J: Right. And the same with our mothers, you know.
We're supposed to be the result of indulgent mothers. Well,
very likely we were seductive to our mothers because we
didn't objectify them. You see, we didn't go the Oedipus
route that Freud likes to talk about, did we? We refused what
Freud calls the "maturation," which is to pick up the harness
and put yourself into the service of the heterosexual modal-
ity—the family and the father and the mother and all that—
which Freud defined as civilization, you know. We wanted to
remain multidimensional, or as he calls it, "polymorphically
perverse."

H: The big problem that we're dealing with now as we
come into our consciousness, as we begin to recognize that
we have our own window, our own way of looking, that we
are different from everybody else—we enter into a new area
of threat to the heterosexual. In Oscar Wilde's time, or even
in 1950, we weren't speaking from a positive, assertive point
of view. We were always defensive, apologetic, attempting to
justify. And when we couldn't do that, we were disappearing

into the woodwork. Now that we are asserting ourselves, we are triggering a backlash of homophobia in the heterosexual in a way that the gay movement never triggered it before.

P: *Let's just talk quickly about how you came to New Mexico.*

J: In 1959, I brought out the telescopic kaleidoscope, which was a great success. It's called the Teleidoscope. And Harry joined me in that enterprise. In 1969, we decided we would leave Los Angeles. We had been hunting in vain for a place to set up a gallery and museum that we'd planned for a long time. We were free to go where we pleased and take our little kaleidoscope factory along with us. Harry had been visiting New Mexico for fifteen years and had some acquaintances here among the Indians. We knew the country was very beautiful, and we also considered it to be a sort of crossroads on the axis of Chicago and Los Angeles—or Denver and Dallas, you know—a place where we could be in contact with the world but also be in the country. We wanted to carry on this great work of studying gay consciousness. So that's why we chose New Mexico.

Sally

LUCY: *How has the women's movement influenced you
as a lesbian?*

SALLY: I think to love myself in a society that does not
want me to do so is miraculous. I think for a lesbian to love
herself or another woman in a society that essentially hates
women is really miraculous. I've been waiting for the women's
movement all my life! I've known since I was a teenager, or
even younger, that my primary emotional, intellectual, and
erotic feelings were toward other women. But I never got to
put it together until the women's movement came along. It's
like the egg and the stone that Mao talks about. You have to
have the internal conditions for the egg to change, and you
have to have the external conditions for change. And if you
have them both, then the egg can hatch, right? But if the egg
is a stone, then it's never going to hatch, no matter how
proper the temperature and moisture is, right? On the other
hand, if you have an egg that has the internal basis for change
but you don't put it in the proper atmosphere, it's never going to hatch. I feel like I've had this internal basis for change
all my life, that I have known who I am and how good I felt
about myself. You know, I've never felt sick. I always felt it
was the rest of the world who was just really messed up.

L: *What was your life like in the fifties?*

S: I spent the fifties essentially either going to graduate
school or beginning my career as a teacher who was very
much in the closet—and very much attempting to hide the
fact that I was a lesbian. And that meant putting down and
holding down a whole part of myself that was really vital to
my being. I have these visions of faculty parties or church
parties or picnics to which I would oftentimes go with a gay
man friend of mine, and we would put on an incredibly good
show. If I addressed heterosexual men, I had to make sure
that I addressed them only so far as to convince them that I
was heterosexual, but not so far as to provoke any kind of
sexual relationship with them. And I guess I was giving off
the image of being the virgin queen . . . I don't know. I don't

know what people really thought. I just know that I felt myself living a dual life and that I put an awful lot of energy into seeing to it that the world did not know what I was actually about.

I was doing all kinds of things in that professional life, when I was being closeted. I was sponsoring sororities, which had a lot to do with the way in which you perpetuate those stereotypes of what femininity is all about. I found myself directing homecoming pageants, I was very close to marching *for* the war in Vietnam, and I was judging Miss Texas contests. A lot of the ways I was in the world were in an attempt to hide the fact that I was a lesbian; I did not want to be discovered. I allowed myself very little feeling when I was in the world and had any kind of attention on me. It was not safe to do so. I became very invulnerable in a lot of ways and a lot of that had to do with hiding.

L: *What part did the Church play in your life?*

S: The Church. That was a big one. The heaviness that came down on me from the Church was the thing that I experienced most deeply. The Church, which theoretically has as one of its values some kind of honesty, turned out to be, for me, the place of my greatest hypocrisy. And that was maybe the toughest to live with. You begin to think maybe you're sick. And certainly the Church is telling you that you're sinful and a blasphemer and all of that. Some of those things that Jesus was saying were really relevant to me—all of the business about love is incredibly important. But what the Church did with that message, or has done with that message, has been so oppressive to women and to gay people that I can't tell you the kinds of things that I used to go through. Like going to a wedding—which would of course be a heterosexual wedding—I would never ever be validated in that way, to have a wedding, you know, in a church, to have the Church validate my concern or care or love relationship to another woman. And you sit there in this pew and you hear either the groom singing to the bride or the bride singing to the groom

or saying to each other the words from the Book of Ruth—
you know, "Intreat me not to leave thee, or to return from
following after thee . . . ," the whole business about "Thy
people shall be my people," and you know it's really a beautiful thing for two people to be saying those words to each
other. And it would just flash on me, just all over me, that
these words were originally spoken by a woman to a woman—
Ruth to Naomi. And then I would flash on all of the incredible relationships out of the Bible, like David and Jonathan.
You know, there were some real love relationships clearly
going on, but the Church has never seen fit to validate those
relationships.

L: *How were you able to get any validation from people?*
Can you think of a particular person that you came out to?

S: I got very little validation in the forties and fifties. I
remember once when I shared information about myself,
simply because I couldn't keep it in any longer, a friend of
mine sort of patted me on the head and said, "Ah, no, you're
not that way—you're really not. Even if you were, it's just
sort of a stage and you'll get better," and "Let me fix you up
with this blind date."

There was even a period of time in which I felt like maybe I
ought to find out what it would be like to be a heterosexual
woman. I had the notion at the time that it all had to do with
sex, right? And so I very deliberately had an affair or two
with some men who were very close to me, who were very
fine men, and although that wasn't a bad experience . . . it
was rather a good experience, but it just couldn't touch the
love relationships that I had had with women. I came out of
that realizing I just was who I was, and that was who I was
going to have to be.

Everybody was so closeted then that the only people you
really could trust were your lovers. The bad thing about this
is that you get into this thing with your lover where it's "the
two of us against the world." And somehow I don't want to
relate to someone out of any kind of fear or the bondage that

comes from being against something else or being different from something else. The hiding part is one of the most devastating, self-hating things that can happen to a human being. Charlotte Bunch [editor of *Quest*] has a game that's a play on "Queen for a Day." She says pretend you're Queer for a Week. Tell everybody that you've really decided that the gay lifestyle is the one that you want to adopt. Just try that for a week. Tell your family, your friends, the people at work. Walk down the street with a person of the same sex, holding her hand or putting your arm around her in some affectionate way, and see what comes down.

But since 1970, when I came to San Francisco and was able to say that word "lesbian" out loud, there has been a real change in my life. I think I'll never forget walking into the first meeting of what we were then calling gay women's liberation. There were something like eighty lesbian women in the room. I had never SEEN eighty lesbians together before in my life—my eyes were out on stalks.

L: *Now there could be a lot more . . .*

S: Yet, I don't know very many forty-five-year-old lesbians who are really concerned about the things that I'm concerned about politically, as far as feminism and the women's movement. There's a difference to me between being a lesbian and being a lesbian-feminist—a lesbian who is committed to women on a political level and not just personally. Though it's getting better. There are more and more who have been lesbians all their lives and who are developing a feminist consciousness. And there are feminists, you know, who suddenly discover that they love women and want to express it sexually and in every other way.

L: *Do you feel feminism is increasing among lesbians?*

S: I think that the women's movement is a great watershed in history. It's a time of incredible change and reversal. Feminism helped me to figure out that what's going on is woman-hatred. And part of the reason that I feel that gay men are as oppressed as they are is that they are, in society's terms, "like women." It seems to me that what lesbians are saying and what gay men are saying is that we've got to take another look at sex-role socialization.

L: *Do you think feminism has influenced gay men?*

S: I think that part of the reason that things have changed so radically for gay men is because things have changed so much for women. When I . . . when a lesbian walks down the street and is identified as a lesbian, that somehow flies in the face of all sexual stereotyping—the nuclear family and all of those things this society wants a woman to be. I think that the women's movement and feminism and gay men are confronting the patriarchy and capitalism.

When I first came to San Francisco, I had the problem of who I was going to identify with—my gay brothers or my straight sisters? Was I going to pick up my picket sign and march in front of Macy's because of the ugly things that had been done to my gay brothers? Or was I going to go to the abortion rally? Now, as a lesbian, I'm not interested in women having abortions so they can have heterosexual intercourse more often. And yet, very deep in me is this desire for everybody to have their human rights. And if women wish to relate to men, then I want them somehow to have that kind of freedom of their own bodies, freedom that this nation didn't give them until we began to do some pushing. So I remember very clearly at one point, having to choose between one meeting or another. And it came down to whether I was going to put my energy with my straight sisters, who in some cases were being very oppressive to lesbians, or with my gay brothers, who had been some of my best allies. My choice on that occasion turned out to be one in which I had to give my energy to women, whether they were straight or gay. And it was really hard for me to do that. And it meant a lot of times that I was splitting myself up in ways that I didn't want to. And yet, if I didn't make some of these choices, I'd find myself spread all over the universe.

I intend to put my energy into changing things for all human beings, but, you know, starting with women . . . I mean, we can have a socialist revolution all over the world and until we confront woman-hatred and what it is that men really think of women and what they think of the woman in themselves, everything else is just a minor skirmish.

L: *So the breakthrough is really with women? Is that where your efforts are going?*

S: I feel like there are four strategies. And I think that different women do different things. For conscious women who believe that capitalism is fucked and that the patriarchy has to go, there's political action—that is, violent overthrow of the system and political organizing. There are women struggling with that, but the sexism of the left has done a lot to hold them back. Or women can work within the system in terms of reform—that is, small incremental changes that say somehow we're going to make room for women here, room for some human vision instead of the usual hierarchical struc-tures. Or creating an atmosphere in which men can find their feminism. Presently I have a job in the system—I teach. And as long as San Francisco State University hires me, then I am part of the reform within the system. Or, you can do alterna-tive organizations—alternative health collectives, alternative schools. And those things are very important too. These first three strategies are very important to me. But the one that I feel is really where it's at these days has to do with women finding their own internal energy source, and in almost a mystical way, learning the uses of psychic energy—in such a way that not only individual realities are transformed but that somehow other people's realities are transformed too. And when you get fed up with the other three strategies, the one that you're usually left with is the last one. Or at least that has been what's happened in my case.

L: *Tell me about how that happened for you.*

S: I had been a heavy Christian, a converted Lutheran.

I was teaching at a small church college, and I had my only religious experience. It was one time when I was being blackmailed. And I was not responding to the blackmail. The woman who was blackmailing me called the college president and said, "You'd better get that lesbian off your faculty." I was called in by the president, and I knew that he was going to ask me the vital question—was I a lesbian. Now, above the president's head there was a picture of the head of Christ— Jesus with a kind of an aura around his head. It's a very famous picture within the Church. The college president leans across the desk and says to me, "Dr. Gearhart, are you a homosexual?" To which I replied, "NO"—at which the head of Christ immediately moves and looks at me for my lie. Anyway, there I was, trying really hard to be a Christian!

L: What did it mean to you that Christ's head turned that way?

S: Even at the time, I considered it really funny. I was trying very hard to understand what connection the figure of Christ had in my life, and I couldn't get any kind of connection. I didn't feel like a sinner. I didn't feel like I was doing anything wrong. All those things that the Church kept telling me—that I was worthless, that I, in the sight of God, had no worth except by his grace, *his* grace, right?—I mean, I was even celibate for five years, not because I thought it was wrong to be a lesbian, but because I was afraid of being caught. And I was actually trying to give Christianity a chance. I really wanted God to move in my heart.

I realize now that I was never converted to Christianity. But what I did was get converted by stages—to feminism. And then the personal conversion came. I very much wanted to develop a relationship with a particular woman and broke the celibacy in order to do that. And felt all the creativity surging back into me that had been left off before her. Then there was a professional conversion. I got involved in a sensitivity group and came out completely drained of all my authoritarian ideas. My teaching changed totally. And then came the political part of the conversion—that was in 1969-70, the year of the Cambodian crisis. In the town that I was living in, we had martial law for a period of ten days, during which time a lot of my hippie friends got beaten over the head by the militia, and it became very clear to me that there was something wrong with this great government of mine.

Maybe the thing that's really important to me is that people do and can change. And the changes that I've gone through in my own life become an example of the way I think that it can happen. If I was who I was ten years ago, and now have changed to the point that I really feel like a rebel against so much of that, then it seems to me that there's hope for the rest of us. And I think that's what feminism means. It sounds like a Geritol commercial, you know—"Before I started taking feminism, I couldn't even spit over my chin."

L: *Are you a lesbian separatist?*

S: . . . ah, yeah, deep in my heart I feel a real need to . . . both for myself and—I sort of feel like it's really important that women separate from men. Okay? I can't be a real absolutist on that, because in the first place separatism is not really possible, you know. How can we separate from the system? You know, it's possible, maybe, to be . . . for women to separate from men but not . . . not from the entire system, and so I have a lot of problems with the definitions of separatism and all that . . . . But I would just . . . the thing that keeps striking me is that I find that women are leaving men by the droves in this country. In greater numbers than statistics probably show. And I suspect that the reason that's happening is that women are coming to some kind of self-love, some kind of sense of themselves. I find them . . . you know, they're leaving men not just to live with other women, or to be lesbians, but sometimes to live alone. I can't find the words for how important I think it is that all of us begin to come to some kind of consciousness of the way that we don't allow each other to *be,* in free ways. And it's that struggle that I spend my life engaged in.

I feel really strongly that separatism is not only viable, but necessary. But I work in the system and not in a separatist way at all. I realized I had to choose a strategy by which to function. I mean, what do you do when you separate off from everybody else? If I separate from men, and then I separate from straight women, and then I separate from lesbians who are under forty, and then I separate from lesbians who are forty who have blue eyes, pretty soon I get down to only myself, right? Which I think is the function. And why it is that so many of us feel the strong separatist thrust and do indeed go through that. But the point is, we can't live by ourselves, and I feel like, for me, there's got to be some kind of political action. And so, in order to get that going, I had to begin to form my coalitions again. I had to begin to relate to straight women and to men, on some levels.

(Nancy joins the interview)

NANCY: *This time you were choosing those coalitions, right?*

S: Yes. That's a good point. I really believe that men have got to get things together in large numbers by themselves. And that's what I see the gift of gay men is. And hopefully the rising of consciousness among some straight men too. I'm not saying that every woman has got to separate from every man. But I think there has to be a large enough separation of women from men to make a qualitative difference in history.

On the one hand we have to be very careful of the kind of backlash that's going to come from that. And, on the other hand, we've got to be reassured that men come to some kind of understanding in themselves that they can take care of themselves. I rarely find a man leaving a woman in order to live with another man or to live by himself or to live without any kind of sexual relationship at all. I don't understand how we can think about relating across sex lines when we are so dependent on each other. And that, to me, points to the necessity for separation. Rita Mae Brown has said that probably the greatest gift of love that a woman can give to a man is to leave him.

L: *Why?*

S: Because then he won't be able to rely on a woman to be his nurturance for him. He won't depend upon a woman to be the intuitive element in his life.

L: *Where will he get this?*

S: He's got it inside himself. I really believe that. I think I have more faith in men than a great many heterosexual women do. Men are not really going to realize this until they begin to miss some of the things that women provide for them, and that to me is the value of separatism.

And, somehow, the whole matter of separatism means that we get to a place where we find ourselves as whole persons. Sex research is beginning to show us that children are probably born bisexual. They are unable to discriminate between a male touch and a female touch. In other words, children, in terms of outreach to other people, probably are capable of receiving love and affection from men and women equally. I call it the treason of the delivery room. The minute a child is born we start to make a half-person out of that child. Every institution in this society goes into high gear to put that child into a sex role. And that child is forced into being exclusively heterosexual. The child gets this shot of "I am a girl," or "I am a boy," right at birth and every day of its life. And never the twain shall meet, except when the two of them get together in the miracle of heterosexual marriage and make one whole person. Divorce statistics, if nothing else, will tell us that that's really a myth.

It's really amazing to me that gay people exist! The media and the institutions promote nothing but heterosexuality. You never see gay couples on TV, you don't find things made for gay people—it's like the world has been made for right-handed people, you know, and you don't find left-handed can openers. The same thing goes for disabled people, for people who are of a different color. We cut across all races, all classes, all cultures—we are anywhere from 5 to 25 percent of the world's population. People don't even know we're there, because we've been hidden so well. And we've become real chameleons. Every gay person has a heterosexual perspective, whether they've had heterosexual sexual experience or not. We're bombarded with it. And I think that the least I could ask of my heterosexual friends is that they somehow cultivate a homosexual perspective.

N: *What do you think you have to offer straight people?*

S: It seems to me that when we're talking about sexual identification, we're talking about all people being able to participate in the whole continuum of feminine and masculine. The more gay people speak out, the more the whole world begins to understand the way all of us are told to fit into a certain role and how that's got to be changed. I've heard other good lesbians say this—that gay liberation may really be the ultimate revolution because when gay people are free, when all people are free to love whomever we wish, where love can be expressed openly to children, to older people, to people of the same sex, to animals, to trees, to the earth, where we can love in the way that I think humans are capable of loving, then that's when we'll be on the road to being a species that is worthy of this planet. I think this is part of the gift that gay people have to offer the world.

N: *How do you relate the struggle of gay liberation and the struggle of feminists to world revolution?*

S: It's real apparent to me that the earth is giving clear signals that we are destroying her. She's been raped and gutted just like a woman. What I'm learning about how this country decimates other countries is an incredible revelation to me. We're destroying a jungle in Brazil that's going to take away half the world's oxygen supply; we're destroying the ozone layer. We can't survive much longer with that kind of mentality. We're all victims of the kind of mindset that runs capitalism, that runs the patriarchy, that says, "I've got to stand with my foot on your neck because there's somebody else with their foot on mine"—competition. I mean, none of us is clean. I believe that all kinds of groups all over the world are beginning to sense the same kind of thing. It's real important that we have the consciousness that says not only "We are oppressed as gay people" but "I am an oppressor as a gay person"—as part of a larger machinery that's doing awful things to the rest of the world.

N: *And I am an oppressor of myself. I mean, I have bought into all those other systems; they're not my own essentially?*

S: Yeah. And I guess the message that the women's movement brings is that where I start is my own experience. It's got to come from where I am personally. Even the early manuscripts of Marx go along with that. But that's what's different about this revolution. Every individual is going to demand consciousness. The attack that is usually made on people who are working in the sex-role arena, like gay people and women, is that we have no class consciousness, that we don't know what material reality is all about. And I don't believe that. I believe that the economic realm is not more important than the psychological realm. And if we don't recognize the fact that there are internal realities, we won't get anywhere as a mass movement. The difference between what's happening now and what happened in past revolutions is that now there is an individual consciousness arising. It isn't just a matter of a leader rising up and leading people to a revolution.

N: *How are you able to maintain your cheerfulness? You're talking about changing thousands of years of attitudes.*

S: I feel a lot of support from other women, from my gay brothers, even from people who are just beginning to tie into what this whole matter of sex roles means. And that gives me an awful lot of strength.

I think I've always been pretty happy with myself, even during those times that I was hiding or playing that heavy schizophrenic game. I always felt myself to be somehow a survivor, and I've always had a real hefty love of people that I think contributes to my feeling good about myself.

N: *Do you think that your mother still loves you?*

S: Oh, yes. I have absolutely no doubt about that. I know there are a lot of things that she disagrees with me on, but I don't think there's ever going to be anything that could break the tie between us. She knows that I'm a lesbian. She doesn't necessarily like it, but I've always been told in my family that you have to be who you are to make yourself happy. There was always a lot of stock put in being honest and having integrity. I was given a sense of my own value and encouraged in my work. This gave me self-love, allowed me to be free in the use of my body.

Of course, my lesbianism wasn't a cause for celebration. I mean, vacations for me, from school or my job, were always the most hideous times of all. Because I couldn't take the person home that I cared most about. Or I couldn't go home with her.

And I think about the other side of it . . . what happens when a lover of yours dies? What part of her family are you? How do you feel being left out of the communal grief? Who commiserates with you at the death of the person that you have most loved? I mean, you feel the anger, the rage, the injustice of all that. Until the gay movement, we had no support.

N: *How do you feel about growing old?*

S: As a lesbian growing older, I don't have to fit into the same kind of sex role that's expected of women in this society. I'm getting a lot more strokes for growing older. There are even little buttons now that lesbians are wearing that say, "I like older women." That's quite an affirmation! The older I get, the better things are getting, and the less fear I have that I'm going to die in some old folks' home by myself. I think there will be other women who will take care of me, just as I think I can commit myself to taking care of some of my sisters. And when that care is spread out among that many women, it becomes much easier and can be much more an act of love and that much less an act of obligation.

I thought my thirties were pretty good, but I have to say that every year of my life has gotten consecutively better.

N: *Is that because you're changing, or is it because of the world?*

S: I don't think the world is changing that much. I'm still worried that we're really going down a path of annihilation, and that's why the women's movement is so important to me . . . because I feel like if we don't make it with the women's movement, as far as this planet is concerned, it's just good-bye, Columbus. I'm really anxious about the state of the world. But in terms of myself, I'm feeling more and more affirmed, and I'm feeling lots of things beginning to come together with women in ways that make some creative, concrete changes in this world.

NANCY'S
STORY

I have worked on and off as a horseshoer, a tow truck dispatcher, and a cab driver. But in the spring of 1975, I was unemployed and restless. My lover worked every day, while I did odd jobs, tended the garden, and had no particular plans. I was more than ready when my brother Peter asked me to videotape several interviews with lesbians for his film on gay people.

Peter, who is a professional filmmaker, had been trying unsuccessfully for two years to raise money from foundations for a documentary on homosexuals. Now he had decided to look for money within the gay community, and he needed visual material to convey his idea to potential investors. He wanted a lesbian to interview gay women while he prepared videotapes on gay men.

I had no previous experience in interviewing or using video porta-pak equipment, but I was interested in Peter's project and was a handy lesbian to ask. I was my brother's sister, and I had plenty of time, but my major qualification was that I was a lesbian—probably one of the few Peter knew.

When did I start feeling like a lesbian? When did I start being one? When did I come out to myself? to my parents? to the world? And, most important to me at the time, when did I have my first sexual experience with a woman? I didn't consider myself a real lesbian before that first experience; for three years, I told myself I was a virgin dyke. I realize now that being gay is as much a state of mind as it is an act of love.

In 1967, my friend Bea was one of the few women I knew who was open with straight people about her lesbianism. I remember seeing her kiss her lover; I felt shocked, repulsed, and fascinated. Fortunately she was open and could be herself with me, so I felt comfortable with her. One day she noticed the boys' basketball sneakers I was wearing and remarked to her lover, "Don't you think Nancy would fit right in at Maud's [a lesbian bar in San Francisco]?" I blushed and tried ungracefully to cover up my size eleven feet.

One night after a party, Bea asked me if I would like to go to Maud's. I was feeling so secure and drunk that I agreed to go—excited but nervous, afraid a bunch of dykey-looking lesbians would start coming on to me. In retrospect, I find it rather extraordinary that I had such a high regard for myself that I was certain that these women would be attracted to me like flies to sugar!

Having picked up society's stereotypes, I thought I would find a group of unattractive, frustrated women. I didn't feel this way about Bea, but she was different! It never occurred to me that the women at the bar would be more interested in each other than in some stranger. Now I understand that my fear of being accosted really reflected my hope that I would be noticed.

As soon as I walked into the bar, my preconceptions disappeared. I was exhilarated, and I thought, "This is the first place I have ever been where women can be themselves." They were not reflecting each other or the dull images projected on them by men. These women were themselves! They were characters, wild in their own particular ways, but not necessarily "butch" or "femme." They were women of every description, enjoying each other. I had always been a "character," and at last I had found a place where I could be myself.

Though I was twenty, I was just beginning to come into my own sense of self and my own sexuality. I'd had little experience with men. I had always felt awkward around them; I didn't know that I was not supposed to be myself, which must have had something to do—thank heavens!—with the lack of "proper" socialization from my parents. Just as I was deciding I was a lesbian, I decided that I was too old to be a virgin, so I went to a gynecologist and got a prescription for the pill. Then I called an old friend and asked him out. He thinks he seduced me! I slept with him twice but continued to go to Maud's and dream about having a woman lover. One was either lesbian or straight then; bisexuality was an option I was unaware of.

A couple of months after I first went to Maud's, I told my mother I thought I was a lesbian. Her response was very calm—as though I were telling her something she already knew. She remembers thinking that it made perfect sense to her, but at the same time she realized how difficult it would make my life. I remember feeling very happy at the time, and I felt then that my mother, whom I call Casey, shared in my joy of self-discovery. I consider myself incredibly fortunate to have a mother who reinforced my choice—unlike the parents of most of my friends, who responded with no support. It never occurred to me that I might be abnormal, because my mother was open when I talked to her—and she had raised me to believe in myself.

When I was six my parents gave me a horse, which I rode off into the desert mesas. Casey would not let me use a saddle. She said that I would learn to ride better without one; I would develop the proper leg muscles. I fell off my horse more than once, but nothing terrible happened; I never thought anything would. My environment was there for me to explore. I was not encouraged to think it malevolent.

As a child, Casey was a competitive swimmer. I was proud to tell my friends that my mother had learned to swim when she was three—the same year she had started first grade. I was sure that my mother was best of all the mothers thrown into the ring by each kid competing in the size-up-each-others'-parents game. In my slow emergence out of childhood I have managed to maintain my belief in her superiority, but rather than brag or show off the newest racing dive she taught me, I grew to hold several theories of child development based on her child-rearing practices.

My mother was my first mentor because of the way she raised me, the way we talked, and the way I watched her talk with her friends—especially my aunt. It was not unlikely, when the two families got together, that Casey and my Aunt Gina would outlast the rest; they could keep each other going all night with their arguments. My aunt was a cynic who did not believe that humankind could improve; Casey believed you had to believe it could or you'd have to give up. I sat in on many of these early sessions, learning to sharpen my wits. I became as adept as they at lying in wait (the image of a vulture comes to mind) for the not-even-slightly-pregnant pause. The only way to stay alive in those conversations was to interrupt—and if you were interrupted, to shout even louder, "Goddam it! Let me finish my point . . . ." It was years before I knew there was another way to talk—and my mother had the nerve to tell me I was argumentative.

As a child I was fascinated by nuns, who were different from mothers or wives. I couldn't believe they wanted to lead the lives they did. I felt sorry for them, but I was attracted to their determination to lead a difficult life. They were the only brave women visible. Boys could identify with cowboys, soldiers, astronauts, construction workers, doctors, and policemen. All kinds of uniforms could set a boy's mind to wondering about who he would grow up to be. I could identify with wives, mothers, and nuns. But rather than playing nun, I played cowboy and doctor and construction worker.

Coming out is a constant process of opening. I started opening when I first thought that I would be a lesbian. Since then I've always insisted straight people know who I am so that they will know that there is a choice; I like to talk about my different lifestyle so that they will not assume theirs is the only one.

In the fall semester of 1968 at San Francisco State, I spoke up at a meeting of the Students for a Democratic Society (SDS) during the now famous student strike. I was disturbed because I found white students arguing about the demands of the Third World students. Although this was my first SDS meeting, I suggested we form special-interest groups and fight for our own demands. I was feeling the need for something that hardly existed at the time: women's and gay liberation. I was quoted in the *San Francisco Chronicle* (November 28, 1968): "An auburn-haired girl reminded students they didn't have to be members of any organization in order to work for the strike. 'You can just represent yourself,' she said. 'The great hue and cry of our generation is self-determination. I'm a member of several minorities: I'm a redhead, a homosexual, and a woman.'" Naively, I didn't realize that to be a lesbian was generally considered unacceptable. Unfortunately, I also didn't realize that in choosing to quote me, the newspaper was probably trying to minimize the legitimacy of the student strike by implying that it was infiltrated by queers and flaky redheads.

As I was beginning to have gay feelings, so was my brother. In our society, it is often as difficult to be a "sissy"—a boy who is not poured from the *macho* mold—as it is to be a "tomboy." I was considered cute when I played football with my male friends. Peter, who shunned competitive sports, was treated like a freak by his schoolmates. I began to think he was gay when a friend said she thought he was, though I wondered how he could be—he had such a nice girlfriend.

By 1973, Peter had been making documentary films for eleven years. In 1967 he had completed *Holy Ghost People,* his award-winning film about an Evangelist church in West Virginia. After freelancing and working as a producer for KQED-TV in San Francisco, he decided he could not make another film until he made one about himself—for and about homosexuals.

When Peter first had gay feelings, he knew no one like himself. He felt that something was wrong with him. He went to a psychiatrist; he tried to have "normal" relationships with women. He thought being gay meant quick fucks in sleazy johns, !imp wrists, and bleached hair; he thought it meant that he couldn't be a "person" and that he would always be relegated by his secret to the fringes of society. Peter wanted to make a film for homosexuals so that other boys and girls—men and women—would learn that the feelings they were having were not unusual. He didn't know then that accepting his gayness was his power.

He decided to make a movie that would help all of us gays believe more in ourselves, come out of our closets, and affirm each other. He wanted the film to recognize and acknowledge the oppression of homosexuals. As a youth with gay feelings, he had no positive role models. He knew no homosexuals, so he

felt he was the "only one." Peter learned by talking to other gay people that their experiences had been similar to his: they too had felt they were the "only one." Many wished they had known someone to whom they could talk about their feelings. Many felt alone and maladjusted because they felt different from their peers. All had to go through years of adjustment before they were able to embrace homosexuality as a positive part of their lives. They found themselves only in themselves. They found no reflection of who they were in society.

Peter planned a short documentary, for use in schools, in which out-of-the-closet gays would talk about their lives and thus offer positive role models for gays having difficulty. We did not realize early in the project that the lack of public information on the realities of homosexuality had created a cultural void which would necessitate our making a much larger film.

Peter asked me to do five or six interviews on the videotape porta-pak machine; he would compile them with his interviews into a composite tape to show investors. He spent an hour showing me how to use the video equipment. I was anxious that I wouldn't be able to work the camera, hold it without jiggling, and ask questions at the same time, so I wrote a list of questions in case my mind failed me. At the time we were not looking for anything specific; we simply wanted people to tell the stories of their lives in terms of their homosexuality. I interviewed a friend from the bar with whom I felt comfortable and who I knew would be supportive. The interview went well, although I did have trouble holding the camera still, asking questions, smoking, and drinking beer. For the next interview I used a tripod and smoked and drank only during breaks.

I soon realized that I really didn't know most of my friends very well. I didn't know how they had come out; we never talked about how we had come to terms with our lesbianism.

In the spring of 1975 I did about six interviews. I met all of the women through Maud's. Whitey was the bartender, and I knew her well—I sometimes stayed after hours to help her clean up. After the work, we would drink and talk for hours. During these marathons she told me about her life, but I didn't think that she would let me interview her; she seemed too shy and vulnerable. Whitey is six feet tall and is the strongest woman I know. I remember telling her that I didn't understand why people were afraid of her; I thought she was like a butterfly. She smiled, blushed, and said that was the way she felt.

Whitey did want to tell her story, and our session went very well. When Peter saw the tape, he was very moved. He felt certain he would want to use Whitey in the film. I was pleased to have a tape of the quality Peter wanted.

Peter was struggling through interviews that didn't excite him until one day he came back to the office very pleased. At a gay rally to protest the beatings of gay men on Castro Street, he had heard Tede speak. Peter described how outrageous Tede was in his flamboyant drag—long, polished fingernails, a 1940s dress, feathers and bangles, topped off with an army helmet or basketball shoes or some equally incongruous final touch. Tede, more than any other speaker, was really socking it to the cops and the straights. Peter had taped Tede, and he felt he had his first good interview.

When I first saw Tede's image, I was amazed at his androgyny. I was moved by his tenacious ability to resist the socialization forced on him. I felt that he owned the part of himself that was female and cherished it as something positive in himself—unlike the more traditional drag queen whose dress often celebrates the archetypical Bette Davis or Joan Crawford type. Strange that Tede could put me in touch with an aspect of myself I had left outside the bar.

The film Peter wanted to make was taking shape in his mind.

A couple of things affected me in those early days. I saw *The Sorrow and the Pity*. That film had so much meaning for me. And that film was doing everything "wrong." It was in black-and-white. It was four and a half hours long. It was full of jump cuts. It had the worst photography. And it was talking heads. But I could have sat there another three hours watching it!

Then I read Studs Terkel's book, *Working.* I realized that to hear other people talk about themselves was fascinating; if what they say is well edited and well done, that format alone is very interesting. *Rolling Stone* magazine had also published an article after asking their readers to submit autobiographies. They got thousands, and they printed many of them in the beautifully edited article. Some of the autobiographies were only a paragraph long; others, a page. But to read what "just people" said about what they did was intriguing. That's sort of how I arrived at the form of the film.

Peter estimated a budget of seventy thousand dollars. Before the film was finished, that figure would grow to over two-hundred thousand. His research had shown not only that no film of this kind existed on the market but that educators were really feeling the need for one. He became convinced that the educational market alone would insure a substantial long-term return. He believed that many gays in his community would invest in the project and that he could earn at least enough to return their investments:

Unfortunately, I'm not the kind of filmmaker who can go off and make a small, "personal" film cheaply. That's just not the kind I make. I'm interested in longer, sync films. So I had to come to terms with my human responsibility and my responsibility to myself. Making your own film—making a film that you care about—is a process divorced from other kinds of filmmaking. The process of writing a book is much closer to the making of such a film than even television is. The areas between art and craft and business are so diffuse.

Making the film would be a long, slow process. I knew people were not going to invest unless I had the act together, unless I approached them impressively. It took a long time to learn how to do that, because no one showed me how. Basically what I learned as we went on was to develop an "approach." We had to convince people that we were creating a significant film. Most people don't raise money for documentaries by such a direct approach. Some films are hustled, but they don't usually turn out well, because the people are more interested in the hustle than in the film. I knew of no good films that had been done through investors.

If the investors genuinely believe that you will make money back for them, without any question they will give you all they have to give, because then they will be making a fortune. So why don't they think that? You have to go through the whole process and figure out why they aren't giving you their money.

Just writing the proposal took me four or five months, because I wrote it and then showed it around to a lot of people and changed it again and again until it boiled down to the final version. People read the proposal and loved it. Almost universally, everyone said it was the best proposal they had ever seen. I thought we'd get the money from the proposal. We didn't get a nickel. I think people felt, "Yes, you can make a proposal. But can you make a film?"

We started doing videotapes partly to raise money. I asked Nancy to help. She was interested, and the trade-off was that she would do it in exchange for learning to use the video equipment. I also wanted to test her to see how we would work together.

I had always felt the film should include both men and women. It would be a better, bigger film if it did. But, politically, I didn't see how we could possibly do it—the climate wasn't right. I didn't see how men could work

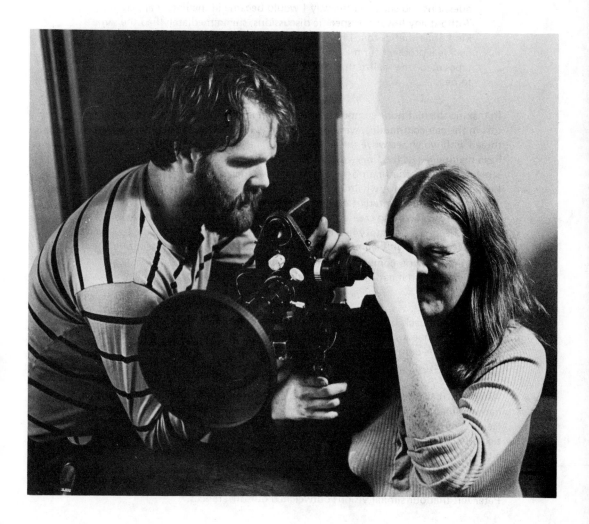

with women, or how I'd even find a woman. Obviously I didn't want to work with a woman who didn't have a strong sense of feminism, a strong sense of lesbianism, a political consciousness. To have made a male-dominated film would have been a mistake not only politically but economically. The film would never have said what it should have said, and it would never have been accepted by women because a strong woman's point of view wouldn't have been represented, because the woman would have been working under me. I didn't see how any really strong feminist would work with me in a situation set up as other than "absolute equals."

Nancy's video interview of Whitey was a knockout. It was so much like the film I wanted. It was what I had imagined the film should be in feeling and tone. Also, a kind of organic connection between the way she asked questions and shot and the way I would became immediately apparent. Without any lessons or specific discussions, she immediately had the same kind of aesthetics that I had. I knew that working with her was going to be a real problem for me. But the immediate sense of what was on her tapes made me realize that it was worth whatever the problems were going to be.

In making the half-hour composite tape which we presented to prospective investors in the gay community, we used Whitey and her story as the major dramatic thread with which we wove the other stories. The general feeling of this tape has been maintained in the finished film. Peter found his first investor through this screening and got the first positive feedback. Neither the audience nor Peter and I expected to be so overwhelmed by the primitive black-and-white compilation. The viewing of these intercut oral histories resulted in the quantum leap of our consciousnesses. We had created a mirror that gave us the affirmation we so desperately needed. Each story had been lived separately, yet each reflected every other. We realized with a great sense of responsibility that we were painting one of the first realistic composite portraits of homosexuals. We hoped that one result would be that gay people would never again doubt their own existence. As Peter said:

The feedback from the first composite screening was really what led me to continue looking for money. I think, too, that's when I realized that its form—continuous intercut stories—would be essentially the form of the film.

After that first screening, I hoped for a chance at the job of co-filmmaker. I was overwhelmed when Peter told me that he wanted to hire me; I had expected, at least, to have to compete with other contenders. Peter and I had never been particularly close. As kids, we had spent most of our time together fighting and, although in recent years we have lived in the same city, we had seen each other only on family occasions, or when one of us needed a favor. When I had a truck Peter borrowed it; when he had a truck, I borrowed his. Despite our relationship Peter felt that our similar visions outweighed our differences.

When I got to the city I took a cab to Peter's for a meeting, though it would have been just as easy to catch a trolley. I had driven a cab in San Francisco for two years, and I had sat in front of the bus station many times a day waiting for passengers. Now I was a filmmaker about to start work on an important film.

As I began to work full-time on the film, I sensed a new self-direction, one based on—"Hey, I *do* have something important to offer." I had based all my actions on the feeling that I wasn't good enough. I had internalized the values our society places on independent women, weirdos, and homosexuals. I saw myself as a freak because my culture saw me as one. I hid in the bar, I hid in my relationships; my sense of self was based on "we" rather than "me." I was not a whole person; I was fractured and devastated like territory occupied by the enemy. Peter's asking me to join him on the film became the means for me to find myself.

Although we had just barely enough money to start filming immediately, we decided to continue with the video process. It was relatively cheap and offered an invaluable method of screening people out for the film itself—and also a less intimidating and more informal way to get people to tell their stories. If we had used audio tape in this initial research, we would not have been able to see people's images. Later, when we had chosen those we wanted in the movie, we would return and reinterview them on film, and they would be more relaxed in spite of the lights, camera, and sound equipment. They would know just what to expect from the interview situation.

We took turns using the video machine and didn't really confer with each other about the people we were taping, or the results. About fifty interviews were done all over the San Francisco Bay Area. We had no particular criteria for choosing people but contacted them randomly through various friends and lesbian and gay-male organizations.

We began to see that the interviews of the women and the men had very different qualities. The men's stories were interesting, but their deliveries were often blah. Many of the men talked about their lives as though they were reading grocery lists. They tended to be less emotional, less vulnerable than the women—probably due as much to the difference in their socialization as to the difference in Peter's and my interviewing techniques.

Peter's style was less involved than mine. He identified with his subjects, but he didn't show it; he maintained a sense of distance. I often participated more by engaging in conversation when something was said that inspired me; I felt that my participation would help the interviewees feel more at ease and that involving them fully in the process would insure an air of informality. I wanted to try not to fall into the prescribed role of interviewer and yet maintain the focus.

Peter's and my working relationship was vastly improved by a ritual we adapted from one I had learned from some country lesbians. They called it "passing the rattle," and it was based on a ritual used by the Native American Church. The person who holds the rattle holds the attention and energy of the group without interruption for as long as he or she chooses. By passing the rattle we were able to get out into the open any tensions or difficulties we were having with one another. One would speak (we soon had to put a time limit on each turn) while the other listened and took notes on what he or she wanted to comment on. I wanted to break down as many traditional roles as possible—those professional situations in which people are not concerned about their personal relationships.

Passing the rattle was the method we used to erase faulty assumptions we had developed about each other. In these sessions, for the first time in our lives, we listened to each other; we bothered to find out how the other ticked. I can hardly believe now that we took the time. Although we called these sessions passing the rattle, my country friends would pale at the comparison. We were in the city, in an office, a man participated, and we did not actually use a rattle! A friend of mine laughed when she heard we used no rattle, but I'm sure she didn't laugh as hard as Peter would have if I'd told him we had to use one.

Peter asked Veronica Selver, a film editor and old friend, to view the tapes with us. He felt her point of view would be unique and invaluable. Veronica is a sound editor and had been working in San Francisco on *One Flew Over the Cuckoo's Nest*. Peter and Veronica had known each other since high school; she had helped him cut some of his first films. We planned to hire two more people, and I suggested that we hire Veronica. Peter was delighted. After the video screenings we also hired Andrew Brown, one of twenty men we had interviewed for the job of camera assistant.

Andrew was an hour late for the interview. He called to find out exactly where the office was, saying that he had left his house three hours early because he knew he would be late. I don't know how we managed to hear what he had to say, because so many words had piled up that day in Peter's office. Peter, who sat behind his desk, identified heavily with the applicants, remembering the days he had looked for work as a filmmaker; he realized how overwhelmed he would have been at this chance. By the time Andrew arrived, Peter was next to useless, and I conducted the interview. I liked Andrew very much. I liked his incredible energy and forthrightness. Rob Epstein was interviewed at the same time. We liked him very much but couldn't hire him right away. We asked him to work as a volunteer, however, and were pleased when he accepted.

When I called to tell Andrew he had the job, he dropped the phone and ran around his apartment screaming at the top of his lungs—I'm surprised he wasn't evicted. Andrew had sung in the chorus of the Philadelphia Opera, and he has one of the most powerful voices I've ever known. Later, when we traveled together in Peter's truck or my car, his voice would reverberate off the roof; it was like standing next to the speakers at a rock concert.

A friend of Peter's suggested we do a book in conjunction with the film. Peter asked Casey, who had had experience as managing editor of the *New Mexico Quarterly,* if she would be interested in such a project. She agreed with great excitement. So while we screened the tapes, we did audio dubs on cassettes. These would later be transcribed to give Casey the written material she would work with.

We spent a week screening the tapes at my parents' home in the country. We set up the small TV and video deck in their living room. With rapt attention, Casey and John also watched the parade of gays on the little television set. Each tape was interesting; we rarely broke our promises to keep silent. The people were diverse: a young anthropology professor; a lesbian mother who worked as a therapist for the city of San Francisco; political organizers, artists, workers, drop-outs, bar dykes, lesbian-feminists, women and men who had just come out; Elsa, a seventy-eight-year-old lesbian poet who had been gay all her life; Tede, an ex-drag queen with a feminist consciousness; a factory worker; Rick, a lawyer who told his beautiful story of an early love and spoke of receiving shock treatments because he was gay. The people were of many races and ages. An ex-school superintendent told of being framed and arrested; a high school student spoke of running away from home.

We watched for about five hours a day—as long as we could before our eyes were crossed from so much concentrated staring at the small black-and-white images on the screen. We were emotionally exhausted from our involvement with the stories. Casey was amazed at how articulate all these people were; she began to think that they were in some way special.

We chose six people: Tede; Whitey; Pat, an ex-WAC and a humorist; Rick; George, the factory worker, who cried as he told his story; and Elsa. Later we added Pam and Rusty, lesbian mothers who had battled custody suits for their children, and by March of 1976, we had filmed eight people. We had also filmed a number of other noninterview sequences: Whitey cutting down a huge madrone tree, a men's bath house, a lesbian bar, and a picnic scene in which Rusty and Pam play football with their kids. A year later we had to make the difficult decision to cut most of these scenes from the film; it had to be shorter, and we felt these sequences took away from the purity of people's stories.

We notified the people we had chosen and scheduled their interviews over a six-week period. I was afraid Whitey would not consent to being included in the film—she might not want to become a public figure; she might not want to expose herself to the pain of telling her story again. I thought it would be a good idea for Veronica and me to drive up to her small cabin in northern California and visit with her. I suggested that we take a transcription of her video interview for her to read so she would have a clear indication of how articulate she was. It would also be a good opportunity for Veronica and me to get to know each other better.

Also, Veronica had never traveled in this country; she was in the West for the first time. She had been raised half her life in France and the other half in New York City. She was wide-eyed at the landscape and at the people she met. We stopped in a small town on the way up and stayed overnight in a friend's converted schoolbus; it sat on a hill among the trees and looked west over the valley. We were surrounded by wild life, and below, near the house, were goats, chickens, cats, horses, and gardens in various configurations and styles of pens and yards. I had always wanted to live the way my friends did; Veronica seemed to be equally disarmed by their lifestyle.

Reluctantly, we left the next morning for Whitey's—another three hours north. Veronica couldn't drive a stick shift, so I did all the driving until we neared Whitey's. Then I tried to teach her. She drove about twenty miles—while I aged at least that many years. I had seen Veronica operate the most intimidating editing tables with a facility that I envied, and I felt certain she could transfer that ability to a clutch and gearshift on a lonely country road. I did not let on that she made me a nervous wreck—I wanted her to feel good about her perform-ance. But I hoped that when she bought a car, she would get an automatic—or find a professional teacher with nerves of steel.

It was wonderful to arrive at our friends' cabin and find Whitey waiting for us. I had not seen her since the video interview the year before. She had moved to the country for good and had built her dream home nearby; she looked wonderful—rosy-cheeked, thinner, and healthy. She beamed when she saw us get out of the car, strutted down the hill, and gave me a big hug—the warmest I'd ever received from her. Veronica told me later that Whitey was even taller, blonder, and stronger than she had thought she would be; her only previous introduction to Whitey had been eight inches of her on a TV screen. We were visiting another beautiful living space, a large cabin nestled among the madrones and pines, goats, chickens, cats, gardens, farm equipment, and piles of lumber and other items that indicated work in progress and lots of dedicated energy.

We spent the evening talking and drinking, and then Veronica and I walked up the hill to the little sleeping cabin where we would stay. Like a ship, it contained all the essentials in a tiny space—a little propane stove, a wood stove, a little sink and mirror, a bed, and bookshelves. The next morning, Veronica reminisced while she took a sponge bath in the tiny sink. The whole place, she said, reminded her of the small room she had lived in in Paris, except the stove was fancier; she and her lover had used canned heat.

We followed Whitey's truck to the top of the trail that led down to her cabin three quarters of a mile away. It is a little frame structure with a slanted roof and a storybook stove pipe coming out of the back horizontal to the ground, then elbowing its way toward the sky, tipping its little tin cap to the clouds. The path ran above and behind Whitey's home, then down to the front of it; we passed piles of wood covered with polyethylene, and trash waiting for the season when Whitey could drive her truck down to haul it out. The cabin was perched above the bank of a stream we had crossed earlier.

Whitey had used a large round section of tree for a doorstep; she opened the over-sized, beautifully built cedar door with a huge padlock on it. The house looked as though it had been built by a cabinetmaker. Every stud was perfectly cut and looked as though it were exactly sixteen inches from the center of the one next to it. Having built the rooms in my mother's barn, I knew how hard it was to be that exact. The inside was still incomplete; silver-backed insulation glared from the reflected sunlight. Whitey was saving her money for the inside siding.

She had read the transcript and listened to the audio dub of her interview, and she agreed to be in the film.

When Whitey came down to the city, we interviewed her in my father's study. Because I was afraid Whitey might be uncomfortable with Veronica in the room while she discussed her early years, I had asked her if this would bother her. She preferred to talk to me alone, which meant that I'd be doing the sound too.

Whitey had decided to quit smoking but put it off one day until after the inter-view. Peter and Veronica were running around taking care of both of us, plump-ing up pillows for Whitey, getting her beer, adjusting lights so that they would not shine in her eyes. Peter spent ages adjusting the shoulder brace so that I would be comfortable. Veronica got the recorder and mikes ready; Peter had two extra magazines sitting in their box next to me so that when the first one ran out, I would be able to pop the next one on the camera myself. This job was normally left to the camera assistant, who would also make sure that the gate in the camera was free of any dirt which could come out on the film's image. While the filming was going on, the assistant would have his or her hands in the black changing bag, removing the exposed film from a magazine and reloading it with new film.

The whole shoot would have made most professional filmmakers' hair stand up on end. We broke many rules. For these first interviews we did not use a tripod, which is why the subjects seem to weave around so much. Peter preferred a shoulder pod, as did I; they feel much more organic, as though the camera is a part of you. The interviewee must talk to you and the camera—not just the cold, hard machine itself. We later sacrificed this intimacy for a steady frame.

The other huge no-no is using the cameraperson as the interviewer. Every film-maker Peter talked to told him he was crazy to try it—and it was unthinkable with amateurs. The problem, they said, is that you cannot shoot as well if you are thinking about what questions you are going to ask, and you cannot inter-view as well if you are trying to think of how you are going to shoot. I feel that Peter's decision to use this method is one of the most important he made.

When Peter and Veronica left the room, there was I and there was Whitey— puffing away on her smokes and slugging down Norwegian beer. I was trying to adjust not only to my new costume, the torturous camera brace—it might have been invented to extract confessions from heretics—but to my various roles: friend of Whitey, interviewer, cameraperson, sound person. I also had to keep in mind the particular viewpoint Peter had suggested I concentrate on.

Whitey didn't want to talk about her mental hospital experiences, yet I knew they were one of the major reasons we were interviewing her. The roles of friend and interviewer are sometimes diametrically opposed. Who am I to insist she talk about a painful episode in her life? One of the major problems I had with making the film was that it demanded this kind of objectivity.

A few days after the shoot, Peter and I picked up the film at the lab where we then screened it. The lighting was beautiful; the set was fine. We had spent a long time with the set, pulling various things out of my parents' house that would look like they'd belong to Whitey, deciding on a picture or mirror or something that would fit on the wall to the left. I learned that setting up a set is very much like painting a picture or taking a photograph. Many of the same aesthetic principles apply. A window frame can't come out of the middle of a head; a huge plant in the lower right part of the frame will throw the whole thing off balance; a huge expanse of wall with nothing on it will seem to go off into space—and carry the viewer's eye and attention with it. We had to be sure we had enough color, but not too much, and not too much of any one color, and not too much of one color in one spot. We had to make sure that a person's clothing was not going to blend in with the background like a chameleon—or clash too violently. We often asked people to change clothes more than once.

I met Elsa at a Country Women's Festival in northern California—a huge, five-day gathering of three or four hundred women. She is a very beautiful woman who broadcasts good health and vigorous energy from every pore. When I first saw her, I wondered if she was a lesbian. I remember Elsa sweeping into the large dining hall with a coterie of friends; she was at the apex of a flying wedge of older women who, undaunted by the numbers of beautiful young women, moved from one end of the hall out the large doorway to a destination unknown to me. I was mesmerized by them. I remember shaking my head and wondering if I had truly seen what I thought I'd seen. This regal court of women seemed so incongruous among this scruffy scene of women, all of whom were searching for the simpler life in the country. I later went to a lesbian workshop held outside in a redwood grove and discovered Elsa sitting on a large rock amidst her friends. Shafts of light filtered through the tall trees and encircled the group while women spoke about coming out. I remember Elsa saying that she didn't understand why it was such an issue.

Although she made me nervous, I wanted to interview her. I drove to her house in the country—a beautiful home surrounded by eucalyptus and redwood trees. When she is not writing, she spends most of her time in a gigantic and prosperous vegetable garden. I was taken aback by her extremely gracious manner of greeting me: She gathered both my hands in hers and gave them a strong squeeze as though I were a very old friend.

Interviewing her initially on video was pleasurable. I often felt I was talking to my grandmother about her early romances, though I knew hardly a granny in the world who would talk about lesbian romances at all, much less as candidly as Elsa.

We returned to film her in February, 1976. We did the interview outside, so we didn't need lights, but we highlighted her face a little with a huge reflector. Before we started, Elsa asked if we were going to make money on the film, and, if so, would she get paid? Peter said it was not customary for a documentary film to pay its subjects but that he had been thinking about giving them a share of the film. Elsa's insistence pressured Peter to have our lawyer draw up a contract for the participants; each now owns a share of the filmmakers' percentage of the film.

I began the interview but felt a tension between Elsa and me; how could I get her to repeat the story she had told me on tape? Veronica, who was doing sound, came out now and then with a suggested question, and she'd talk to Elsa during magazine changes. Clearly, the rapport was being established between Elsa and Veronica, not Elsa and me. Veronica was surprised when I suggested that she take over the interview, while I monitored the sound. She drew out some very good responses, but we never did get Elsa's story for the film (fortunately we had it on videotape for this book).

Pat, an ex-WAC, is in her early fifties. In the videotape interview with Pat, I talked so much that one can judge by her expression that she was quite annoyed with me: "Whose interview is this, anyway?" Peter and I shared the film interview with Pat. Peter began, so that Pat would be talking to someone to whom she had not already told her jokes, to someone who could give her a fresh response.

I knew Pat was funny. I had sat many times with her at Maud's and listened to her crack one joke after another. But I had never heard her talk about her early gay life in San Francisco. I was going to try to move Pat out of her humor and into some more serious feelings—try to get her to talk about who she really is and what she really feels about being a lesbian and about being oppressed. I knew that Pat had a hidden warehouse of feelings. I could tell by watching her face in the mirror when she sat at the bar and thought no one was looking. I knew because I have a similar store of feelings.

When I took over the interview, Pat was already tired and hot from the lights. It was getting dark, so that the window next to her eventually became pitch black— another uncontrollable variable that adds to the emotional impact of the film. I used about two mags and felt I was getting nowhere with her.

I decided to be more responsive and more challenging, feeling that we had nothing to lose. Pat had answered negatively when I asked a question about lesbian support, so I asked a question which developed from her negative response: If she had had no support, how could she stand it? It elicited an emotional response, a frustrated response, and a long silence following it. In those few seconds she expresses for all of us our sense of powerlessness, our resignation, and our alienation. Pat stopped telling her jokes and showed a part of herself that was protected by them.

I am repeatedly moved by this part of the film because I identify so with Pat. Filming her silence, without interrupting her, was the most difficult thing I did during the making of the film. I wanted to get up and hug her, I wanted to get angry, I wanted to scream, I wanted to console her—the last thing I wanted to do was film her. As she was exposing her emotions, I was forced, for the sake of the documentary, to control mine.

Our only intention in the interviews was to create the question, to build an atmosphere that would allow each participant to feel comfortable enough to be herself or himself. It was most important to us to be true to the individual's personality and sensibility. Six thousand watts of light and a huge film camera are not conducive to the creation of this atmosphere. The interviewers were forced to do whatever they could to counterbalance these obtrusive elements. Besides working the camera and asking the questions, we had to respond in a meaningful way so that the subjects would feel that they were being listened to and supported—the meanest trick of all. We had a 16-millimeter camera covering our faces. One hand was busy focusing the camera, and the other was operating the zoom lens. We thought then that we wanted the audience to hear our verbal responses; we thought they would identify with us and, in this sense, we would be responding for them. Though many of the interviewers' comments were eventually cut, we have left many—so the audience will know we exist, so they will know that we are fallible. My question to Elsa—"How old were you when you were born?"—never fails to get a huge laugh, and I never fail to flinch.

The Rick shoot was the only filming of a man in which I participated. I did the sound. Andrew loaded magazines, and Peter conducted the interview. We had become so adept with the lights that we could do the lighting and the set in a couple of hours on the day of the interview. Rick, who is an influential lawyer, an early gay activist, and a city commissioner, had helped Peter put together the very first videotape screening to be used in raising funds.

Rick dashed home from work, took off his sports jacket and tie, tried on a series of different shirts for our inspection, sat down, and got interviewed: one! two! three! let's get this thing on the road, let's get down to the nitty-gritty, I'm a busy man, no silly business, no chit-chatting, nothing superfluous. His tone never varies in the film, whether he is talking about his first romantic love or his terrible shock treatments. He does, however, change in a very subtle way his basically set expression—his eyes light up and a very slight smile begins to form—when he talks about his relationship with and love for his lover David.

When David joined him later in the interview, Rick's manner softened considerably. Despite his efficiency and drive, Rick is a very mild-mannered, soft-spoken man. When I first saw his video image and heard his voice, I was certain he was a Wyoming cowboy in business suit drag. On the other hand, David's sports shirt doesn't disguise what appears to be his shy banker nature.

A friend had given me the names of two lesbian mothers who lived together in San Mateo, both of whom had to fight the courts for the custody of their children. I spoke to Rusty, who said she would be delighted to be interviewed, and she was sure that Pam would be also. They lived in a very pleasant working-class suburban home on the central peninsula south of San Francisco. I walked into the small, crowded living room where Pam was having her hair dried by a friend while they watched a football game on television with one of the kids.

When I took the videotape back to the office everyone was astounded by their contrasting images, by their articulate perspective and awareness of their plight as two women, each of whom had children, who were madly in love with each other after years of being together and months of agony fighting the county for custody of their kids.

For the film session, I interviewed Pam first, then Rusty, then the two of them together. Veronica monitored the sound, while Peter loaded magazines. It was the most comfortable and casual of all the interviews I participated in.

Rusty and Pam have the ability to make everyone feel at home, including three filmmakers with their tons of equipment and, unfortunately for us, every neighborhood kid in the area. While we were in the midst of filming, kids came to the door every few minutes. Locking it was useless. Then they would ring the bell, which would be picked up by the microphones. Pam and Rusty could not easily answer the door; they were wired to the tape recorder; I was the most encumbered with camera and microphone. Veronica was connected to the recorder by her earphones, so Peter sat out in the car to waylay any startled children who, no doubt, would run and tell the others about the strange goings-on at Rusty's and Pam's house—"Hey, Rusty and Pam are going to be in the movies!"

Indeed one would have thought the two women were professionals used to so many lights and the concentrated staring of the camera lens. They were a good deal less nervous than I, and they followed to the letter our instructions to look at the lens, rather than at our encumbered faces, while they spoke.

After lunch, we rearranged some furniture to create the set for the interview with both of them. Peter wanted to do an interview with a mirror on the set reflecting the cameraperson/interviewer so that the audience would realize where the voice came from and see that the interviewer was also the person shooting. Over their couch Rusty and Pam had a long mirror set in a deep frame. Little shelves on either end were filled with knick-knacks, souvenirs, and Pam's perfume bottle collection. We had to move the mirror down so that it would reflect me, and when we took the valuables off, Pam insisted on washing it. Lighting ready, kids under wraps, camera ready, sound ready, slate . . . we were ready to shoot.

Pam and Rusty's was the last shoot at this stage. Peter was certain we could assemble this material into a very rough cut which we could screen to raise more money. He had shown a videotape composite to WNET-TV, the New York PBS station, and they wanted to buy the television rights, pending their review of the film material. We were fast running out of funds. We were going to have to start taking rich gays to lunch again. I had done no fundraising to speak of, and I wanted to learn. So while the others put together a rough cut, I was on the phone organizing a screening for potential investors.

At first I found it difficult to talk to strangers. But I soon discovered that it was not difficult at all; most people were very interested. I also quickly got over the sense that it was little ole me asking for money for the film. It was not me—ex-horseshoer, bar dyke—asking people to invest; it was Nancy Adair, co-producer of a seventy-five-thousand-dollar film. Although I lived in what most people would consider a ramshackle apartment, I would imagine myself speaking from a large desk, and although I was wearing overalls and sneakers, I'd picture myself in a gabardine suit. I'd have a cigarette holder in my hand, be wearing a large pinkie ring. I began to feel like our stationery looked—swank.

I am astonished at the number of steps involved in the filmmaking process. There is so much to learn. No wonder they call it an "industry." I wonder if people in the far distant future will be baffled and amazed by the number of hours and the hordes of workers it took to put together a three-hour film, as we are amazed by the construction of the pyramids.

We shot a total of about fifty hours of film, which is a little more than one hundred thousand feet—about twenty miles. That equals four million frames—the separate little pictures strung together in front of a little light to give the illusion of movement. Ordering all this chaos was the editor's job. What is the old saying?—"A picture is worth a thousand words." At this rate, our footage is worth four billion words!

When the track was transcribed, we made six photocopies of each interview. Casey, Rob, and Dale, a volunteer, joined Veronica, Andrew, Peter, and me in this initial screening process. We viewed one interview a day on the screen at the office. We each followed the interview on our copy of the transcriptions, and we took notes in the margins. In this way we were each able to give Peter our input; we were able to respond in writing to everything everyone said. Peter then began the editing process.

Peter was working out a rough dramatic format based on his first ideas of what the format should be: a dialectic—thesis, antithesis, synthesis. He has strong ideas about how to build drama. He knew that in order to get the most power out of Rick's story, he'd have to use his first very positive love story, and that Rick's early positive experiences would counterbalance George's and Whitey's and Elsa's negative stories. He knew he couldn't deliver all the heavy stuff in one constant rhythm; he needed to counterpoint with humor. Pat serves this purpose. Just as we have been told something heavy, Pat makes us laugh. Then when she stops laughing, we get the clue that things are really getting serious, and the drama builds to a peak around Whitey's hospital experience, Pat's long silence, and George's tears. Peter did not want a dry eye in the theater.

We drew up a questionnaire so we could have input from the audience and invited members of the gay community, filmmakers, friends, our families, and the people we had interviewed on film. We were all extremely nervous that Sunday morning in March, 1976. What would people think of our film in its infant stage? How could they possibly understand what it would become? Would they sit through three hours of talking heads? And how many would get up so early on a Sunday morning?

I was a nervous wreck. Standing in the lobby I almost turned inside out when I saw some of the staunchest lesbian-feminists I knew walk in. I thought, "I'm not going to be able to live through this—I'm bound to be trashed!" I had been so careful not to invite them; Veronica, on the other hand, had not. I was afraid they would not accept the film because at that time we didn't have a lesbian-feminist in it.

Peter and Veronica knew from past experience that early screenings are usually disastrous, because people are not seeing the final version. Viewing a work print is like looking at piles of brick and lumber for a house rather than at the finished building itself.

Peter introduced each of us, gave a brief sketch of the history of the project, and described what a work print was. I had the jolly task of explaining who would and would not be in the film. "We will be traveling to New Mexico to interview Chicanas and Native Americans. Andrew will be traveling back East to look for a black man, Rob will look for young men, and I will be going South to find a lesbian-feminist." There I was in a haven of lesbian-feminists—scads of them right there in the audience! I knew I couldn't explain myself, and my heart was thumping in my chest; I was turning red and stammering. When we were ready I sat in the aisle so I could watch the audience. They came to watch the film; we came to watch them. They were quiet, then they laughed; Pat came on and they *really* laughed—they had hysterics! Then they were quiet; they were really listening. I left to have a cigarette, and when I came back I could see faces transfixed by the people talking on the screen.

We had planned to watch the three hours of film without a break, and we could hardly stand the tension. Then, miraculously, just after George cries, something happened to the projector, and the film was out of sync—the sound didn't match the picture. Peter yelled for a short intermission, and everyone went to the lobby. People were crying and embracing each other. A lesbian friend of mine, who disliked men, went up to George (whose eyes were also red) and told him how wonderful he was. Another friend who is normally intimidated by the likes of Pam and Rusty told them how marvelous they were. People who were in the film but who did not know each other met and hugged like long-lost friends. Gays from various political factions were talking with each other. If getting us together were the only thing the film was to accomplish, it would be a success as far as I was concerned.

We started again. I was beaming and feeling very different about the feminists. At the end we walked down to the front and received applause. We asked the people in the film to stand, and they received a huge hand; then we opened the floor for discussion. Besides many questions about future plans for the film we received many compliments. George said that he loved Pat; he had learned a lot that day about the problems lesbians face. A straight woman said she had known nothing about gay life but felt that she had learned not only about gays but about human liberation. Perhaps straights could identify with the people in the film because they are familiar with the trauma of adjusting to the puritanical values of this culture, and they too would receive affirmation for their struggles. Other gay men and women whose lifestyles were so very different said that for the first time they had seen a film that taught them about each other. Tede said that he felt good being filmed by us, that our casualness and shared roles were inspiring to see in a project of this scope, and that he felt he could trust us.

At one point I turned to Peter and thanked him for asking me to work with him. I had rarely thanked Peter for anything—and certainly not in public. Casey cried. She was so moved by the overwhelming reception, and by the film, but she was especially affected by my expression of gratitude. She had always felt pain at the distance between the two of us. Now she felt she had finally seen us touch—seen the two of us grow up.

Peter's inspiration gave birth to the project, the film crew nurtured it, and the gay community supported it. It became what its birthright required: no longer

Peter's film, but a film for all of us, and by all of us. It now had its own momentum and had initiated the shape of its own destiny.

We hired Lucy Massie Phenix to help Peter with the business of producing and to manage the office, and Rob, who had been working as a volunteer. Lucy had a lot of experience editing films and some experience in production. She had one of the most enthusiastic responses to the film and asked me if there was any work she could do for us. We were looking for someone to run the office while we were traveling. At first Lucy was reluctant to take this job because she had had little experience with bookkeeping and so on, and she was more interested in the filmmaking itself. I told her that I thought that the seemingly strict classification of the job would soon dissolve and that she might, before she knew it, find herself behind a camera or in an editing room. Lucy remembers how she felt when she first saw the film, and how she became involved with the project:

> I just happened to be in San Francisco when the first rough-cut screenings of the early film were going on. I had come to California to bring a film I had just finished editing in New York and was staying with friends who were part of the lesbian community. I was thinking and reading and talking with women about a film I wanted to make on the early emotional and sexual experiences between women. It was at this point that I went to the screening of what was then being called *Who Are We?*

> Like everyone around me, I was very very moved by it. I cared about these people, and they pulled me into many issues that I was feeling drawn to explore. I was outraged at the oppression they felt from without—and within. I knew that this was an important film about something I wanted to learn more about, and I was hoping that there was need for an editor to work on the film.

When we first interviewed Rob, I was struck by his gentle qualities and by his understanding of the concepts of feminism and lesbian-feminism. He strongly identifies with this politic—a difficult position for him to be in, I imagine, since many lesbian-feminists do not give the time of day to men and seem sometimes to be most turned off by gentle men—the quality of "gentle" was forced on us, so we reject it. Rob, on the other hand, embraced it.

Lucy and Peter flew to New York for the final negotiations with WNET regarding television rights. We were counting on this money to pay for our next expenses. Veronica and I rented a videotape machine and drove to New Mexico—always a happy trip for me. I enjoy going back to my home state, and I like to visit all my relatives and friends. I was eager for Veronica to meet all these people. While I traveled north to look for Native American and Chicana lesbians, Veronica stayed in Albuquerque and interviewed minority women there.

I soon discovered how different the reception to me and the project would be outside the San Francisco Bay Area. I visited many relatives and friends, and I found it interesting to see who would ask about my work and who wouldn't. Straight people who were secure with their sexuality had no problem talking about the film, but people who had had homosexual experiences or feelings and were afraid of those feelings could not ask about it. Gays who had been closeted for years were especially reticent to bring up the subject. Many were afraid I was going to stir up the settled pot and cause trouble. They felt they had led good lives; their friends accepted them. They saw no reason to make a big stink.

I was not interested in talking to anybody who didn't want to talk to me. I don't believe in opening anybody else's closet. That very personal decision we must each make on our own. I know your secret, and I will keep it.

When I got back to Albuquerque, Veronica said she had a surprise for me. She took my hand and pulled me through the doorway. Sitting there with a cigarette in one hand and a beer in the other was Nadine—the first lesbian I had ever known. If I had not known her as a child, I would not have known that lesbianism existed. She was in my cousin's class, and five or six years older than me, so I didn't know her well. I remember people's thoughts about her; they thought she was kind of crazy. Veronica had interviewed Nadine's lover, Rosa, that day; we decided I would interview Nadine the next.

Peter had asked me to look up John and Harry while I was in New Mexico. Peter said that many people had told him that they should be interviewed. I spoke to John on the phone, and he was extremely friendly and very interested in talking to me about the film.

John gave me excellent directions to their house near the San Juan Pueblo in the Rio Grande River Valley. Direction-giving in rural New Mexico has been elevated to a subtle art. There are few street signs, and one has to have a trained eye to spot natural—and not so natural—landmarks. "You'll cross an arroyo, then turn left on the first dirt road past the cottonwood tree on your right about a quarter of a mile past the old bridge over the ditch. You will see an old Studebaker pickup on blocks. Turn left there." I found their home with little trouble—after a short detour to the local dump. As I came around the bend, it was raining slightly. In the distance I could see a little man holding a large umbrella of the type I am more accustomed to seeing in the hands of Homburg-hatted New Yorkers. People don't use umbrellas in New Mexico except to keep the sun off during the Corn Dance—which always brings rain, so they come in handy then. As his voice had foretold, John was older by thirty years than I had thought he would be.

His style of dress was as incongruous to the umbrella as the umbrella was to the desert. He wore sandals, khaki pants, a bright shirt, and a little grey pony tail—and a cheery smile and twinkly eyes. I pulled up to him and let down the window; he stuck his hand in and gave me a very warm handshake, then opened the gate and told me to drive to the end of the compound. John and Harry shared this particular piece of land with numerous other homes. They are close to their neighbors and very involved with community affairs. I was offered herbal tea and dried fruit while we waited for Harry to get back from town.

When he came, I was struck by his stature. Harry is very tall, also in his sixties. He wore the same sort of clothes John did and had his steel-grey hair tied back in a pony tail at the nape of his neck. I soon knew why I had to interview them.

Harry had helped start the Mattachine Society, the first homophile organization in the United States. John was an inventor—which amused me greatly, since he looked so much like Benjamin Franklin. He had been working on an optical machine that projected kaleidoscope images, and he showed me what his little invention could do. It was one of the most beautiful visual experiences I have ever had.

John and Harry share in each other's work. Harry takes an active interest in John's inventions, and John does much of the writing they publish in the name of The Circle of Loving Friends—the name they had chosen for themselves. I had read one of their papers and had been impressed with the philosophical content; its radical nature was what had led me to believe that The Circle of Loving Friends was a group of young gay men—not two older, politically experienced men.

When I returned to their home a few days later for the interview, we began outside, but the mosquitoes got to be quite a bother. We moved into their crowded dining room, lined with shelves filled with jars of preserves, herbs, books, and odds and ends of optical glass, bolts, and nuts which had drifted in from John's work table. Again, I was served homemade goodies—dried fruit and bread. Harry makes bread once a week.

I stayed on for a while after the interview. We talked on and on about the history of gay liberation and the significance of gay people in our society. I felt I had been talking to the Horse's Mouth—the grandfather of gay liberation. I had received an invaluable outline for further study about gay people. I mentioned that someday I would like to explore their library. They invited me back warmly and told me I was now part of their circle.

After we had completed our interviews in New Mexico, Veronica flew to New York to look for professional women, and I flew to Atlanta. I was looking for a woman who could represent the *spirit* of lesbian-feminism rather than the rhetoric. I wanted someone who could translate, through the lens of her life story, the feelings I had had at women's events in California. Was I looking for the impossible? Wasn't so much of the spirit I was searching for brewed only within a *group* of women? Could one person represent it? Didn't the film itself have to reflect this spirit—and how could it if it was also about men?

I was looking for the most articulate spokeswoman (with a southern accent). I loved the South, and I loved the people. I felt that I was at home. The texture of slowness and the cadence of speech is much more my speed and style than the plastic-edged tongue of northern California and the rest of the country.

The woman I was looking for didn't have to be an intellectual or a movement leader. I talked to many women who belonged to the Atlanta Lesbian Feminist Alliance (ALFA). I went to a meeting; I went to a softball game, to a bar. A large city was not quite the atmosphere I was looking for.

I stayed for a week and became very close to them both. I had been running around like a maniac interviewing and filming people for months. I needed this time to reflect—to stop and talk about other things. It was difficult for me to leave.

Then, in North Carolina, I found a farm where women were living together. One of them, Ann, was a veterinarian in private practice. The women were beginning to get involved with the local lesbian organization. It was there that Ann had met her lover Dilly.

I interviewed them, and we talked about feminism, lesbianism, separatism, coming out, telling your parents. I was so excited that I decided to erase a tape I had already done to get more of our discussion. I felt I had found what I was looking for: a group of women who expressed the spirit of lesbian-feminism. But how could we film a group? I felt that we had to somehow.

I called Lucy at the office in San Francisco after the interview to tell her I had found the women; I had found the spirit I was looking for. Lucy was wonderful to talk to on the phone. She always got excited as soon as I was excited. She was a perfect ear. She had in a way become a mother hen to all of us—a role she had managed to avoid all of her life until she became involved with us. We had a huge phone bill those two months. Apparently I was not the only one calling the office to freak out. Andrew, Rob, and Veronica had their spells too. Lucy had become the point where all our paths converged; she was the spoke of the wheel. "Tell Peter that I would like him to . . ." "How is Andrew doing, and Rob?" and "By the way, how are things in San Francisco? How are you?"

On the train to New York I thought about my travels—about all the places I'd been and all the new people I'd met. I had met many different women and a few men. I had met new lesbians, young lesbians, older lesbians; I had met lesbians of different classes and different colors, and I had fallen in love with several of them. I thought about how easy it was for me to travel among these people, how friendly and open they were. Everyone I talked to was interested in the film. Almost everyone I asked consented to be interviewed, but everyone supported the idea. I thought about the ways these women were willing to share their lives with me, about how candid each was. And I thought about how they are with each other, how they love each other, how open they are.

I had put my trip to New York off as long as possible. I did not want to be in the murky heat of the Bicentennial crowds. I took a train to the city about two days before a planned screening. As soon as I stepped off the train, I felt a tremendous surge of energy and exhilaration. My rhythm seemed to pick up with the fast pace of the city. I went to our friend Susan's apartment, where Peter was staying. I was so eager to see everybody again. Peter had not yet signed a contract with WNET, but he had wrangled an office there, and we spent the next few days there calling people for a New York screening.

The New York screening was very different from those in the San Francisco Bay Area; the New York audiences were much more critical. Peter and I stood up at the end and fielded the questions. I felt I had really held my own with the tough "political gays."

We began sharing our tapes at Susan's apartment and finished them at Veronica's mother's summer house on Cape Cod. Each person presented his or her tapes to the group in whatever order he or she chose.

Before we began looking at tapes, we had several pass the rattle sessions in which we planned the strategy for the next few weeks and did some criticism/self-criticism. These meetings marked the beginning of the transformation of the group—the beginning of the move toward more collectivity. I think that everyone was a little unclear as to his or her role. Whose film was it? How would roles be defined? Peter was not into making unilateral decisions involving the format, but he did make the major business decisions. Peter was producing the film, but he did not feel that he was directing it. Although he and I had done most of the interviewing up to this point, this would no longer be true. I feel that we became more collective because we had to, even though I believed in doing it and pushed for it. But I also had a tremendous emotional resistance to the collectivization. Peter had the most power, and he had given me more than the others. I felt I would be lost in the group, that I'd lose my role as Peter's assistant. I would become part of the group, but Peter would not—not in the same way.

I was unable to trust the group because they threatened me. I had too much ego attachment to the idea that this was Peter's and Nancy's film. I liked being associated with the project as Peter's equal, as I was viewed in the eyes of those outside the group. I was not, at this point, thinking of the best interests of the film.

We sat in a circle at one end of Susan's large living room—Andrew, Veronica, Rob, Lucy, and I on foam couches formed in an L, Peter opposite in a chair. I remember Peter's anxiety and tears. I do not remember the particulars of the conversation.

These early New York meetings were a beginning—with each of us wondering what our roles would be, each struggling with power, Peter trying to be clear about giving up power, not wanting to do it because of guilt. Was he remembering another group he had worked in, when he had given all his power away until none was left, and the film he was working on and the group he was working with were destroyed because they weren't clear with each other? Was he finding himself in a similar situation, or could he trust us? Could he trust himself?

I was remembering all the times I'd had difficulty working in groups. I wondered if Lucy was remembering the last film collective she had worked with—a group that called itself a collective, but really wasn't. And who was she in this group? What could she bring to us in terms of her group experience, her filmmaking experience? She was frustrated as she tried to speak. We stopped passing the rattle, and the meeting broke down into hysterical interruptions and misunderstandings and raised voices. When Lucy tried to speak, the words were jumbled, she became muddled, she was interrupted by me or Peter. She rocked back and forth on the couch, tried to forget a raging headache. It was hot, and we had to solve the group and individual problems before we could make any decisions.

Andrew was jerking his leg up and down; he seemed dizzy, confused with the speed and volume of conversation. He could not break in. Rob, too, was confused, finding it difficult to make his contribution. Veronica was rubbing her forehead and grimacing—she looked like she had been in a battle. Peter and I managed to stay above the mire of all the words better than the others because probably most of them were ours. We were accustomed to interruption and yelling—it was our family dynamic. As was usual whenever we didn't pass the rattle, he and I dominated the meeting. Each member of the group would have to learn to fight to be heard, each would feel manipulated into using the style Peter and I were used to. The others would begin to challenge this style, and the overabundance of Peter's and my input.

Six volatile people struggling to be heard. From the tone of things, one would think that we could never possibly work together—as one would think, if one heard an Adair family fight, that we hated each other. On the contrary. The level of angry tones is a direct measure of the family's strength, because we eventually come to an understanding and move to the next plateau.

So it was with the Mariposa Film Group, as we later named ourselves. (Mariposa is the name of a street near the office. It means butterfly in Spanish. We found out later that it is used derogatorily in Mexico to mean homosexual.) We were honest with each other; we got our feelings out, and we developed a familial trust for each other. Each meeting would end with some kind of resolution. We would meet again the next day and start all over. In this way, we began to know each other better; we began to work and fight together. We became a unit, a group—and we shared the tasks of making the film. We began to recognize who we were and where we had to go. We stayed together because we recognized the importance of the film. We worked as a group in making decisions about the content of the film because this film could not have been made in any other way. The process of videotaping alone necessitated group decisions. This film had to reflect diverse viewpoints, and the varied points of view in our group would guarantee this reflection.

We had to learn to listen to each other and to let each person flow at his or her own rate. Sometimes we made mistakes because we didn't listen. Just as the film was being finished, we may just have begun to really listen to one another.

After screening some of our tapes in New York, we drove to Cape Cod, to Veronica's mother's beautiful little frame house—a paradise in which to spend a hell of a week. We would swim naked early in the morning in one of the fresh-water ponds. I would lie on my back, feel the water glide along my body, close my eyes. I would be lost in a kind of floating spacelessness. My legs would start to sink, I'd kick a little to keep them floating, the sun would try to pry my eyes open. I would wonder where I was; I would wonder if I was where I thought I was. I would open my eyes and discover that I was in a different place. Hair dripping, we'd come back to breakfast, a feast on the lawn in the sun—eggs, bacon, cereal, fruit, coffee. What a lucky bunch of queers we were . . . .

After cleanup Peter would usually herd us together— he is a natural sergeant-at-arms—with each of us wanting just a little more conversation, a little more time to be in the sun, more time to think about anything at all. Even after the first call—"Hey, come on, we said we'd meet at 9:30, and it's already 10:00! We have a lot to do!"—somebody would have to go to the bathroom, or find cigarettes or pen or notebook. By the time we had settled down, it would be 10:30. Fortunately we still didn't have the corporate executive's sense that time is money. We'd be ready to screen the tape and then inevitably something would be wrong with the machine. Another delay. Finally we'd settle in—coffee, smokes, pen, paper—and we'd watch tape after tape.

We looked at tapes in a small upstairs sitting room. We planned to look at all of them in four or five days, then have two days to discuss them and choose whom we wanted to add to the film. Veronica, Rob, Andrew, and I had each done at least ten hours of tapes apiece, and we would each have to select from these to show the whole group. In New York, we had seen Veronica's tapes of professional women and had already made a tentative choice. Veronica and I showed the tapes we did in New Mexico first.

The people we chose for the film are a reflection of the film we have unconsciously made. They are like desert cactuses; despite the lack of nurturance from society, they are hearty survivors, and they have very thick skins. Many are alone; they are lonely; they are sensitive in direct proportion to the strong defenses which they have had to develop to protect themselves. The couples also reflect this strength. They are each other's defense against the hostile world, each other's port in the storm. We kept responding to the people who were like the ones we already had in the film—people who, despite the odds, are as self-actualized as they can possibly be.

After we had chosen all the people to be filmed, we went back to the city and worked out the filming schedule, which was especially complicated because we had to film people all over the country, and Peter, the only one with enough

experience, had to be at each shoot. Coordinating all of the film equipment and Peter and seventeen pieces of luggage for twelve shoots in twelve parts of the country, with the five of us, was no easy task. By the end of six weeks, we were all exhausted.

Rob describes the final filming of David, a college graduate he had met in Amherst:

I went to Amherst to scout a location in which to film David; it was to be my first full interview. David was in transition. He had just finished school and hadn't decided where he would be living next, but he wanted to be filmed in Amherst since he had spent his most recent years there.

Judy suggested we ask Mrs. Dee, her employer and a high-level administrator at the University of Massachusetts, if we could use her property. She had a lovely farmhouse with wooded land and a quiet pond in back that sounded ideal.

When Peter and Andrew arrived, Judy took the three of us to see the location and to meet Mrs. Dee, who told us we were welcome to use her property. In our brief conversation we did not discuss the film other than to say we were interviewing a university student. And Mrs. Dee did not ask.

That evening as Peter, Andrew, and I were having dinner with David, the waiter told me I had a phone call. "Who and why would anyone call me here?" I thought. It wasn't like the Hollywood movies where one feels very important getting such an urgent phone call; it felt more like being paged at McDonald's.

It was Judy. "Hi! Don't worry. No one died," she warned me, knowing that family tradition views unexpected phone calls and disasters as synonymous. "I can't get something off my mind. I never told Mrs. Dee what the movie's about. Did you guys?"

"No, I guess we assumed you did when you first called her and told her we were making a film."

"I suppose it doesn't matter. I just wouldn't want her to think we were intentionally withholding anything from her so she'd let us use the property."

"Oh, no. That's silly. Besides, she never asked!"

My next instinct was to call Mrs. Dee and blurt out, "WE'RE MAKING A FILM ABOUT A BUNCH OF QUEERS."

As foolish as the possibilities might seem, and as homophobic and anti-gay as their implications are, we were responsible for involving unwilling people. Suppose someone recognized Mrs. Dee's pond, or the horse that kept getting in the way. "Isn't that Mrs. Dee's property?" they might ask. "Do you think she's . . . ?" Or suppose Mrs. Dee's dog Rover ran in front of David while we were filming. Someone might think, "Oh, my! That's Mrs. Dee's dog! I never would have suspected *he* was gay!"

David was very direct and honest about his experiences and his feelings. I found him moving; he had a sensitivity, an awareness, a sweetness, and a quiet strength that was unique in contrast to the other men in the film.

We filmed him by a daisy patch near the pond on Mrs. Dee's back property. Her horse kept getting in the way; we were either in *his* corral or *his* pasture, neither of which he seemed willing to share. Every time we tried to set up, one person had to be on guard to shoo the horse away from the equipment. Finally we let the horse have his way and gave him free access to his territory.

Mrs. Dee did eventually find out what the film was about. She was quite angry at first. She held Judy accountable for not telling her the explosive subject of the film. I wrote her a long, detailed letter apologizing for our oversight: "I thought Judy told you, and Judy thought I told you. Besides, you didn't ask." I agreed with her—it was negligence, but not with bad intent—and I told her all about the project.

A few weeks later, we got a note from Mrs. Dee. She agreed it was a misunderstanding. She said she didn't like being in a position of potential controversy without being given a choice in the matter—particularly on an "issue" for which she had strong opinions. In closing, she said her choice was to offer her complete support, and her opinion was that she thought the project sounded worthwhile and important. With that, she wished us luck.

The decision to include Mark in the film was made without videotape: he was the only person who was not preinterviewed. Rob describes the filming, which took place at Mark's New York office:

We made a last-minute decision to film a New York male, and Mark had the qualities we were looking for: he was urbane, involved in the executive-corporate world, gay identified, and successful.

His interview took place high above the streets of New York City, where Mark is an executive vice-president of a market research firm. Mark got permission from the company's president for us to film him in his office, and we did the interview during business hours.

The day of the shoot Andrew, Veronica, Peter, and I left the WNET building where we had an office and loaded the equipment into the cab, squeezing ourselves in too. As we rode down Avenue of the Americas, Peter told Andrew, Veronica, and me that he thought we should approach this shoot differently. Given the location, and the fact that it was during working hours, we should be less informal and more professional. We kidded him about his attitude and—since Peter was the only one who had met Mark and seen his office—reminded him of how easily he was impressed.

We stepped out of the elevator into a plush entranceway, lined with impressively plaqued doors leading to various corporate suites. Veronica bellowed loudly—which seemed out of character—"We're here!" Peter's face reddened; he turned toward us and said, with a squished up facial expression, "Sssssshhhhh!" His arms flapped at us to be quiet. The three of us began to giggle like schoolchildren caught in the act of defiance by the teacher.

When we walked into Mark's suite, all giddiness was left in the hallway. We were greeted by a receptionist, and secretaries made way for us to come through and unload equipment. Mark was there to greet us warmly. Suddenly, Peter's attitude was the one we all assumed.

Caught in the tangle of our own objectives, we may have set limitations to the focus of Mark's interview. He is a warm and friendly person—and I'm not sure we captured that aspect of who he is.

As we were setting up in Mark's office, I sat once in his big swivel chair, behind his big desk, and looked out at the big view. I felt like a little pea. It caused me to think two thoughts: first, documentary film is glamorized voyeurism, taking me into situations where I might otherwise never be; second, to have a chance to hear from a person who is in many ways different from myself is, in some ways, more worthwhile than to hear from someone who is in many ways like me.

In Washington, Lucy and Peter and I filmed Cynthia, as Lucy recalls:

When Nancy showed her tapes of Cynthia and Helaine, Cynthia had us all in stitches. Her eyes rolled, and her hands talked, and as her rippling laughter pulled us into her stories, we realized she was doing to us what no one else had yet done in the interviews: she was talking about her first sexual feelings toward a woman and drawing us into the excitement, the nervousness, the tension, the feeling of it. She was the first woman on film or tape who had talked comfortably and directly about sex.

After Lucy interviewed Cynthia, I took over and interviewed her and Helaine, her roommate and business partner whom I had met in 1970 when she was a sixteen-year-old high-school runaway. We wanted to point out in the film that gay people have strong friendships with each other, which do not necessarily involve sex. Both interviews are included in the book, although only Cynthia appears in the final version of the film.

We had decided at the Cape that we had to try to film a group, because so many people talked about being able to accept themselves because they had group support. In the South Lucy and I had preinterviewed many women who were active in Triangle Area Lesbian Feminists (TALF). We thought we'd treat this group as though it were an individual; we would handle its history and development similarly to the growth of a personality and fit this into the dramatic flow of the individuals in the film. Lucy, Peter, and I filmed twelve or so women sitting in a circle talking about their involvement with TALF and its influence on them.

We later discovered that the form of this footage could not conform to the other material, and we were unable to use it. Any sense of group solidarity in the film comes through people's stories, and from the illusion the film gives that, although they don't know each other, the people in it are the best of friends.

Ann is the woman who I feel more than any other represents me in the film. She is also a role model for me; she represents a spirit of the new lesbian that I so strongly respond to and identify with. Her profession, her interaction with the small community she lives in, and her relationship with her family made her decision to be in the film very difficult for her. She felt that gay liberation and our project were more important than any of the other considerations. I feel she weighed her decision more carefully than some of the other participants precisely because her work, her home, and her family are of such primary importance to her.

Ann is a highly respected veterinarian who worked for years in the local stock auction doing blood tests on wild cows and wilder bulls. We interviewed her in her farm yard. Every few minutes, another dog or cat would come to her for a comforting pet and caress.

After the filming we were treated to a feast her lover had cooked to celebrate the conclusion of a hard day's work. Ann wore a long, red satin boxer's robe emblazoned "Baby Ruth" or "Sugar Daddy" or something of that nature.

After dinner I challenged Ann to an arm-wrestling match—I figured her costume indicated she was in for a fight. Everybody pulled back from the table and cleared the dishes in our path. We squared our positions, took each other's hands; each of us pushed the other with all our strength. We were deadlocked; there was complete silence from the others. Then we looked at each other's eyes and started to laugh. I gave way all of a sudden, and we both fell over backwards onto the floor. I figured I had met my match.

Lucy flew back to San Francisco, where she, Rob, and Andrew would begin the laborious task of syncing up the footage, transferring sound, and supervising the lab. Meanwhile Peter and I flew to New Mexico where we would meet Veronica and film John and Harry, then Nadine and Rosa.

The last scene we shot there was Nadine and Rosa cooking enchiladas on their wood stove. We sat down to eat the food we had filmed and celebrated the end of our expedition. Peter flew back to San Francisco. Veronica and I completed our circle; we packed up the equipment and drove back.

So much of the process of this film hinged on the development of Peter's own relation to it. It became clear to him that although he had established the initial structure of the interviewing procedure in both videotaping and filming, he had to have creative and active input from all of us. He did not see himself as director in the traditional sense, but Peter made it clear to us while we were in production that he would edit the film with an assistant and would expect our regular collaboration. We repeated the earlier editing process and screened all the material, with each of us marking what we liked on our verbal transcripts.

At this point I joined Casey to work on the book, preferring an active role in its creation to an essentially inactive or reactive role in the cutting of the film. It was a difficult decision to make, because I wanted to learn about the editing aspect of filmmaking.

I moved up to the country, where Casey had been editing videotape material for almost a year. Casey and I were constantly frustrated by our efforts to collectivize the book work. I soon realized that we would have to see the project as our own.

I am the only lesbian I know who is working with her mother. The fact that I am working with her on a book about homosexuals is entirely unfathomable to most of my gay friends. "Working with your brother? And your mother? That's amazing! My mother won't have anything to do with my being gay." I have just recently started calling Casey by her first name. It is a pity the English language does not have a word that describes this new relationship, a word that would encompass working companion/mother/friend.

Meanwhile Peter was discovering that he could not cut this film himself. After he had established the initial dramatic form for the film, Veronica joined him as coeditor. Then, later, Lucy and Rob would join them, so the ongoing work of editing was accomplished by a group of people. Andrew worked on and off in the small, dark editing room—winding film, unwinding film, splicing and unsplicing—work we all considered tedious. Andrew couldn't stand it. When I came into the back room, I could feel his impatience. Andrew worked half-time at editing and at transferring the sound from tape to 16-millimeter magnetic stock, using the tape machines at Fantasy Records. He also helped Peter cut the music sequences in the film.

Veronica relates the difficult decisions involved in the editing:

> The editing process began in the camera. We had videotaped, so we had an idea of what we wanted to focus on with each person the second time around. Our filmic interviews were already selective in their questions. What we chose to ask related to two things: the particular person's story or angle on things, and the overall structure we had already thought out for the film. This was not to be a film about theory. We wanted to stick to human experience: "What happened and how did you feel?" We had worked out what Peter calls a "dramatic curve," which began with the first feeling of gayness and included childhood, or when one started to feel different: initial self-awareness. The downhill part of the curve then moved to the difficulties encountered in being gay: the external difficulties and the internalizing of the oppression. The final part was to be self-realization: the

awareness that one can be fulfilled, that one can grow. Hopefully it would reveal the rejection of the internalized oppression by an awareness of its external source—in other words, the articulation of a social consciousness.

We organized each person's material into sequences; after the first pull, each portrait was roughly fifteen minutes long. That portrait was once again transcribed, and the text was cut up into the sequences we had arrived at. In the first cut, we wanted to tell eight stories simultaneously. You hear the beginning of Rick, then Whitey, then George. You go back to Rick, then Pat comes in—you are following all the stories at once. You can imagine the complexity of cutting up twenty-six stories and trying to keep a coherence to the whole as well as maintain a concern for each individual. The editing board got very full!

(Author's note: the editing board was a bulletin board—the size of the fifteen- by eight-foot wall—set up in the middle room of the office. Each piece or sequence in the film was typed on colored paper—each person in the film had his or her own color—and arranged on the board. The editing board offered the best means for us to see the development of the story at a glance. Using the slips of paper, which were numbered to correspond to the relevant pieces of film, the editors could change sequences around very easily and quickly, compared to trying out the same sequences using the actual film.)

The third chapter, "Love," was about coming to pleasurable terms with being gay and some first positive experiences of gayness. That third chapter began an hour and a half into the movie and introduced a series of new characters: Cynthia, David, and Ann. We discovered that an hour and a half into the film is too late to introduce new people. Nobody wanted to see a new face. Nobody wanted to say, "Now, wait a minute. Am I going to find out this person's story too?"

The most difficult editing problem we had was to integrate, introducing all the characters early in the film so that the viewer wasn't distressed with seeing them appear for the first time much later on. We were also concerned with the ongoing considerations of pacing, of how long to stay with someone at a given time, and at which point to pick up his or her story again. We cut up the bits of paper, we moved from movie to editing board; we went time and again to the outs, because our original portraits of the people changed as the needs of the film changed.

One of the major editing concerns was the balance of women and men. Lesbians had been for too long slipped into films or books about homosexuals as a token gesture. There was no question that this film, like the film group, would have equal participation of men and women. Often people (usually men) have told us that the film is more heavily weighted toward women. Rob expresses his concern from a male point of view:

> The male consciousness was never as clear or directed as the female consciousness. There was a feminist personality and analysis for the group to assume—one that included all women—but there was no larger male personality that included all gay men in the same way. It would be oversimplification to say this was merely a reflection of the men working in the film, or the men working on the film. It is rather a reflection of most gay men and the gay men's movement which limits itself, for the most part, to dealing with "rights" without a broader overview. As a unit, the goals of the men in the group were less clear and less defined than the women's, and I think the same holds true for the men in the film: for the most part, we were resistant to making footprints in ground that had not yet been broken.

> In the final editing stages, Peter and I began to see the men as being overshadowed. We thought it was a simple question of male/female balance. Lucy and Veronica, as editors, tried to be sensitive to what we were feeling, but they didn't understand what we meant. In retrospect, I think we were asking them to understand something we ourselves did not fully comprehend.

We were also concerned with the delicate balance between interview material and the verité sequences. It was often very difficult for us to let go of this sometimes very beautiful visual material, which we had spent so much time thinking about, setting up, and shooting. Most of these sequences are not in the film. At one point, about six months into the editing, a rough cut was assembled using all of these verité pieces. After a screening of this version, we realized that we had to return to the original form—predominately talking heads with occasional music and visual breaks.

Those of us who were not editing would give Peter, Lucy, Veronica, and Rob our input about once a week. I had felt for a long time that we still had inadequate feminist content in the film. One day I was rereading Sally's video transcript for consideration for the book and realized that we needed her, an articulate spokesperson representing the lesbian-feminist view, in the film. In this way, my working on the book influenced the film.

When we got back from our travels, we had no intention of filming anyone else. But after several screenings and criticism from friends, we decided that we had to interview an Asian person. This decision may seem like tokenism if one looks at it from a negative perspective, as though we were using the people in the film for our own purposes. Indeed I often felt that we were dancing along a fine line of what many would consider racism. We would all look to Andrew, who would be overwhelmed in trying to explain his point of view to five whites. I would identify with him, thinking about how I felt trying to explain sexism to a group of men. Everyone in the film becomes a token symbol representing a spectrum of the audience. We wanted the film to influence people to stop objectifying individuals, yet ironically we had to objectify them in order to make the film. The people in the film reflect the biases of the Mariposa Film Group and the individuals within it.

Andrew found Dennis:

> I found Dennis through an Asian support group. Such groups are developing within the gay community to help deal with minorities' "double oppression." In spite of his apparent ostracism in being a gay Asian male, Dennis crosses numerous ethnic and social lines in reflecting the common struggle that most gay males encounter in maturing sexually.

I am always disappointed to find that gay men and women are just as racist and sexist as many of their straight brothers and sisters. Dennis grapples with his struggle to be himself while trying to deal with being a symbol. His parents, who were born in Mainland China, were diplomats in this country at the time of the revolution and chose to become grocers in Seattle instead of returning home. Dennis has always had to deal with being a minority, and this sort of struggle or detachment is what he puts into perspective for me.

As he implies, when you're already removed, it becomes less of an adjustment to deal with not being a part of a group. This is what support groups are starting to realize—that in reality their members have a unique strength: the determination to live and feel happy about themselves.

Dennis is able to reach and speak to many people because he talks about alienation. This experience is one that many of us go through, but all of us don't escape its crushing blows to our personalities. Being gay can be viewed by Dennis as just another one of the adjustments to one's personality one has to make during a lifetime.

Each of us seemed drawn toward one person who represented us in the film—for me, as I've described, it was Ann. Peter found himself missing until very late in the process:

> At the last moment, after editing the film for about eighteen months, I became aware that a whole range of experience was missing from the film—basically, mine. Although I could relate to and identify with almost everyone in the film, there was no male who was about my age, no one who I felt really represented my experiences. I expressed my feelings to Andrew and Rob, who agreed. The women supported our feelings. About a month

before, I had shown a rough cut of the film to an old college friend whose work as a visual (or poetic) filmmaker I had always admired. He liked the film, basically, but he made some very harsh—and, as it turned out, correct—criticisms of its current state, including the fact there was no one like me in it. When it came time to do more videotapes for this last person, I asked Nick if I could tape him, which I think genuinely surprised him. I said, "Put up or shut up." He put up. We videotaped him and a number of other "thirtyish, openly gay men, perhaps Jewish, professionals, or involved in the arts." We felt that Nick's interview would most add to what the film lacked.

Nick was easily the most nervous of any of the subjects. Part of the reason, I'm sure, is that he is a filmmaker. He was all too aware of the power we had over him to distort his image. Further, with all the other interviews, a fair amount of time had lapsed between the videotape trial and the actual filming, so the participants had time to forget what they had said and could be less self-conscious. Nick had only a week or so between the two.

Matters were made worse because my usual preshoot nervousness was heightened by having another filmmaker watch me set up—one who was so nervous that he had to relax by occasionally, with profuse apologies, making suggestions as to how the interview should be lit!

Casey and I have been working together for over a year. Casey's major focus has been editing the interviews, while mine has been working on this narrative. It has been difficult at times because I have had to withdraw my energy from the book and drive down to the city to attend meetings about the film.

As I was driving down to San Francisco I would slowly change my thinking from the problems of the book to film problems. I would wind down from thinking about what I was going to have to write about the history of the project and begin to deal with the project itself. I had to look at its past while I was still involved with its present. When I had parked in front of the office, I would often sit in the car for a few moments and take several deep breaths to prepare myself for an entirely different reality. I would quickly review whatever problem we might be dealing with that day: How could we make the film shorter? Which two people would I be willing to cut out? Should the filmmakers be in the film and, if so, how? How would we deal with the visual sequences? How would we figure out what percentage each of us owned? (We were each paid one hundred dollars per week and owned a portion of the film based on how much time we spent on it.)

When I felt ready I would walk slowly up the stairs. I'd be confronted with a great deal of energy, which was always changing. Sometimes it signified a break-through, and everyone would be laughing and feeling good. Or perhaps people would be frustrated because they couldn't find a solution to a sticky problem. Always people were exhausted, oftentimes working on twenty-four-hour shifts. For weeks at a time they would get little more than four hours of sleep a night.

One day I walked in to discover that Peter had hired a new office manager, Kathy Glaser, who ended up doing a little of everything, including helping with the book. She was a whiz on the phone as well as on the typewriter. She held creditors at bay in one moment and encouraged investors the next. She stayed overnight to splice film together for early morning screenings. She kept us all in good spirits with her fantastic sense of humor, which helped us (and her) keep perspective amidst what was often the chaos of frustrated editors battling it out with each other. Kathy would come into the office with a funny grin on her face to tell a new tale about her cat who had fallen out the window and whose personality had taken a turn for the worse. Or about how amused she was, being a gay woman, that the boy who worked in the corner store where she bought one can of cat food every day had a crush on her. At first Kathy had a hard time defining her role. I felt she should become a part of the "collective"; others, particularly Peter, felt that we had to set a limit somewhere, and the group should be defined by the six of us who had worked on production.

Kathy captures the mood of the final days of editing:

> I began as a savior, just out of the shower. It was February, and Rob called me at the office from New York to see if I could be on a plane in half an hour with the reel of film he and Veronica had left in the editing room—it was to be screened in a few hours on Broadway. "I don't see why not," I said. "I have my hairdryer here." In half an hour I was on the plane in my Earth Shoes and a trenchcoat with no buttons, a silver can at my feet. I got there just in time—freezing, serious mission all over my face (although Rob claims to have caught me looking up at buildings with my mouth open).

> "That's beautiful, just what we needed, perfect, about time somebody had the ingenuity to do that, looks nice." They came in one by one to comment on the row of message clips with names (theirs) on them that Peter had asked me to pushpin to the door. They smiled a lot. They paid me more. They brought me Kahlúa and rubbed my back as I typed. Their immediate acceptance made me nervous. It secured me in a position I didn't want to be known for. I wanted always to have been involved in the whole thing, the impossibility of which kept me vaguely anxious and made it difficult to be comfortable with my account books when burning and compelling issues were under discussion in the next room (for example, is a lesbian who is not actually from Lesbos a "lesbian" or a "Lesbian"?) Their delicacy ("Should we include Kathy in the meetings? Does that mean we are accountable to her? Does she want to have anything to do with us?") became assumption ("Goddamn it, Kathy, get in here").

Toward the end of the editing I walked into the office and found another new face—Amanda Hemming, who had just graduated from college and wanted to become a filmmaker. She was looking through the yellow pages one day, calling up all the film companies listed. Adair Films was the first one she called. She was told that there wasn't a job, but when she asked if there was any volunteer work to be done, whomever she spoke to must have paused, and Amanda insisted on stopping by. Little did she know about what she was getting into—a straight woman who soon began to learn more about gay people than she could have imagined, not only from the film itself but by working so closely with us. Although she joined us as a volunteer she was later put on the payroll. The editors told me they didn't know how they could have done it without her.

Despite the seemingly helter-skelter nature of the project, despite the confusion of editing, fundraising, and, at one point, new filming, I was always impressed by how smoothly and professionally things were being done. I would walk into the back room, small and dark, with film reels and film cans and film boxes stacked on several shelves, with loose film hanging on hooks—hundreds of feet falling down in a spaghettilike mass in a bin below—and see Veronica sitting intently at the huge editing machine, with earphones on, listening to a particular segment over and over again, trying to decide how to cut it. I would stand watching for a long time before I would tap her on the shoulder to say hello. She would take off her phones, smile, ask me how I was, and hope, I'm sure, that I would not engage her in conversation which would interrupt her concentration—I rarely did. I would turn around to see Lucy tucked away behind the bookshelf in the middle office, which had been converted to make room for the editing machine she was working on. She too would be so involved that she would only be able to wave hello. Amanda Hemming had been hired to help edit the film, and Kathy Glaser was now office manager. Then I'd see Rob intent with a segment he was working on, or Peter and Andrew cutting a music sequence, or one of the two other women, Pat Jackson and Jennifer Chinlund, who were hired toward the end of the project to cut sound.

I would often try to tell all of them about my experience in writing, would wish that they could have a glimpse of what I was doing. But words could never do it, and they were all working so hard that they could not drop in on me while I was intently working at my table.

Peter generally worked at night so he would not be interrupted by phone calls and the business of producing. He would stay long enough in the morning to take care of some of this, talk to Kathy about what needed to be done, what letters to write, what phone calls to make, and which ones to expect. Often I would come by in the morning long enough to catch a glimpse of Peter—bleary-eyed and stumbling around looking for his coat—on his way home to bed. Veronica, Rob, or Lucy might just have arrived a little more refreshed after a few hours' sleep. I was witnessing the shift change.

We had long used the working title *Who Are We?* for the film. No one was satisfied with it; we spent months trying to come up with a better one. We even had a contest at one of the final screenings of the film at the Archives. We were going to give the winner a crate of Texas oranges and a juicer. *Word Is Out* is a title many people helped create. I first picked up on it when we filmed Sally's speech at the Gay Freedom Day parade—now one of the last scenes in the film. Sally repeated the refrain "... and the word might get out that ...." When her speech was over, I was talking with Casey and other friends. We realized then that *The Word Is Out* might be a good title; when I suggested it, everyone screamed, "That's it! That's it!" I said I didn't think the other filmmakers would like it. Casey bet me dinner out that they would. She won. We decided to drop the word "the." The others felt we needed a subtitle and came up with *Stories of Some of Our Lives.* Because *Word Is Out: Stories of Some of Our Lives* was named by many of us, no one received a crate of oranges.

As the film began to assume its final form, Lucy found herself dealing with the question of its message:

My hope is that the power of the film can be in its inclusiveness. We are not talking about change in the sense of a radical break from who we are; we are talking about becoming free—as men and women, as humans—to move along a continuum where most of us have been stuck in one place or another. The power of the film is in its double-see, a validation of experience which in some measure we can all identify with, and at the same time a sense that something is wrong, that we cannot stop here, and that we are all implicated as oppressors and as oppressed. We feel this because of what we have each come through, because in some way we understand that, however great the external pressures are to form us and to shape the way we live and grow, our own strength against our own selves—what we know ourselves to be from the inside—is the most effective and insidious oppression.

The film casts questions on the health of us all, on the very possibility of heterosexual and maybe homosexual relationships without role inequality. The film intimates that what has been considered "sick" by society might actually be more healthy than what society encourages, fosters, pushes upon us. Because of how imbued we all are with self-images that incorporate sex roles and expectations inextricable from our physical sexuality, we are left with a turnabout: women relating with women, men relating with men.

Do we stop here? Will sex, then, in either case, define how close we can get to another human being in a total way? Will we accept the definition that has formed our characters and which we work, in this film, to reject—a finality of the separation between being male and being female, and, therefore, a finality of the separation between being gay or straight?

Androgyny is a concept in human evolution that means a transcendence of male and female, including both. We have no equivalent word for relationships that transcend our sexual definitions. Can we even conceive of these possibilities?

Andrew, too, considered the effect of the film on his life and his perceptions:

This group had a definite purpose: to spread the word about gay America. We allowed our lives to be affected by the people in the group and film. Both have been a positive experience for me.

Being interviewed automatically puts one in a strained position. You're representing whatever group the viewer chooses to associate with you. I hope this film will help show the universal experience of sexual growing

up in America. The experience of making this film has moved me toward a crucial time in my own career. To think that most films are created by one or two people after struggling with five has made me see the merit in creating space for numerous perspectives.

The major lesson I have learned from meeting most of the people interviewed and hearing people who see the film is how universal and similar our sexual experiences are in America. This commonality helped us realize the need to let the world know about a few gay experiences, while at the same time letting other gay people see themselves.

Tracy Gary joined us in the fall to take care of the fundraising. She had been at the early Berkeley screening; she loved the film and became an integral part of the project. Without her, we would probably have had to stop the editing and spend all our time raising money, and we would still be working on it as I am writing this—five months after the San Francisco opening. I have often felt that this project is blessed—just as we need something done, the right person comes along to do it. As crazy as we would get, everything always worked out.

Tracy's indefatigable energy for the film often reinspired us after bouts of depression over it. While she worked on several other projects, she became more involved with ours until she was working full time on promotion and distribution and became Peter's invaluable business associate. She would come flying into the office, briefcase overflowing with papers, arms overflowing with papers, eyes twinkling, a bright smile despite too little sleep the night before. Tracy spent most of her time on the telephone. Peter discovered that the best way to talk to her was to use line one and call her up on line two. She has even cast her statement for this book in terms of the telephone:

> —Hello. All the filmmakers are in a meeting now, but I'd be glad to answer any questions you might have. . . . This is Tracy. I work at the office on promotion. . . . Oh, yes, we're eager to get a piece about our film in *New West* magazine. Can you help us, Jeff? . . . Hold just a second. The other phone's ringing. . . .

> —Sarah! Oh, hi. Can you get some volunteers from the Coalition for Human Rights to do some publicity for the Castro opening tomorrow night at Harvey Milk's speech at Horace Mann Junior High? . . . Oh, and we should meet soon to put together a contract for your group's percentage of the grosses opening night and a statement for the emcee and press. How's Tuesday at six at the Cafe Flore? . . . Good! See you then. Thanks.

> —Jeff? Sorry. OK, let's think of an angle. Perhaps the financing of the film—the incredible belief of the investors, some of whom have borrowed money in order to put money into the film, the necessary hustle that we've needed to do in order to get the film out in any way that would make it visible beside the biggies of Hollywood. . . . Sorry, it's the phone again.

> —Kathy? Sure, just a sec. Who's calling, please? Oh. Kath! Are you there? It's Ryder Sound Company about our bill! No, we can't possibly now. Try to stall them for another thirty days, I guess. What? Nadine and Rosa are flying in on Wednesday for the opening? Great!

> —Jeff, are you still there? OK, Kathy's available to help with the phones now, so let's go. We're this group of people who believe in the film, the issue—that it's time to get people talking about being gay or feeling oppressed or different or whatever. Four and a half years ago when Peter started, nobody took him seriously; now there's a credibility to the project, and we've found supporters. But we're still having problems. Marine's Memorial turned down our request to use their auditorium because they said the film was "too controversial." "People might get excited in their seats," the assistant manager said. And today one of the top radio stations in the city—whose owner is gay himself, incidentally—turned down our

advertising because their listenership, they claimed, would be displeased by words in our spots like "gay" and "lesbian." It's incredible! Sure, I'll check schedules out with the filmmakers, and hopefully we can all make it tomorrow at four. Thanks.

—Hello, Don, this is Tracy Gary of Adair Films. We really need your help in planning advertising for *Word Is Out*. We've got to get this thing off the ground but don't have or believe in spending the hundreds of thousands that are wasted in most print campaigns. Mostly we've planned to have prescreenings in each city with press and organizations and key individuals. We're getting what we can free, hoping for major grass-roots effort, and borrowing what we can. Could I come in and discuss nationwide rates with you for newpaper and magazine ads? Great!

—Kath, let's do the investors' letter. OK, we'll take *all* four lines off the hook.

Out of the corner of my eye the phone loomed like some big eye—was it still blinking? Each call meant a question answered or an idea in motion, but was I really becoming like some dog passing a hydrant in relationship to the phone?

We all had a good time together mostly. We shared a lot of respect and terrible anger but incredible trust at times too. We got things done—that's what I loved. And we were all educated in the process—and we educated others too. It is hard to imagine going forward to other projects without the opinions, criticisms, and stimuli of these friends.

The editors had told me how exciting the mix would be; I had been looking forward to it. Mixing meant that as each reel was "locked" for picture, the sound editors took over and worked on all the tracks—an incredibly complex procedure of which I have only a meager understanding. The separate tracks are "married" onto one track to fit the picture at the mix. This significant process symbolized the very last input we would all have in completing the film. After the mix, the labs would take over. We were now working toward a deadline; the film would open in San Francisco on December 1 in a benefit showing to raise money for gay rights organizations.

I walked into the huge, dark studio at Fantasy Records to witness this exciting and magical event and discovered after half an hour or so that I was bored to death. A professional mixer had been hired to work the board—the instrument panel, which looked as though it had been borrowed from a *Star Wars* set. The large booth, or desk, was filled with rows of buttons, switches, and lights. The panel faced a huge movie screen on which the film was projected; behind and above the panel was the control room from which the movie was projected and where the huge, upright tape machines were located. Each of the three or four sound tracks was threaded onto a machine; the master tape which recorded the tracks was threaded onto another; the film was threaded onto the projector. All of these machines worked in synchrony with one another and were controlled by the mixer at the panel below.

The control room also held shelves of cassettes with recorded sounds and noises that filmmakers might want to use for their sound tracks: bird chirps from various parts of the country, dog howls, dog barks, dog growls, rain in the city, rain in the country, traffic sounds in a city (Baltimore, New York, Podunk). We also had several cassettes of our own which would be used as filler for blank spots in the track.

A young woman sat in the control booth; she would be called on to play various cassettes, and she operated all the machinery.

The mixing process is a long and tedious one of recording the sound inch by inch, foot by foot, section by section. Each interviewee's voice level was set for tone and quality with the level varying as to whether a shot was a closeup or a long shot. A person could be made to sound older, breathier; the ambience of a room could be changed to make it softer or it could be given more echo. Once these qualities were established, the recording began. Forwards and backwards, forwards and backwards—the picture on the huge screen in front was moving forwards and backwards. Seeing the picture move backwards while hearing the backwards sound—English backwards sounded like Swedish to me—made me feel giddy after just a few minutes. People appeared to be eating their words—it made me very nervous.

While they were mixing the visual sequence of Whitey walking down the hill, Peter wanted to put in some extra bird chirps. I thought this suggestion was ridiculous; there seemed to be plenty. We must have watched Whitey walk down—and then backwards up—the hill a dozen times before Peter was satisfied with a bird. He'd press the intercom button and tell the woman in the room above, "Try the oriole again." She'd play the oriole cassette; then the recorders and the film would all be put in reverse, and the scene would repeat with the new bird sounds. Peter would be dissatisfied and call for another and another until one for some reason or other resonated with his ear, and he'd choose it. Whichever one he used, I hated, which I told him. He said, "You just wait. You'll like it in the film." He was right. I do.

After the mix, the track would be transferred at the lab to an optical track and put on the film stock itself.

The very last day of the week-long sessions, we all sat in the studio and saw the film with the mixed track, experiencing it for the first time in its final form. We are a funny group of people, always thinking about the next job to be done, rarely stopping to celebrate any particular landmark event. I don't think we ever were, as a group, able to congratulate ourselves. Some of us were thinking about what needed to be done to promote the opening; others were thinking about the lab work. Individually, we may have stopped for a brief moment to take a deep breath and say, "Whew! We did it!" But I don't suppose the "whew!" was any more significant than the one a jogger utters when the daily run is finished.

I spent most of the day before the San Francisco opening picking people up at the airport. Nadine and Rosa came to see the opening; Ann arrived with her lover, and Helaine and Cynthia flew in from Washington, D.C. It was all a dream I could not quite fathom. The morning *Chronicle* carried a half-page article about us and *Word Is Out.* I began to wonder what it would be like to have people know my name, my face. I was so numb it was difficult for me to react to anything. I was picking up women at the airport who had decided to come just hours before. I met Holly Near, a West Coast singer whom we had asked to emcee. I was such a space case that Holly offered to drive back to the city. I hoped we would sell out the fifteen-hundred seat Castro Theater, situated in the heart of San Francisco's "gay ghetto." Much to my surprise, when I arrived with Nadine and Rosa a huge line was already curling around the block. We sold out. I could not sit through the film, which was being so enthusiastically received that you couldn't hear most of the punch lines to the jokes; people were laughing too hard. I got up and down from my seat several times, went to the bathroom where I thought I would find some peace but ran into several friends who were also unable to stay still in their seats because of the overwhelming energy and excitement.

At the end, Holly introduced George, who then called up to the stage each person in the audience who was in the film. He first called Pam and Rusty and their kids, then Tede, Elsa, Whitey, Dennis, Pat, and Nadine and Rosa—who were so nervous during the film they were unable to watch most of it. They all received enthusiastic applause. Nick came up, and Trish Nugent, whose music we had used in the film, and Buena Vista, who provided the men's music. Cynthia, Freddy and his daughter, each climbed up to the narrow stage and walked down the line of the others there, hugging each one as they went. Most of those so closely allied in the movie had never met. For ten minutes or so, the audience was giving a standing ovation.

Then George introduced us, and we each came up to the stage. Standing on a stage with fifteen-hundred people applauding is quite an experience. Veronica asked George for the microphone to thank all our parents for their support; many of them were in the audience. Peter, who had run out during the showing to get a paper to read the review, announced that he was embarrassed and was *not* the director of the film; the Mariposa Film Group had made it.

The film has opened to rave reviews in San Francisco, New York, Los Angeles, and other cities all over the country. Peter and Tracy have proved that a small company can get a low-budget film distributed, that independent filmmakers can make it. The Mariposa Film Group has proved that a meaningful film can be made by a group of people working without clearly prescribed roles. And individually I have learned that I have something to offer the world.

I don't want our efforts and this document to become a drop in the bucket. It frightens me that voters in so many cities are repealing gay rights initiatives—or even that gay people's love for one another frightens others so that we have to fight for such laws in the first place. Intolerance in the name of God, in the name of Love, is so profound that people are repealing basic human rights initiatives.

I believe that if people will see *Word Is Out* and read the book, many will change their minds—though if people were open-minded enough to have the experience of the film, the hostile feelings toward us probably would not exist.

A lesbian mother came up to me the other day to tell me that her son, a Baptist who had rejected her, had seen the film and been very moved by it. A few hours of sitting in a theater where he need not feel threatened gave him the strength to validate his mother. He told her the film had changed his feelings about all human beings he felt to be different from him; it had made him feel more love for people. Conversations like this make me realize how important it is for everyone to see *Word Is Out.*

Selected Bibliography

Note: Where an author is more commonly known by a pseudonym, he or she is listed alphabetically by the pseudonym, followed by the given name in parentheses.

Fiction and Poetry

Aldridge, Sarah (Anyda Marchant). *Cytherea's Breath.* Bates City, Mo.: Naiad Press, 1976. A slightly old-fashioned love story about two women active in the feminist movement of the early 1900s.

Arnold, June. *The Cook and the Carpenter.* New York: Daughters, 1973. A novel exploring many situations and concepts basic to feminism: multiple relationships, communal living, power, political action. No gender-specifying pronouns are used, forcing the reader to examine the stereotypes of male- and femaleness.

————. *Sister Gin.* New York: Daughters, 1975. An unusual book dealing with menopause and aging from a lesbian-feminist perspective.

Baldwin, James. *Another Country.* New York: Dial, 1962. A novel, by one of America's foremost black authors, which deals with a wide variety of races, sexualities, and sexual relationships. Homosexuality is presented in a basically positive manner.

————. *Giovanni's Room.* New York: Dial, 1956. The first of Baldwin's novels to deal with homosexual themes. Concerns a white bisexual adrift in Paris.

————. *Tell Me How Long the Train's Been Gone.* New York: Dial, 1968. The most positive of Baldwin's work with regard to homosexuality. Concerns an actor involved in a homosexual relationship with a well-adjusted, younger gay man.

Bannon, Ann (Ann Holmquist). *Odd Girl Out.* New York: Arno Press, 1975. The first book of a fifties pulp series that has become a classic. Laura goes to college and is seduced by her roommate, Beth. Beth eventually rejects Laura for a man and marriage; Laura flees to New York City. First published in 1957.

————. *I Am a Woman.* New York: Arno Press, 1975. Laura arrives in New York City, falls in love with her straight roommate, then meets Beebo Brinker, butch *par excellence* of Greenwich Village. The seduction scene is yet to be topped in lesbian writing. First published in 1959.

————. *Women in the Shadows.* New York: Arno Press, 1975. Two years after the events of *I Am a Woman,* Laura and Beebo are undergoing the ghastly process of breaking up. Violent and negative. First published in 1959.

————. *Journey to a Woman.* New York: Arno Press, 1975. After nine years of marriage, Beth wants a woman. Deserting her husband and children, she goes to New York City in search of Laura. But first she meets Beebo. Contains strong feminist precepts. First published in 1960.

Barnard, Mary. *Sappho: A New Translation.* Los Angeles: University of California Press, 1958. Very little is known about the woman whom the Greeks regarded as one of their greatest lyric poets. She may have been exiled to Lesbos; she may have formed a women's literary circle there. One of the better translations of the remaining fragments attributed to Sappho.

Barnes, Djuna. *The Ladies' Almanak.* New York: Harper & Row, 1972. Delightful caricature and satire of Natalie Clifford Barney's lesbian circle of the twenties by one of its members. First published in 1928.

————. *Nightwood.* New York: New Directions, 1961. Complex story of an affair between two women, one of whom often disappears without notice. Set in Left Bank Paris and New York City of the 1920s. First published in 1937.

Barr, James. *Derricks.* New York: Greenberg, 1951. A collection of short stories by one of the most prolific authors to come out of the gay subculture of the fifties.

————. *The Occasional Man.* New York: Paperback Library, 1966. Barr's second novel follows a forty-year-old man through a series of homosexual affairs after the breakup of a long-term relationship.

————. *Quatrefoil.* New York: Greenberg, 1950. Two navy officers fall in love and are forced to deal with the consequences. The novel portrays gay pride, though it ends in tragedy. One of the classic gay-male novels of the fifties.

Bernikow, Louise, ed. *The World Split Open: Four Centuries of Women Poets in England and America, 1552-1950.* New York: Random House, 1974. Poetry.

Bissert, Ellen. *The Immaculate Conception of the Blessed Virgin Dyke.* New York: Violet Press, 1977. Poetry.

Boucher, Sandy. *Assaults and Rituals.* Oakland, Calif.: Mama's Press, 1975. The major theme of these four short stories is the reconciliation of the past with the present. Two are specifically lesbian: one details the remembrance of a first lover; the other, an encounter with that same lover fourteen years later.

Bowles, Jane. *Feminine Wiles.* Santa Barbara, Calif.: Black Sparrow, 1977. Stories and sketches.

————. *My Sister's Hand in Mine: The Collected Works of Jane Bowles.* New York: Ecco Press, 1977. Expanded edition of Bowles' *Collected Works,* including the novel *Two Serious Ladies,* in which Christina and her companion Lucie, with whom she has an ambivalent relationship, move to an island with the ever-present Arnold.

Bowles, Paul. *Things Gone & Things Still Here.* Santa Barbara, Calif.: Black Sparrow, 1977. Nine short stories by the American expatriate who lives in North Africa.

————. *Let It Come Down.* New York: Random House, 1952. A novel of intrigue set in Tangiers.

Brown, Rita Mae. *The Hand That Cradles the Rock.* Oakland, Calif.: Diana Press, 1974. Poetry.

————. *In Her Day.* New York: Daughters, 1976. The story of two women who attempt a relationship despite a multitude of differences. Covers nearly every issue of relevance to feminism.

————. *Rubyfruit Jungle.* New York: Bantam, 1977. The now-famous adventures of Molly Bolt, an up-front lesbian from the wrong side of the tracks who accepts flak about her lifestyle from no one. A classic. First published in 1973.

————. *Songs to a Handsome Woman.* Oakland, Calif.: Diana Press, 1973. Poetry.

Bulkin, Elly, and Joan Larkin, eds. *Amazon Poetry.* New York: Out & Out, 1975. Poetry.

Burroughs, William S. *The Wild Boys: A Book of the Dead.* New York: Grove Press, 1971. A satirical fantasy in which roving packs of homosexual boys attack the established culture and eventually destroy the entire world. Burroughs, one of the principal avant-garde writers of the fifties, is known best for *Naked Lunch.* Nearly all of his works concern homoeroticism.

Capote, Truman. *Other Voices, Other Rooms.* New York: Random House, 1948. A novel concerning the relationship between a thirteen-year-old youth and an older man.

Carpenter, Edward, ed. *Iolaus: An Anthology of Friendship.* London: Allen & Unwin, 1902. An anthology of short stories on friendships collected by gay pioneer Edward Carpenter. The first true gay anthology.

Charnas, Suzy McKee. *Walk to the End of the World.* New York: Ballantine, 1974. A science-fiction novel set in post-holocaust Earth where sexual apartheid is the rule, homosexuality is the norm, and women hold the lowest social positions. But the women are planning a rebellion. Ranks with Russ' *The Female Man* in importance to science fiction. *Motherlines,* a sequel, is due from Berkley in 1978.

Clausen, Jan. *After Touch.* New York: Out & Out, 1976. Poetry.

Cocteau, Jean. *The White Paper.* New York: Macaulay, 1958. Published anonymously, but obviously a fictionalized autobiography. The awakening of a young Frenchman to his homosexuality.

Colette (Sidonie Gabrielle Colette). *Claudine at School.* New York: Farrar, 1930. Colette, a prolific French writer of the twenties and thirties, is famous for her analytical studies of women. The story of a sixteen-year-old French girl, written as a diary. The lesbian content is fairly major; detail is lavished on her crush on one of the school assistants, on an affair among the teachers, and on a young girl's crush on the narrator.

————. *Claudine in Paris.* New York: Farrar, 1931. The main focus of this book is Claudine's move to Paris and her pending marriage. Most of the lesbian content is presented through recollections of her schoolgirl days.

————. *Claudine Married.* New York: Farrar, 1935. Claudine can't figure out what is wrong with her marriage until she has an affair with a woman. Unfortunately, the woman is having an affair with Claudine's husband at the same time.

————. *Claudine and Annie.* New York: Farrar, 1934. More feminist than lesbian, this last book in the Claudine series describes how Claudine helps her friend Annie to escape the tyranny of a cruel husband. The two women fall in love but decide not to pursue their passion. (All four Claudine books have been reprinted in one volume: *The Complete Claudine,* New York: Noonday, 1976.)

————. *The Pure and the Impure.* New York: Farrar, 1975. This work presents a series of narrated portraits in novel form of several well-known lesbians, including the Ladies of Llangollen and Renée Vivien. First published in 1933.

Cory, Donald Webster, ed. *21 Variations on a Theme.* New York: Greenberg, 1953. The first anthology of gay short stories to be published in the United States. Includes stories by Christopher Isherwood, John Horne Burns, Stephen Spender, and Paul Bowles.

Covina, Gina, and Laurel Galana, eds. *The Lesbian Reader.* Berkeley: Amazon Press, 1975. Short stories, poetry, and nonfiction from *Amazon Quarterly.*

Craigin, Elizabeth. *Either Is Love.* New York: Arno Press, 1975. One of the first novels to deal fairly with bisexuality; an autobiography. First published in 1937.

Dickinson, Emily. *Collected Works.* Many editions available. Poetry.

Dowd, Harrison. *The Night Air.* New York: Dial, 1950. A fictionalized autobiography revolving around a homosexual actor's search for security. His journey takes him through a marriage, several homosexual affairs, and finally back to his old home town.

Duffy, Maureen. *The Microcosm.* New York: Simon & Schuster, 1966. An English lesbian pub is the backdrop for sympathetic, realistic stories of three lesbians from different walks of life.

Ford, Charles Henri, and Parker Tyler. *The Young and the Evil.* New York: Arno Press, 1975. Follows the madcap adventures of Karel and Julian as they wander through the lively gay subculture of New York City's Greenwich Village in the thirties. First published in 1933.

Forster, E. M. *The Life to Come.* New York: W. W. Norton, 1972. A collection of short stories, none of which were published during the British author's lifetime, probably because of the homosexual nature of most of the plots. Forster was a member of the famed Bloomsbury group, which included Lytton Strachey, Leonard and Virginia Woolf, Roger Fry, and others.

————. *Maurice.* New York: W. W. Norton, 1971. A posthumously published homosexual love story complete with a happy ending.

Foster, Jeannette, and Valerie Taylor. *Two Women.* Chicago: Woman-Press, 1976. Poetry.

Garland, Rodney. *The Heart in Exile.* New York: Coward, McCann, 1954. A psychiatrist searches for the reason behind a patient's suicide. Presents an insider's knowledge of London's gay life.

————. *The Troubled Midnight.* New York: Coward, McCann, 1955. Two British diplomats get involved in a homosexual scandal. Based on an actual incident.

Genet, Jean. *Miracle of the Rose.* New York: Grove Press, 1966. Semi-autobiographical study of criminality and homosexuality by one of France's most important literary figures. Insightful look into role-playing and power.

————. *Our Lady of the Flowers.* New York: Grove Press, 1963. A mixture of autobiography and fiction. Concerns "Our Lady of the Flowers" and his assorted associates (thieves, transvestites, pimps, and prostitutes).

————. *Thief's Journal.* New York: Grove Press, 1964. Probably the most autobiographical of Genet's works. Concerns his adolescence and entry into the world of crime.

Gide, Andre. *The Immoralist.* London: Cassell, 1930. A novel by a well-known man of letters. Semi-autobiographical. Deals with a married Frenchman who, during a vacation in North Africa, comes to realize his gay potential.

Gidlow, Elsa. *Sapphic Songs: Seventeen to Seventy.* Oakland, Calif.: Diana Press, 1976. Poetry.

Ginsberg, Allen. *Howl & Other Poems.* San Francisco: City Lights, 1956. Poetry. Now one of America's best-known poets, Ginsberg first became prominent during the "Beat" era of the fifties.

————. *Journals: Early Fifties—Early Sixties.* Edited by Gordon Ball. New York: Grove Press, 1977. Ginsberg sees journals as a "dream repository, poetry register & random thought-form-bank." Unpublished poems and political ravings.

————. *Kaddish & Other Poems 1958-1960.* San Francisco: City Lights, n.d. Poetry.

————. *Planet News.* San Francisco: City Lights, n.d. Poetry, including "This form of life needs sex" and "Kral majales."

————. *Reality Sandwiches.* San Francisco: City Lights, n.d. Poetry.

Goodman, Paul. *Making Do.* New York: Macmillan, 1963. A wide-ranging novel concerning a bisexual anarchist and the problems which he and his friends face.

————. *Parents' Day.* Saugatuck, Conn.: 5 X 8 Press, 1951. Novel concerning a homosexual teacher in a prep school.

Grahn, Judy. *Edward the Dyke and Other Poems.* Oakland, Calif.: Women's Press Collective, 1971. Poetry.

————. *She Who.* Oakland, Calif.: Diana Press, 1977. Poetry.

————. *A Woman Is Talking to Death.* Oakland, Calif.: Women's Press Collective, 1974. Poetry.

Greenspan, Judy. *To Lesbians Everywhere.* New York: Violet Press, 1976. Poetry.

Grier, Barbara, and Coletta Reid, eds. *The Lesbians Home Journal.* Oakland, Calif.: Diana Press, 1976. A collection of short stories by Jane Rule, Isabel Miller, Dolores Klaich, and many others, reprinted from *The Ladder,* a lesbian periodical.

Griffin, Susan. *Like the Iris of an Eye.* New York: Harper & Row, 1976. Poetry.

―――. *Voices.* Old Westbury, N.Y.: Feminist Press, 1975. A play heard as the individual "voices" of five women, one of whom once had a woman lover.

Hall, Radclyffe. *The Well of Loneliness.* New York: Simon & Schuster, 1975. The classic of lesbian novels. A barely disguised autobiographical plea for the social acceptance of lesbians. The book was banned in Britain as "obscene" until the 1950s. First published in 1928.

Hall, Richard. *The Butterscotch Prince.* New York: Pyramid, 1976. An exciting murder mystery with a gay liberation ending. Cordell McGreevy searches for the killer of his friend Ellison.

Hansen, Joseph. *Fadeout.* New York: Harper & Row, 1970. The first in a series of mystery novels revolving around Dave Brandstetter, a gay insurance investigator-detective. Other books in this series are *Death Claims* (1973) and *Troublemaker* (1975).

Harris, Bertha. *Confessions of Cherubino.* New York: Harcourt Brace, 1972. An unusual novel about two long-time friends who are apparently lesbians, although their relationship is never consummated. Both are insane by the end of the book; sexual oppression is implied as the cause.

―――. *Lover.* New York: Daughters, 1977. Stories of women's lives, told not as history but as creation.

Hellman, Lillian. *The Children's Hour.* New York: New American Library, 1962. Two women who run a school are accused of being lovers by a vicious pupil. The charge is false, but one of the women realizes that she is latently gay and hangs herself. A sympathetic portrayal despite a tragic ending: this play clearly places the blame on social mores.

Howard, Elizabeth Jane. *Odd Girl Out.* New York: Viking, 1972. Arabella comes to live with a married couple, sleeps with the husband once, then falls in love with the wife. The inevitable confrontation portrays Arabella as the only loving, honest person of the trio.

Isherwood, Christopher. *The Berlin Stories.* New York: New Directions, 1946. First published as two volumes in Britain during the thirties, the book is the author's thinly veiled autobiographical account of Berlin during the rise of the Third Reich.

―――. *A Single Man.* New York: Simon & Schuster, 1964. A beautiful autobiographical novel. The hero is a professor at a large southern California university. His homosexuality is understated and unsensationalized.

Jackson, Graham. *Gardens.* Scatborough, Ont.: Catalyst, 1976. Eleven fine short stories, most of which are explicitly homosexual in content.

Jackson, Shirley. *Hangsaman.* New York: Popular Library, 1976. A horror tale of a woman gone mad. Natalie is seduced by another woman at college. The author does not make clear whether her seducer is another person or a fragment of Natalie's own personality. First published in 1951.

————. *The Haunting of Hill House.* New York: Popular Library, 1962. A chilling suspense/horror novel about four people invited to live in a haunted house as an experiment. One of the women has a "roommate" of unspecified gender; another has clear lesbian tendencies. First published in 1959.

————. *We Have Always Lived in the Castle.* New York: Popular Library, 1964. The lesbian content in this mystery/thriller is allegorical but closely tied in with the mystery that surrounds two women shut away in a house.

Jordan, Robin. *Speak Out, My Heart.* Bates City, Mo.: Naiad Press, 1976. A woman brings her lover home to meet her family, knowing they will not approve of her lesbianism. A "coming out" novel.

King, Francis. *A Domestic Animal.* London: Longmans, 1970. Dick Thompson, a gay, middle-aged British writer, falls in love with a dashing heterosexual Italian man. Most of the work of this well-known English novelist is pertinent to gay readers.

King, Louise. *The Day We Were Mostly Butterflies.* New York: Doubleday, 1964. A series of delightful short stories whose characters are a stereotypically gay male and a lesbian couple. A sympathetic comedy.

Kirkwood, James. *Good Times/Bad Times.* New York: Simon & Schuster, 1968. The ambivalent sexuality of adolescence is dealt with in this book as it examines the personality of a young man, Peter Kilburn, and his relationship with his friend, Jordan.

Kleinberg, Seymour, ed. *The Other Persuasion.* New York: Random House, 1977. An excellent collection of many out-of-print short stories about homosexuality. Most of the authors are gay, and the selections are balanced between lesbians and gay men.

Klepfisz, Irene. *Periods of Stress.* New York: Out & Out, 1976. Poetry.

Knudson, Roxanne R. *Fox Running.* New York: Avon, 1977. A young adults' book about the developing deeper-than-average friendship between two women track runners preparing for the Olympics; their sexuality is not made explicit.

————. *You Are the Rain.* New York: Delacorte, 1974. A suspenseful young adults' novel with lesbian overtones. Two teenage women become attached to each other when they are lost together in the Florida swamps.

Larkin, Joan. *Housework.* New York: Out & Out, 1977. Poetry.

Leduc, Violette. *La Batarde.* Translated by Derek Coltman. New York: Noonday, 1976. Slightly fictionalized autobiography about the author's childhood and youth, including a detailed account of her progression toward lesbianism. First published in 1965.

————. *Ravages.* New York: Panther, 1972. The story of two French girls in a boarding school and their passionate affair. A fictionalized autobiography that offers great detail about the author's affairs, primarily with women. Originally titled *Therese and Isabelle.* First published in 1967.

Leyland, Winston, ed. *Angels of the Lyre: Anthology of Gay Poetry.* San Francisco: Panjandrum Press and Gay Sunshine, 1975. The first in-depth anthology of gay poetry, an exploration of gay consciousness and the poetic being. Includes work by Allen Ginsberg, Frank O'Hara, Jack Spicer, Harold Norse, and many others.

Lynn, Elizabeth. *A Different Light.* New York: Berkley, 1978. A science-fiction novel that is wholly gay, extremely sympathetic, and never inclined to preach. The central characters are two male lovers; several minor lesbian characters also figure in it.

McCarthy, Mary. *The Group.* New York: New American Library, 1964. A novel following the lives of eight graduates of Vassar's class of 1933.

McIntosh, Harlan. *This Finer Shadow.* New York: Dial, 1941. A gloomy view of the gay men's culture of the late thirties. A bisexual seaman, Martin Devaud, roams New York City and meets some interesting people, mostly gay.

McIntyre, Vonda, and Susan Anderson, eds. *Aurora: Beyond Equality.* New York: Fawcett, 1976. A collection of short stories on a theme of "after equality . . . ?" Two by Alice Sheldon are specifically lesbian: "Houston, Houston, Do You Read?" (which won the Hugo and Nebula Awards for 1976) and "Your Faces, Oh My Sisters! Your Faces Filled of Light!" Relevant to gay men is Joanna Russ' "Corruption."

Mallet, Francoise. *The Illusionist.* Translated by Herma Briffault. New York: Arno Press, 1975. A novel focusing on a young woman's passage into adulthood and her affair with her father's mistress. Excellent study of the conflicts that occur when youthful dreams meet adult realities. Somewhat autobiographical.

Mariah, Paul. *Letter to Robert Duncan While Bending the Bow.* San Francisco: Manroot, 1974. Poetry.

———. *Personae Non Gratae.* San Francisco: Manroot, 1977. Poetry.

———. *Selected Poems 1960-1975.* San Francisco: Manroot, forthcoming. Poetry.

Maugham, Robin. *The Link: A Victorian Mystery.* New York: McGraw-Hill, 1969. A mystery novel which takes place in Victorian Australia. Homosexuality, viewed positively, is an integral part of the plot.

———. *The Wrong People.* London: Heinemann, 1970. First published in 1967 under the pseudonym of David Griffin. On a vacation in Tangier, Arnold Turner discovers that he's attracted to young men, and his attachment to one of them, Riffi, leads him into some dangerous dealings.

Mayne, Xavier (Edward J. Stevenson). *Imre: A Memorandum.* New York: Arno Press, 1975. One of the first American gay novels ever written (1908), this romantic homosexual love story is filled with gay pride. Written by one of America's earliest gay defenders, the book is a joy to read.

Meaker, Marijane. *Shockproof Sidney Skate.* Boston: Little, Brown, 1972. The author's one book that doesn't portray lesbians destructively. Sidney Skate's mother is a lesbian, and his girlfriend is more interested in his mother than in him.

Melville, Herman. *Billy Budd, Sailor: An Inside Narrative.* Chicago: University of Chicago Press, 1964. Research has unearthed evidence leading to speculation that Melville had more than a passing interest in men. Nowhere is this more evident than in this tale of the "handsome sailor," Billy Budd, and his love/hate relationships with two other men.

Miller, Isabel (Alma Routsong). *Patience and Sarah.* New York: Fawcett, 1973. A romantic story about two women in the early nineteenth century who contrive an independence from their male relatives and go off to live on land of their own. Based on conjecture about the lives of painter Mary Ann Wilson and her companion, Miss Brundidge. Originally titled *A Place for Us.*

Mishima, Yukio. *Confessions of a Mask.* New York: New Directions, 1958. In an autobiographically based account, Mishima depicts a young man coming to terms with his homosexuality.

————. *Forbidden Colors.* New York: Berkley, 1974. Mishima is regarded as Japan's most outstanding novelist. All of his work finds the protagonist faced with a moment of significance. In this novel, Yuichi is faced with an anguished homosexuality.

————. *The Sea of Fertility.* New York: Pocket Books, 1975. Mishima's major work—a tetralogy concerned with reincarnation. After its completion, he committed suicide by ceremonial *seppuku.* The four books included are *Spring Snow* (1968), *Runaway Horses* (1969), *Temple of Dawn* (1970), and *Decay of the Angel* (1970).

Morgan, Claire (Mary Patricia Highsmith). *The Price of Salt.* New York: Arno Press, 1975. Two women meet, fall in love, and build a relationship, despite obstacles. The ex-husband of one takes their child away when he discovers that his ex-wife is a lesbian. First published in 1952.

Nachman, Elana. *Riverfinger Women.* New York: Daughters, 1974. The adventures of Inez Riverfinger and her friends. A tale of radical lesbian-feminism from the viewpoint of women in their teens during the late 1960s.

Norse, Harold. *Carnivorous Saint: Gay Poems 1941-1976.* Berkeley: Gay Sunshine, 1977. Poetry.

————. *Hotel Nirvana: Selected Poems.* San Francisco: City Lights, 1974. The first comprehensive selection of Norse's best work, drawn from books written during fifteen years of wandering.

O'Hara, Frank. *The Selected Poems of Frank O'Hara.* Edited by Donald Allen. New York: Knopf, 1974. Poetry.

Olivia (Dorothy Strachey Bussy). *Olivia.* New York: Arno Press, 1975. Fictionalized autobiography of a young English girl's year in a French boarding school. She develops a crush on her headmistress, who has a woman lover of many years' standing.

Parker, Pat. *Child of Myself.* Oakland, Calif.: Women's Press Collective, 1971. Poetry.

———. *Pit Stop.* Oakland, Calif.: Women's Press Collective, 1972. Poetry.

Piercy, Marge. *Small Changes.* New York: Fawcett, 1974. A realistic novel that details a woman's slow progression toward feminism and then lesbianism. Covers many issues important to the women's movement.

———. *Woman on the Edge of Time.* New York: Knopf, 1976. A novel of feminist futurism.

Rader, Dotson. *Gov't. Inspected Meat.* New York: Paperback Library, 1972. A story about a young man's struggles with being gay in a repressive society.

Reade, Brian, ed. *Sexual Heretics: Male Homosexuality in English Literature from 1850 to 1900.* New York: Coward, McCann, 1971. An anthology of poems and prose produced during a time of tremendous growth in gay-male literary culture. The author's long preface analyzes the selections.

Rechy, John. *City of Night.* New York: Grove Press, 1963. One of the best of the sixties' "exposé" novels. This one deals with the bleak world of hustlers.

———. *Numbers.* New York: Grove Press, 1967. The sequel to *City of Night.*

———. *The Sexual Outlaw: A Documentary.* New York: Grove Press, 1977. An Orwellian drama of sexual oppression in an American city.

Renault, Mary (Mary Challans). *The Charioteer.* London: Longmans Green, 1956. Finely drawn portrait of a young Englishman's coming-out process during World War II.

———. *The Last of the Wine.* New York: Simon & Schuster, 1973. The story of Alexias, a young Athenian of good family, who reaches manhood in the last phases of the devastating Peloponnesian War. What gives him strength and imparts life to an otherwise purely historical novel is Renault's sensitive and respectful portrayal of his friendship with another youth.

———. *The Middle Mist.* New York: Popular Library, 1972. A young woman, tired of her family, runs away to be with her elder sister, Leonora, who is a lesbian—and one of the most memorable characters in lesbian fiction.

———. *The Persian Boy.* New York: Pantheon, 1972. Beautiful fictionalization of the life of Alexander the Great. A large portion of the plot deals with his love relationship with Bagoas, a slave boy. Positive and romantic.

Richmond, Len, and Gary Noguera, eds. *The Gay Liberation Book.* New York: Ramparts, 1973. A collection of articles and poems which came out of the early gay (male) liberation movement. Includes pieces by Allen Ginsberg, Paul Goodman, Allen Young, William Burroughs, and Harold Norse.

Rossetti, Christina. *Goblin's Market.* 1859. Poetry. Available in many English poetry anthologies.

Rule, Jane. *Against the Season.* New York: Manor Books, 1975. A story about an unwed mother who falls in love despite herself. The setting is a small town; several of the numerous characters are lesbians.

————. *The Desert of the Heart.* New York: Arno Press, 1975. The author's best novel. A gentle, slow-moving story about the love that develops between two women living in Las Vegas. The obstacles they must overcome are internal rather than external; their commitment to each other is not made until the final pages.

————. *Theme for Diverse Instruments.* Vancouver, B.C.: Talon Books, 1976. A collection of short stories, some of which were originally published in *The Ladder.*

————. *This Is Not for You.* Vancouver, B.C.: Talon Books. Kate loves her, but is determined that Esther remains heterosexual. Esther's relationships with men are destructive, as is Kate's refusal to consummate their relationship; Esther finally joins a convent.

————. *The Young in One Another's Arms.* New York: Doubleday, 1977. A group of people living in a boardinghouse decide they will remain together even though their house is sold and they are forced to move. Several of the characters are lesbians.

Russ, Joanna. *The Female Man.* Boston: Gregg Press, 1977. A first-of-its-kind book that made lesbian-feminism in science fiction something to be dealt with. Four women from different planets and times are brought together to settle a very literal war between the sexes.

————. "When It Changed." In *Again Dangerous Visions,* edited by Harlan Ellison. New York: Doubleday, 1972. Also in *Nebula Award Stories 8,* edited by Isaac Asimov. New York: Harper & Row, 1973. Men land on a planet inhabited only by women and find that the women neither want nor need them. The women view the arrival of the men as an event that will destroy their way of life. Awarded the Nebula Award for 1972.

Sackville-West, Vita. *The Dark Island.* New York: Doubleday, 1934. A novel of the love between two women.

Sarton, May. *The Fur Person.* New York: New American Library, 1970. A delightful story told from the viewpoint of a cat who lives with a lesbian couple.

————. *Mrs. Stevens Hears the Mermaids Singing.* New York: Norton, 1975. Autobiographical novel in which a writer recalls the love affairs which inspired her writing and concludes that her best work was prompted by love for women.

Selby, Hubert, Jr. *Last Exit to Brooklyn.* New York: Grove Press, 1974. A very harsh side of homosexual life. A powerful novel.

Spicer, Jack. *The Collected Books of Jack Spicer.* Edited and with a commentary by Robin Blaser. Los Angeles: Black Sparrow Press, 1975. Poetry.

Stein, Gertrude. *Fernhurst, Q.E.D. & Other Early Writings.* New York: Norton, 1971. Both "Fernhurst" and "Q.E.D." are relevant in this collection. The first is a fictionalized account of a love triangle between Stein and two other women; the second, the story of her first affair with a woman.

Sutherland, Alistair, and Patrick Anderson, eds. *Eros: An Anthology of Male Friendship.* New York: Arno Press, 1975. A superb collection of homoerotic literature throughout the ages. Includes selections ranging from the Bible and classical sources to the twentieth century.

Suyin, Han. *Winter Love.* New York: Panther, 1973. Story of a college woman's affair with another woman.

Taylor, Valerie. *Love Image.* Bates City, Mo.: Naiad Press, 1977. Modern pulp novel about a movie star who deserts Hollywood in order to be with her woman lover. Valerie Taylor published seven other novels during the late fifties and early sixties; all, unfortunately, are out of print.

Tey, Josephine (Elizabeth MacIntosh). *Miss Pym Disposes.* New York: Berkley, 1971. A British murder mystery set in a girls' college. Two of the students are lovers; their relationship holds the solution to the crime.

––––––. *To Love and Be Wise.* New York: Berkley, 1972. A mystery about a disappearance and an attempted murder. The lesbian content is minor but central to the solution.

Van Vechten, Carl. *The Blind Bow-boy.* New York: Knopf, 1923. A delightful campy novel from the twenties. Young and gay Howard Prewitt, straight from a small Midwest town, goes to New York in search of a mate.

Vidal, Gore. *The City and the Pillar.* New York: Dutton, 1948. Jim Willard makes love with his best friend while still an adolescent. It's a one-time experience, and both boys grow their own ways: Bob becomes straight, while Jim remains gay. Yet their evening together is not forgotten. Vidal wrote *The City* when he was twenty-three but changed the ending and issued a revised edition in 1965. An extremely important book for its day.

Vivien, Renée (Pauline Tarn). *Muse of the Violets.* Bates City, Mo.: Naiad Press, 1977. Poetry.

––––––. *A Woman Appeared to Me.* Translated by Jeannette Foster. Bates City, Mo.: Naiad Press, 1976. Fictionalized autobiography of the author's relationship with Natalie Clifford Barney. Includes a detailed historical-biographical introduction by Gayle Rubin.

Warren, Patricia Nell. *The Fancy Dancer.* New York: Morrow, 1976. A tough, proud, and gay man becomes the lover of a priest in a small Montana town.

––––––. *The Front Runner.* New York: Morrow, 1974. Emotional novel about a gay track star, his coach/lover, and their trip to the Olympics. A tragic ending.

Waters, Chocolate. *To the Man Reporter from the Denver Post.* n.p., 1975. Poetry.

Weirauch, Anna Elisabet. *The Scorpion.* Translated by Whittaker Chambers. New York: Arno Press, 1975. The story of a woman's search for love and happiness. After a long affair, complicated by tragedies and family pressures, Metta's lover kills herself, and Metta seeks solitude among strangers. Some editions titled *Of Love Forbidden.*

————. *The Outcast.* New York: Arno Press, 1975. A continuation of *The Scorpion.* Metta meets and is attracted to Corona, but discovers that they once had a mutual lover. Several editions and translations of the Weirauch books exist; the Greenberg volumes (1932 and 1933) may also be relied upon for accuracy.

Wilde, Oscar. *The Picture of Dorian Gray.* London: Ward Lock, 1891. A fantasy story about a man and his unique painting. Shades of the occult and the supernatural intertwined with hints of homosexuality.

Wilhelm, Gale. *We Too Are Drifting.* New York: Arno Press, 1975. Beautiful story about two women who fall in love despite all sorts of complications and pressures. A lesbian classic. First published in 1935.

————. *Torchlight to Valhalla.* New York: Arno Press, 1975. Novel about a woman artist who lives alone with her father until his death. Offered a heterosexual marriage, she instead chooses to love a woman. Less explicit than *We Too Are Drifting.* First published in 1938.

Winant, Fran. *Dyke Jacket.* New York: Violet Press, 1976. Poetry.

Winsloe, Christa. *The Child Manuela.* New York: Arno Press, 1975. The German classic from which the movie *Mädchen in Uniform* was taken. Manuela makes public her love for one of the boarding school teachers and the results are disastrous. First published in 1933.

Wittig, Monique. *The Opoponax.* New York: Daughters, 1976. On the surface, this novel is an account of the day-to-day life of a French schoolgirl; actually it is a tale of a one-woman revolution. Attention is given to the protagonist's first relationship with another girl. The book was awarded the French Prix Medicis in 1964.

————. *Les Guerilleres.* New York: Avon, 1973. The story of a community of women living without men. Impressionistic, heavily symbolic, and mythological; more often feminist than lesbian.

————. *The Lesbian Body.* New York: Avon, 1977. A tribute to the specifically lesbian body, done within the framework of several lesbian relationships. Couched in medical terms.

Wollstonecraft, Mary. *Mary, A Fiction.* New York: Schocken, 1977. The first known novel with a theme of lesbianism (1788). A thinly disguised autobiographical account of the author's relationship with Fanny Blood.

Woolf, Virginia. *Orlando: A Biography.* New York: Harcourt Brace, 1956. Virginia Woolf's tribute to her friend and sometime lover, Vita Sackville-West, who was also a writer. The life of the protagonist spans four centuries; she changes sex every hundred years or so.

Nonfiction

Abbot, Sidney, and Barbara Love. *Sappho Was a Right-On Woman.* New York: Stein & Day, 1972. An examination of lesbian lifestyles before and after the lesbian-feminist movement. Includes historical documentation of the New York movement in the early 1970s and of the gay/straight split within the National Organization for Women.

Altman, Dennis. *Homosexual Oppression and Liberation.* New York: Dutton, 1971. Excellent basic book on gay liberation. A political analysis. Provides a clear picture of the hows and whys of homosexual oppression.

Austen, Roger. *Playing the Game: The Homosexual Novel in America.* New York: Bobbs-Merrill, 1977. Austen not only documents the existence of the homosexual novel but provides a history of it. An important reference and bibliographic tool.

Birkby, Phyllis, et al., eds. *Amazon Expedition.* Albion, Calif.: Times Change Press, 1973. A collection of essays on lesbian thought and experience by Bertha Harris, Jill Johnston, Joanna Russ, and others.

Boyd, Malcolm. *Am I Running with You, God?* New York: Doubleday, 1977. Prayers, meditations, and random jottings by Boyd, an Episcopalian priest.

Brown, Rita Mae. *Plain Brown Rapper.* Oakland, Calif.: Diana Press, 1976. Politically astute essays by the author of *Rubyfruit Jungle,* many of which were originally printed in *The Ladder* and *The Furies,* a lesbian-feminist newspaper.

Carpenter, Edward. "The Intermediate Sex: A Study of Some Transitional Types of Men and Women." 1908. Reprinted in *Homosexuality: A Cross Cultural Approach,* edited by Donald Webster Cory, pp. 139-206. New York: Julian Press, 1956. Writing during the Victorian era, the author attempts to find a place in a moral society for the homosexual. This is to be accomplished, he believes, by condemning all sexual acts of any kind and subscribing to what he calls "true" homosexuality—a nonsexual love relationship with a person of the same gender. Other Victorian writers dealt with the phenomenon of homosexuality. (See Krafft-Ebing and Lombroso in this bibliography, for example.)

Clarke, Lige, and Jack Nichols. *Roommates Can't Always Be Lovers.* New York: St. Martin's Press, 1974. Subtitled *An Intimate Guide to Male-Male Relationships,* this book consists of letters sent to the authors when they were the editors of *Gay* magazine and their responses.

Cordova, Jeanne. *Sexism, It's a Nasty Affair.* Los Angeles: New Ways Books, 1974. Humorous articles on sexism, lesbianism, and feminism by the long-time editor of *The Lesbian Tide.*

Cory, Donald Webster. *The Homosexual in America: A Subjective Approach.* New York: Greenberg, 1951. Though containing some dated views of homosexuality's "causation," this book was one of the first widely read books on homosexuality written by a gay man. Takes a "civil rights" approach.

Covina, Gina, and Laurel Galana, eds. *The New Lesbians.* Westminster, Md.: Moon Books, 1977. Interviews of lesbians from across the country by the editors of *Amazon Quarterly.*

Damon, Gene (Barbara Grier). *Lesbiana.* Bates City, Mo.: Naiad Press, 1976. A reprint of the book-review column of lesbian literature that ran in *The Ladder* from 1966 to 1972.

Damon, Gene (Barbara Grier), et al., eds. *The Lesbian in Literature.* Bates City, Mo.: Naiad Press, 1975. A scholarly and thorough listing of all the known books with lesbian content published prior to January, 1975. About 2,500 listings. One of the two books necessary to any research into lesbian literature, history, or culture. (The other is *Sex Variant Women in Literature.*)

Dover, K. J. *Greek Homosexuality.* Cambridge, Mass.: Harvard University Press, 1978. A scholarly examination of the nature of homosexuality during the Classical Period as evidenced in the comedies of Aristophanes, legislation and law, the dialogues of Plato, and Archaic and Classical poetry. The author is one of the world's foremost Hellenists.

Elbert, Alan. *The Homosexuals.* New York: Macmillan, 1977. Edited interviews with seventeen gay men. Revealing work similar in approach to *Word Is Out.*

Falk, Ruth. *Women Loving: A Journey toward Becoming an Independent Woman.* New York: Random House, 1975. One woman's definition of love expanded by thoughtful personal accounts and interviews with other women.

Fisher, Peter. *The Gay Mystique: The Myth and Reality of Male Homosexuality.* New York: Stein & Day, 1972. An in-depth look at gay-male life. Awarded the Gay Book Award of the Task Force on Gay Liberation of the American Library Association.

Foster, Jeannette. *Sex Variant Women in Literature.* Oakland, Calif.: Diana Press, 1976. The in-depth, milestone study of the lesbian portrait in literature; ranges from the sixth century B.C. to 1955.

Gearhart, Sally, and William Johnson. *Loving Women, Loving Men: Homosexuality and the Church.* San Francisco: Glide, 1974. An examination of the Church's relationship to homosexuality. Clear and concise, with equal time given to both women and men.

Gearhart, Sally, and Susan Rennie. *A Feminist Tarot.* Watertown, Mass.: Persephone Press, 1977. Feminist commentary on the Waite-Smith tarot deck. Traditional interpretations tend to stress a sexual hierarchy.

Gibson, Gifford. *By Her Own Admission.* New York: Doubleday, 1977. A thorough and sympathetic account of Mary Jo Risher's fight to maintain custody of her son, this book deals with the fears a lesbian mother must live with.

Gidlow, Elsa. *Ask No Man Pardon.* Mill Valley, Calif.: Druid Heights, 1975. A short philosophical treatise on the importance and place of lesbianism in the larger culture by the author of *Sapphic Songs* and *Moods of Eros.*

Ginsberg, Allen. *Allen Verbatim: Lectures on Poetry, Politics & Consciousness.* New York: McGraw-Hill, 1975. The poet in prose.

————. *Gay Sunshine Interview.* Berkeley: Grey Fox Press, 1974. Extracts of interview in *Gay Sunshine,* January-February, 1973.

Grier, Barbara, and Coletta Reid, eds. *The Lavender Herring.* Oakland, Calif.: Diana Press, 1976. A collection of essays and articles from *The Ladder.*

Hodges, Andrew, and David Hutter. *With Downcast Gays: Aspects of Homosexual Self-Oppression.* Toronto: Pink Triangle Press, 1977. Reprint of a leaflet that has circulated for some time. Controversial examination of the ways homosexuals reinforce their own oppression.

Hyde, H. Montgomery. *The Love That Dared Not Speak Its Name.* Boston: Little, Brown, 1970. A fascinating history of homosexuality in Great Britain. Manages to be very informative despite its omissions and emphasis on male homosexuality.

Jay, Karla, and Allen Young, eds. *After You're Out.* New York: Pyramid Books, 1975. A collection of essays about the day-to-day problems of living a "liberated" life.

————. *Out of the Closets: Voices of Gay Liberation.* New York: Pyramid Books, 1974. A collection of essays on gay liberation, coming out, and other related topics.

Katz, Jonathan. *Gay American History: Lesbians and Gay Men in the U.S.A.* New York: Crowell, 1976. A collection of original documents dealing with homosexuals from colonial times to the present. Pertinent for both lesbians and gay men. An invaluable reference source.

Klaich, Dolores. *Woman Plus Woman: Attitudes towards Lesbianism.* New York: Simon & Schuster, 1974. An examination of various lesbian lifestyles, done mostly through interviews. Explores some of psychology's myths about lesbianism and looks at some lesbian authors from a historical and biographical perspective.

Krafft-Ebing, Richard von. *Psychopathia Sexualis: A Medico-Forensic Study.* Translated by Harry E. Wedeck. New York: Putnam, 1969. A Victorian view of the psychological aspects of sexuality. First published in 1894.

Kuda, Marie. *Women Loving Women.* Chicago: WomanPress, 1976. An annotated bibliography of lesbian literature.

The Ladder, 1956-1972. New York: Arno Press, 1975. The reprinted and bound set of the first and longest running lesbian periodical, in sixteen volumes.

Lauritsen, John, and David Thorstad. *The Early Homosexual Rights Movement (1864-1935).* New York: Times Change Press, 1974. A basic reference source regarding the first stirrings of homosexual awareness, pride, and organization. Short and concise.

Lombroso, Cesare. *Crime: Its Causes and Remedies.* Translated by Henry P. Horton. Criminology, Law Enforcement, and Social Problems Series, no. 14. Montclair, N.J.: Patterson Smith, 1968. A Victorian postulation that deviations are of genetic origin. First published in 1911.

McNeill, John. *The Church and the Homosexual.* New York: Simon & Schuster, 1976. Supported by the latest psychological research and study of scripture, discusses the homosexual's relationship with his or her religion.

Martin, Del, and Phyllis Lyon. *Lesbian/Woman.* San Francisco: Glide, 1972. The first general nonfiction work on lesbianism written by and for lesbians.

Myron, Nancy, and Charlotte Bunch, eds. *Lesbianism and the Women's Movement.* Oakland, Calif.: Diana Press, 1975. Essays on lesbianism and feminism from *The Furies.*

Rule, Jane. *Lesbian Images.* New York: Doubleday, 1975. An overview of lesbian images in literature. Includes biographies of twelve lesbian authors, critical analyses of their work, and an overview of recent fiction.

Sanders, Dennis. *Gay Source: A Catalog for Men.* New York: Coward, McCann, 1977. A sourcebook and directory for gay men.

Steakley, James D. *The Homosexual Emancipation Movement in Germany.* New York: Arno Press, 1975. Gives a clear view of the rise of the German homosexual-rights movement in the nineteenth century to its destruction by the Nazis in the 1940s.

Teal, Donn. *The Gay Militants.* New York: Stein & Day, 1971. A play-by-play account of the birth of the gay liberation movement from the Stonewall Riots of 1969 through its infancy.

Tripp, C. A. *The Homosexual Matrix.* New York: McGraw-Hill, 1975. Controversial book which astutely examines almost every aspect of homosexuality and its relation to society.

Vida, Ginny, ed. *Our Right to Love: A Lesbian Resource Book.* Englewood Cliffs, N.J.: Prentice Hall, 1978. Produced in cooperation with women of the National Gay Task Force, this book embodies the spirit of basic human-rights issues of all women and presents a stimulating exploration of the nature and scope of lesbian lifestyles.

Weinberg, George. *Society and the Healthy Homosexual.* New York: Doubleday, 1972. An insightful basic book in the understanding of homophobia: the abnormal fear of homosexuality.

Young, Ian. *The Male Homosexual in Literature: A Bibliography.* Metuchen, N.J.: Scarecrow Press, 1975. A 3,000-item bibliography of fiction, poetry, drama, and autobiography of gay-male interest. Includes four articles on gay literature.

Biography

Acosta, Mercedes de. *Here Lies the Heart.* New York: Arno Press, 1975. An autobiography by one of the lesser-known members of lesbian expatriate Paris. Fascinating accounts of the literary and artistic circles of the 1920s and '30s, including a detailed description of the author's relationships with Greta Garbo and Marlene Dietrich.

Anderson, Margaret. *My Thirty Years War.* New York: Horizon, 1970. Humorous account of the first thirty years of the author's life, focusing on her relationship with Jane Heap and their struggle with *The Little Review.*

————. *The Fiery Fountains.* New York: Horizon, 1970. The second of a three-book autobiography by the founder and publisher of *The Little Review.* This volume details her life with Georgette Leblanc until Leblanc's death in 1941.

————. *The Strange Necessity.* New York: Horizon, 1970. A recounting of the author's life and escapades from 1942 on. Includes, among other things, her relationship with Dorothy Caruso, widow of the famous opera singer.

Bell, Anne Olivier. *The Diary of Virginia Woolf: 1915-19.* Vol. 1. New York: Harcourt Brace, 1977. Last of the major works of Virginia Woolf to be published. The diary was continued for most of Woolf's life, "written after tea, written indiscreetly," and possesses the same precise characterizations and fluid style that we find in her novels and essays. An intimate look at a complex individual.

Bell, Quentin. *Virginia Woolf: A Biography.* 2 vols. New York: Harcourt Brace, 1974. Biography of the novelist by her nephew. Much previously unpublished material, including her letters to Violet Dickinson, Vita Sackville-West, and Ethel Smyth. Only passing mention is made of her homosexual relationships with women.

Bunch, Charlotte, and Nancy Myron, eds. *Women Remembered.* Oakland, Calif.: Diana Press, 1975. A short collection of biographies originally published in *The Furies.* Includes portraits of Susan B. Anthony, Dona Catalina de Erauso, and Queen Christina.

Carr, Virginia Spencer. *The Lonely Hunter, A Biography of Carson McCullers.* New York: Doubleday, 1976. Biography of the author of *The Heart Is a Lonely Hunter, Member of the Wedding,* and *The Ballad of the Sad Cafe.* Doesn't hedge about McCullers' lesbianism.

Casal, Mary. *The Stone Wall.* New York: Arno Press, 1975. Autobiography by a woman born in New England during the 1860s. The author claims that only lesbians are capable of a "pure" relationship, but her account is almost wholly heterosexual and demonstrates the failure of her affair with another woman.

Colette (Sidonie Gabrielle Colette). *Earthly Paradise.* Edited by Robert Phelps. New York: Penguin, 1974. A selection of Colette's writings, arranged to form an autobiography.

Dickson, Lovat. *Radclyffe Hall at the Well of Loneliness: A Sapphic Chronicle.* New York: Scribner's, 1976. A disappointing book but, barring Una Troubridge's *The Life and Death of Radclyffe Hall* (a fine, uncomplicated book that is nearly unobtainable), it is currently the only biography of Radclyffe Hall.

Grier, Barbara, and Coletta Reid, eds. *Lesbian Lives.* Oakland, Calif.: Diana Press, 1976. Biographies of famous and infamous lesbians, reprinted from *The Ladder.*

Isabel, Sharon. *Yesterday's Lessons.* Oakland, Calif.: Women's Press Collective, 1974. Autobiography of a working-class lesbian.

Isherwood, Christopher. *Christopher & His Kind.* New York: Farrar, 1976. Personal memoirs of Isherwood's youth.

Johnston, Jill. *Gullible's Travels.* New York: Music Sales, n.d. Autobiographical writings, many of them first printed in *The Village Voice,* about the travels and adventures of the author.

———. *Lesbian Nation.* Simon & Schuster, 1973. Key autobiographical and political writings that include an account of being gay in the 1950s and the process of becoming a lesbian-feminist.

Laguardia, Robert. *Monty: A Biography of Montgomery Clift.* New York: Dutton, 1977. The biography of the tormented actor.

Mavor, Elizabeth. *The Ladies of Llangollen.* New York: Penguin, 1974. Biography of the famed companions who lived in Llangollen, Wales—although the author avoids any direct mention of lesbianism.

Mellow, James R. *Charmed Circle: Gertrude Stein and Company.* New York: Avon, 1974. A fine biography of Gertrude Stein and the members of her circle in Paris.

Millet, Kate. *Flying.* New York: Ballantine, 1974. Autobiographical detail about the period following the author's sudden vault to media and movement "stardom."

———. *Sita.* New York: Farrar, 1976. Documents the breakdown of a relationship.

Nicolson, Nigel. *Portrait of a Marriage.* New York: Bantam, 1974. A biography of Harold Nicolson and Vita Sackville-West—best known for her relationship with Virginia Woolf—by their son. Includes portions of Sackville-West's diary.

Nicolson, Nigel, and Joan Trautmann, eds. *The Letters of Virginia Woolf: 1888-1912.* Vol. 1. New York: Harcourt Brace, 1975, and Vol. 2 (*1912-1922*). New York: Harcourt Brace, 1976. An intimate look at the complex British writer.

Nin, Anais. *The Diaries of Anais Nin.* Vols. I-V. New York: Harcourt Brace, 1966-74. Almost all Nin's work incorporated lesbian themes, and her famous diaries, an account of her entire life, are no exception. The greatest lesbian emphasis is found in Volume I.

Patterson, Rebecca. *The Riddle of Emily Dickinson.* Boston: Houghton-Mifflin, 1951. States in print what many have known for a long time: that Emily Dickinson's poems found their inspiration in her love for women. Contains a detailed analysis of some of the poems and includes an extensive history of "Katie," the woman on whose account Dickinson went into seclusion.

Secrest, Meryle. *Between Me and Life: A Biography of Romaine Brooks.* New York: Doubleday, 1974. The first biography to discuss the importance of an artist's sexual orientation and relate it to her art work. Romaine Brooks, although she was famous in her own day, is a now-forgotten painter. She also maintained a fifty-year relationship with Natalie Clifford Barney, the infamous literary mentor and seducer of many European women. Offers a view of Paris artistic circles in the 1920s.

Stein, Gertrude. *The Autobiography of Alice B. Toklas.* New York: Random House, 1955. The life of this early twentieth-century American author, written as if it were an autobiography of her lifelong companion, Alice B. Toklas.

Toklas, Alice B. *Staying on Alone: Letters of Alice B. Toklas.* Edited by Edward Burns. New York: Random House, 1974. Gertrude Stein relied on Alice for the emotional equilibrium that released her creativity. This collection, letters written after Stein's death in 1946, provides insight into Alice's personality and their life together.

Williams, Tennessee. *Memoirs.* New York: Bantam, 1976. The famous playwright describes his family relationships, love affairs, and struggle to achieve recognition.

Bibliography Compiled by: Sue Critchfield, Fran Haselsteiner, Eric Garber, Linda Gunnarson, Gail Larrick, and Lyndall McCowan

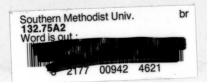